# RAYMOND ARON

# RAYMOND ARON

## The Recovery of the Political

### BRIAN C. ANDERSON

ROWMAN & LITTLEFIELD PUBLISHERS, INC.
*Lanham • Boulder • New York • Oxford*

ROWMAN & LITTLEFIELD PUBLISHERS, INC.

Published in the United States of America
by Rowman & Littlefield Publishers, Inc.
4720 Boston Way, Lanham, Maryland 20706

12 Hid's Copse Road
Cummor Hill, Oxford OX2 9JJ, England

British Library Cataloguing in Publication Information Available

**Library of Congress Cataloging-in-Publication Data**
Anderson, Brian C., 1961–
    Raymond Aron : the recovery of the political / Brian C. Anderson.
       p.   cm.
    Includes bibliographical references and index.
    ISBN 0-8476-8757-0 (alk. paper).—ISBN 0-8476-8758-9 (pbk. :
alk. paper)
    1.  Aron, Raymond, 1905–    —Contributions in political science.
I. Title.
JC261.A7A54    1998
320'.092—dc21                                           97-24239
                                                            CIP

ISBN 0–8476–8757–0
ISBN 0–8476–8758–9

Printed in the United States of America

∞ ™ The paper used in this publication meets the minimum requirements of
American National Standard for Information Sciences—Permanence of Paper
for Printed Library Materials, ANSI Z39.48–1984.

*To my Wife and my Parents*

Brian C. Anderson is senior editor of *City Journal*. Formerly, he was a research associate in social and political studies at the American Enterprise Institute and literary editor of *Crisis*. With Daniel J. Mahoney, he is the editor of Transaction's Aron Project, publishing new editions of Raymond Aron's greatest works. Dr. Anderson's reviews and essays have appeared in *First Things, Review of Politics, Interpretation, Salisbury Review,* and many other journals and magazines.

# CONTENTS

# ACKNOWLEDGMENTS

Writing this book has been a joy, and an education. Many people need to be thanked. First, I owe a profound debt to three scholars, from whom I have learned just about whatever I know about things political (they may have reason to be disappointed!): Hilliard Aronovitch first suggested the study of Aron as a way beyond some of the impasses in contemporary political theory; Daniel J. Mahoney's brilliance, enthusiasm, and measured judgment have been a source of unending satisfaction and classical friendship; Michael Novak has offered a model of civic responsibility, deep learning, and wisdom from which I will benefit for the rest of my life.

Various people have read and commented on the manuscript. In particular, I would like to thank Adam Wolfson of the *Public Interest* and Peter Augustine Lawler of Berry College. I've always felt Wayne Norman's skeptical eye looming over my shoulder. AEI has been a hospitable, challenging, and exciting environment. Steve Wrinn of Rowman & Littlefield has been a model editor, and I am deeply honored that this study will appear in a new series edited by Kenneth L. Deutsch and Jean Bethke Elshtain on twentieth-century political thought.

My parents have been what parents should be: loving, patient, and kind. To my wife, Amy, I owe something inexpressible; virtually every word was written with her in mind.

# 1

# INTRODUCTION: RAYMOND ARON
# AND THE DEFENSE OF
# POLITICAL REASON

There is a certain irony in the fact that Raymond Aron's reputation currently is ascendant everywhere except in the English-speaking world, since for many years his sober defense of political reason was received far more favorably there than in his native France.[1] The resurgence of philosophical rigor and political responsibility among the Parisian intelligentsia, led by Pierre Manent, Luc Ferry, Alain Renaut, Marcel Gauchet, and many other philosophers, social scientists, and historians, owes much to Aron's lifelong resistance to the temptation toward totalitarianism and the literary politics that usually attended that temptation.[2] Aron is now recognized by the French as the preeminent political thinker of the postwar years.

Aron's achievement was truly remarkable. Among modern political thinkers his work stands out both for its range and for its quantity. The breadth of his work is staggering: it covers numerous disciplines, from the philosophy of history and the critique of ideology to sociology and nuclear strategy; from political economy to the study of power in international relations. Though intellectual life throughout the twentieth century has been characterized by fragmentation and specialization, Aron consistently resisted such tendencies, harking back to an older tradition of reflection that sought to organize and integrate the disparate facts of the human world under the umbrella of reason. At the same time, Aron recognized the impossibility of accomplishing any final synthesis and noted the sharp limits to the power of reason to gather together the varied dimensions of human learning and experience. He was,

1

after all, a participant in a twentieth century that gave birth to monsters both rationalist and irrationalist and that forever bore witness to the dangers of any attempt to build utopia with the hands and tools of mortal men and women.

As for the quantity of his work, Aron published during his lifetime over forty books, along with countless articles and editorials—enough, as his former student Stanley Hoffmann has written, to drive "his commentators and disciples to despair."[3] But whether writing on the philosophy of history, the critique of Marxist and leftist ideology, peace and war, or the nature of the liberal democratic regime, it is in part the *consistency* of Aron's thought, as well as its analytical rigor and lucidity, that make it of continuing relevance. This rigor, and the deep meditation on the nature of politics that grew out of it, prevented Aron from succumbing to the seduction of totalitarianism that mesmerized so many intellectuals in our time; it thus provided the basis for his disenchanted conservative liberalism during a period when such a sober viewpoint had few friends.[4]

It is for these various reasons, intrinsic to his stature as one of the century's giants of political reflection, that I have undertaken the following study of Aron's thought. There is another reason, however, and it relates to the state of contemporary political theory, particularly in its Anglo-American form. Liberal theorists (but not just liberal theorists) operating in the long shadow cast by John Rawls's *A Theory of Justice*, have developed a method of reflection on politics that distances itself from the *reality* of political life, resulting in an abstractness in much contemporary political theory—its divergence from the common understandings of citizens and statesmen that make up the texture of the political and human world in our time and in any time.[5] That is, Rawls, Ronald Dworkin, and their many students have developed a model of thinking about politics often sundered from political, economic, and social reality, undermining the mutuality of theory and practice.[6] This is the case even though many of these theorists have addressed, often with theoretical rigor, current political and moral controversies (i.e., international justice). They have done so, however, by abstracting away from convictions alive in the human and political world, preferring to operate through a jurisprudential or rationally deductive model of political philosophy often contemptuous of common understandings as expressed in the reality of political life. It would be only a slight exaggeration to refer to contemporary liberal political theory as political theory without politics.

One of the underlying tasks throughout the chapters below will be to bring out what is essential to Aron's work: its distinctively *political* nature, Aron's *defense of political reason*. Aron's recovery of the political provides an articulation of theory and practice, an understanding of the role and method of political theory, and a historically based defense of the liberal democratic regime that is at least a partial corrective to the methodological and political inadequacies of the main currents of contemporary political theory. Two problems obviously need further elaboration for this belief in Aron's continuing relevance to take on the appropriate weight: First, what, exactly, is meant by "political reason" and how is it exemplified by Aron's thought? Second, in what way has contemporary political theory rendered itself so unpolitical? The former question will be our focus in the remainder of this introduction. The latter will be addressed in the concluding chapter, where Aron's disenchanted conservative liberalism is confronted by contemporary political thought.

## 1. WHAT IS POLITICAL REASON?

What does it mean to *think politically*, to defend political reason?[7] How did Aron embody this stance and how does it provide the interpretive key to his work, allowing him to avoid the errors of so many of his contemporaries as well as a later generation of thinkers? These are questions we will address in a preliminary way now and will flesh out in later chapters.

Aron's first real experience with politics took place when he was a young scholar, making a teaching sojourn in Germany during the 1930s. What he saw there shook forever his faith in the naive rationalist liberalism of his teachers Leon Brunschvicg and Alain (Emile Chartier). Both were progressivist representatives of the rationalist philosophy dominant in pre-World War II France. Brunschvicg was a philosopher of science, convinced of the march of human progress toward a rational future; Alain, a fierce moralist, deeply suspicious of the compromises and "dirty hands" of politics. Neither thinker helped Aron grasp what was happening in Germany during the rise of Nazism. As he was to recall later,

"Once and for all, I ceased to believe that history automatically obeys the dictates of reason or the desires of men of good will."[8] Brunschvicg's Kantian rationalism and the overt moralism of Alain were inadequate in the face of the irrational political forces that would soon sweep away Europe, then the world. Other methods were needed, and the political world would have to be examined for what it *was*, not confused with what we might hope it to be.

The method Aron adopted to grapple with the political upheavals of his age is expressed succinctly in his reply to the journalist Dominique Wolton, who interviewed Aron almost a half century after his German experience. Wolton had queried Aron about the meaning of a comment he made earlier in the interview, in referring to Merleau-Ponty, Sartre, and other French radical philosophers, that the left failed to "think politically." Here is Aron:

> It [their failure to think politically] means two things. First, they prefer ideology, that is, a rather literary image of a desirable society, rather than to study the functioning of a given economy, of a liberal economy, of a parliamentary system, and so forth . . . And then there is a second element, perhaps more basic: the refusal to answer the question someone once asked me: "if you were in the minister's position, what would you do"?[9]

Together, these two conditions, here negatively expressed, form the foundation of political reason; they amount to the "categorical imperative" of Aron's entire project.

The first condition can be reconstructed as follows. Aron held that if one wanted to adequately conceptualize the political, it was essential, above all, to avoid "literary" politics. By literary politics Aron meant a manner of engaging with political life that deliberately or otherwise ignored reality and that preferred to remain on the level of an abstract theory or a kind of pure, contentless moralizing. The archetypal example of such thinking—which can be seen as a kind of intellectual solipsism—is found in the political writings of Jean-Paul Sartre, who dismissed empirical analysis entirely and replaced it with his prodigious imagination.

The double standard practiced by Sartre and other radical theorists was marked, Aron felt, by bad faith: Western societies were excoriated for their every injustice (and what society, Aron would ask, has not been unjust?) while the socialist world was judged on the basis of its ostensibly good *intentions*.[10] The radical philosophers failed to understand the constraints and dangers—and the awesome responsibility—of politics. Neither the functioning of democratic capitalism nor that of "actually existing socialism" was deemed worthy of investigation by Sartre or Maurice Merleau-Ponty. Yet it remained tellingly the case that Sartre would have had no adoring public were he ever to have found himself, through some terrible misfortune, behind the Iron Curtain. More likely, so Aron believed, Sartre would have been sent, like so many other independent minds, to the Gulag.[11]

Implied by this rejection of literary or ideological politics is Aron's rejection of utopian speculation: Aron does not provide a model of the good society, nor does he specify in any dogmatic way the principles according to which such a society might be built. As political philosopher Pierre Manent has noted, "Aron's point of departure is what our societies say about themselves, the ideals which they profess, principally liberty and equality."[12] Instead of assuming the reconciliation of these principles—ideals opened up and extended by the democratic revolutions of the nineteenth century—Aron explored their meaning, how they might conflict, where conflict is unavoidable. Manent adds, this method of analysis "moderates the exaggerated hopes born of the illusion of being able to multiply in all circumstances the advantages of liberty by those of equality."[13] Aron's refusal of literary politics pushed him in the direction of a phenomenology of political life.

There are two important points worth making at this stage. First, Aron's approach suspends or brackets the broader, and more deeply philosophical, question of what is the best regime. While he referred from time to time to a Kantian ideal of a reconciled society, this ideal remained completely formal—so formal that it served as only a minimal universal (that is, certain societies can be rejected as inhuman without positing a model of an ideal society). Aron was not unaware that a distorted version of the same ideal—the reconciliation of man with man—had also been at the core of one of the twentieth century's worst barbarisms, and was often used by Merleau-Ponty, among others, to exculpate those responsible for that barbarism. Similar to two of his intellectual heroes, Montesquieu and Tocqueville, Aron had too profound a sense of the diversity of history to admit easily to a strong notion of an ideal society or best regime, or to succumb to the extreme generalities favored by literary political thinkers.

In this we can offer a slight disagreement with Allan Bloom's otherwise perceptive reading of Aron. Bloom argues that Aron "was persuaded of the truth of the theory of liberalism, that for him its practice was not only the best available alternative but the best simply, and that his personality fully accorded with his liberal beliefs."[14] While the first and third parts of Bloom's statement are correct, the second—that liberalism was "the best simply"—goes too far, although under modern conditions Aron would surely agree. But to suspend the question of the best regime does not, after all, entail that one cannot draw distinctions between actually existing regimes regarding their effects on human flourishing. Again showing his affinity with Montesquieu, Aron was keenly aware of political *evil* and dedicated himself to opposing it, and to exposing the lies through which it gained its hold over human sensibilities. In this, Aron's liberalism might be seen as similar to Judith Shklar's "liberalism of fear," where the goal of liberal institutions is primarily negative: to mitigate those myriad obstacles—ineradicable in any absolute sense because of the human propensity to vice—to living a decent human life, but to refrain from any comprehensive metaphysical view of human nature.[15] This rendering of the purpose of political institutions is to understand politics as, in Kenneth Minogue's apt description, "the activity by which the framework of human life is sustained; it is not life itself."[16]

Aron was not a relativist, and his "skepticism" has usually been overstated. Indeed, it would make a mockery of Aron's entire intellectual career, his defense of the achievable goods of the common human world against the surreality of the utopians, to see him as a philosophical skeptic. Aron's bracketing of the question of the best regime does mark a difficulty, however, and raises the question of the philosophical status of Aron's reflection. Leo Strauss, the philosopher who provided the most enduring and powerful critique of the entire tenor of modern political thought, argued that for political philosophy to be possible, a distinction between the real and the ideal must be made—a distinction whose coherence, he believed, had decisively collapsed as a result of the subjectivist and historicist erosion brought about by the upheavals of modernity.

Strauss held that if we are constructing our own "values," or if they are solely a product of historical contingency and refer to no natural order of the world, then the idea of the best regime dissolves. If the best regime no longer exists in thought, however, then political thinking can only be pragmatic. In the end, Machiavelli or Nietzsche triumphs over Aristotle.[17] The only alternative for the political thinker, on Strauss's view, is to return to ancient thought—the classical teaching of natural right—where the possibility of distinguishing the real and the ideal, the "is" and the "ought," will once again make sense against the backdrop of a conception of human nature richer, and more morally laden, than that available to moderns. While Aron was sensitive to this argument, and indeed sympathetic to a degree with it (he admitted, for example, that the question of the best regime, *pace* positivistic social science, retained meaning and was ultimately inseparable from man's political nature), he refused to take the step into the realm of pure political philosophy as understood by Strauss.[18]

In Aron's judgment, the answer to Nietzsche and Marx had to be advanced *politically*; thus his defense of political reason was concerned, above all, with enlightening the conditions of *political practice*. While Marx himself saw his project as doing exactly that, the essential turns on how political practice is actually understood. For Aron, it was crucial to take seriously the role of the political actor, something Marx viewed as secondary or even *un*essential. The political thinker who abandoned the playing field of politics was of little help to statesman or citizen; he failed, in Allan Bloom's evocation, "to understand the political beast."[19] Although Aron's political philosophy was not fully developed or articulated, however, it remains implicit: there *is* a conception of the common human world, natural goods, and a "thin" view of human nature—in short, a positive teaching—that can be found in his work. Even as he avoided the metaphysical controversies which are inseparable from premodern thought—as in controversies over different "thick" conceptions or images of human nature—Aron's phenomenological description of the political world allowed him to reconnect with the various frameworks through which our humanity is expressed and thus enabled him to orient thought and action in a way far more in keeping with the goods of our common human world than could be found among most of his contemporaries.[20]

The second point is that Aron's suspension of the philosophical question of the best regime rests in a deep sensitivity to the antinomical structure of the political world, a structure that assures that certain goods cannot be maximally combined. In Aron's words, "every advance in liberation carries the seed of a new form of enslavement."[21] As an example, or series of examples, that captures this antinomical structure, it is sufficient to call to mind the conflicts among the regnant ideals of modern societies. Not only is it the case that liberty and equality are often at odds, but these notions, in turn, are both in tension with another modern ideal: the Promethean demand for the mastery of nature and society. Modern Prometheanism dictates, among other things, economic efficiency and its attendant hierarchical social relations, none of which easily reconciles with equality or liberty.[22] This acknowledgment of the condition of *political scarcity* might be compared fruitfully with the notion of the incommensurability of values associated with philosopher Isaiah Berlin.

Berlin, in a series of influential studies, rejects what he views to be the dominant illusion of the Enlightenment: that a rational morality and a science of politics can be either discovered or constructed. Ultimate goods, on Berlin's view, conflict with each other and cannot be combined in a single life or single society.[23] Berlin professes that there is no standard whereby the claims of ultimate "values" could be rationally arbitrated, and thus such conflicts are conflicts among incommensurables. This means, however, that we are forced to make tragic choices in political life, that no choice is without loss, and that the Enlightenment project, at least in its most hubristic construals, is rooted in an insupportable mystification. Aron departed from Berlin, nonetheless, in his refusal to abandon a reasonable foundation for political moderation—"prudence, 'the god of this world below'"—when confronted with such tragic dilemmas.[24] An *accurate* description of the common human world told Aron that tragic conflict was not unamenable to the moderating influence of reason. While tragedy could not be abolished, its impact, and its frequency, could be limited. This difference between Aron and Berlin is of some interest, and we shall explore it in our concluding chapter.

As noted above, the rejection of literary politics requires the patient empirical study of existing institutions and regimes. Without such an effort, political thought remains detached from historical, political, and social reality and hopelessly abstract. Aron often made the observation that most twentieth-century Marxists, particularly of the French variety, had abandoned the study of economic, social, and political reality and replaced it with philosophical formulas derived from Marx. Perhaps the most instructive example of this type of *ideological* thinking can again be found in the political writings of Jean-Paul Sartre, writings whose influence was for a time extensive, not just in France but throughout the world. Aron was much more of a Marxist, if to be a Marxist meant to analyze economic, social, and political reality, than Sartre, Louis Althusser or, for that matter and writing out of a different tradition, analytic Marxists G. A. Cohen and John Roemer, whose work, while philosophically more exacting and clear than Sartre's or Althusser's, remains just as distant from the most powerful truths and dilemmas of our time.[25]

Aron's study of the nature of modern industrial societies led him to dramatically different conclusions than those Marx anticipated would hold as capitalism made its long march through the institutional and social life of the West. The concept of industrial society, for which Aron is often remembered, included several components: the scientific organization of work; the necessity to invest; the desire to increase productivity and pursue economic growth.[26] It served Aron well as an analytical tool, demystifying the Marxist-inspired regimes of their radical otherness and disenchanting the magical politics of the radical French intelligentsia by setting up a ground for comparison between the liberal democratic capitalist world and that of actually existing socialism. A comparison of the two species of industrial society—the Western and the Soviet—quickly revealed feasibility constraints to economic and political organization that limited the realm of the politically viable, ignorance of which rendered political thought insensible and potentially ruinous. It also revealed something else: that the fundamental difference between modern societies, all sharing traits from the standpoint of industrial organization, rested on the *political regime*. Aron's defense of the dignity and importance of politics grew in part out of a painstaking and multileveled empirical analysis of modern society.

We have been looking at several of the implications contained in the first of the two conditions of political reason forwarded by Aron in response to the questioning of Dominique Wolton. In particular, we have focused on the rejection of utopianism; the bracketing of the question of the best regime; the acknowledgment of the tragic conflicts which often rend the fabric of the political world; and the necessity for concrete analysis of the conditions of modern political life. But what of the *second* condition suggested by Aron in the passage quoted above?

Aron described it as "more basic" than what we have been exploring. To recall it now, the second condition requires the following: when one thinks about politics, when one seeks to *think politically*, it is essential to ask the question: "If I were in the Prince's position, what would *I* do?"[27] We might call this the *principle of political responsibility*.[28] This deceptively simple question opens on to the entire problematic of political judgment, the philosophy of history, and the theory of action.

It is worthwhile to trace the biographical motivation for Aron's adoption of this principle, which can be found in his *Memoirs*. In 1932, Aron was introduced by a well-placed friend to an undersecretary in the French Foreign Ministry. He sought to convey his anxiety over political developments in Germany, which he had witnessed first hand. The young Aron, filled with intellectual passion, in possession of the formidable education of a student from the École Normale Supérieure, and fresh from Germany, proceeded to deliver what was no doubt a superbly crafted lecture to the undersecretary. The reply he received, polite but devastating, would stick. As Aron remembered it, his interlocutor responded:

> Meditation is essential. Whenever I find a few moments of free time, I meditate. So I am grateful to you for having given me so many subjects for meditation. The prime minister, minister of foreign affairs, possesses exceptional authority, he is a man out of the ordinary. The moment is ripe for all initiatives. But you, who have spoken so well about Germany and the dangers appearing on the horizon, what would you do if you were in his place?[29]

*What would you do if you were in his place?* This question would be the first question Aron would ask, both himself and of others, whenever political judgment was required. Bloom referred to it as Aron's "statesmanlike prudence."[30] From this early moment of his adult life on through to his death in 1983, Aron would uphold the imperative of political responsibility—to put himself in the position of those confronted with fateful political decisions; to place himself at once *within* political life and at the same time, in Aristotelian fashion, attempt to see *further* than its contending participants. Elsewhere in the *Memoirs*, Aron underscored this pivotal idea: "To think about politics is to think about political agents, hence to analyze their decisions, their goals, their means, their mental universe."[31] Much is contained within this imperative or principle, so let us expand on it in an effort to grasp exactly what Aron means.

First of all, to think about politics in a responsible way comprises, among other things, a theory of action. Action is at the heart of politics but carries an essential *incertitude*: it depends on human choice and thus is not yet real but only possible. Manent has perceived clearly the problem as formulated by Aron: "he asks himself what kind of theory will enable us to understand and shed light upon action without falling into doctrinairism which dissolves the incertitude and therefore the liberty of action in a false necessity or rationality but without admitting either that the world of action is pure confusion unamenable to reason."[32] There are two enemies that Aron wanted at all costs to avoid in theorizing action, the heart of politics; both render political thought impossible. The first assumes that human choice—action—is entirely determined in advance, that freedom is only a mirage, and that the *real* stakes are elsewhere, in the economy, or in the unconscious, or in the "social," or in any of the other subpolitical determinants which have so often been evidenced in modern reflection as characterizing the life, particularly the political life, of man. The second ascribes a radical freedom to human action, assuming that the world of action is solely what we make of it, that reason is only a mask for power, and that "truth" is nothing more than what we construe it to be. Between determinism and relativist nihilism—the twin doctrinairisms that have dominated philosophical thought in this century—Aron sought a middle way, the *only* legitimate way for genuine political thought. As Manent comments, Aron "wants to reconquer the field of practical philosophy or practical reason, not by a return to the Aristotelian doctrine but by using the conceptual tools forged by those authors whom we might situate on the frontier between philosophy and social science, such as Montesquieu or Max Weber."[33] Between determinism and relativism, then, what Aron sought was a theory of *reasonable action*. The very asking of the question, "what would I do in the minister's place?" is an admittance that reasonable action is possible, that human *freedom* is possible. To place oneself in the Prince's or the citizen's place, however, is to recognize that freedom is also *constrained*, that the number of choices or options available to the political actor is not unlimited. This in turn leads us to another implication of political reason and to Aron's writings in the philosophy of history.

Aron's philosophy of history, or, more appropriately, his attempt to determine the *limits* of historical objectivity, is bound up with the quest to identify the conditions for reasonable political action. In order to determine the range of political options available to the Prince or citizen, one has to ask what of history it is conceivable to *know*. Aron's first major work, *Introduction to the Philosophy of History*, which we will look at in depth in the next chapter, contains certain ideas that would mark his thinking from then on. The project of the *Introduction* was to move from reflection on the limits of theoretical objectivity in historical knowledge to the question of action. In this dense book, Aron rejected on the epistemological level *both* Hegelian or Marxist determinism—philosophical systems that presume to know the history of the world in advance—*and* Nietzschean relativism, where historical knowledge is replaced with a perspectivism that denies all epistemological warrant to historical truth. The first approach swept away human freedom in a torrent of historical force, although it retained, in a dogmatic fashion, a certain conception of historical truth; the second rendered freedom meaningless by untethering it from any substantive content.

The sociologist J. A. Hall has argued that Aron, in rejecting these two alternatives, placed himself between Isaiah Berlin's "hedgehog and fox."[34] Berlin's classification, borrowed from the Greek poet Archilochus, describes "hedgehogs" as striving to interpret everything by locating phenomena within an all-embracing system. A "fox," on the other hand, operates descriptively. In Berlin's account, the fox "expresses himself in many directions, as the spirit takes him."[35] Hall's assessment is basically sound: Aron's philosophy of history involved discerning the historical necessities, often massive, that constrain human choice in order to articulate the degrees of freedom available to the political actor and to render the contingencies of decision less onerous. The unique historical condition of man for Aron was that both determinism and relativism were exaggerated, *epistemologically* and *practically*. The political actor was free but limited in his freedom; the interpreter of history was capable of attaining *partial* knowledge of an *indeterminate* history. Aron's *probabilistic* philosophy of history was therefore in the service of his moderating defense of political reason against the twin threats of determinism and relativism.

Before concluding this introductory chapter with a brief outline of what follows, there is one important question relating to Aron's defense of political reason that has yet to be initially addressed. This is the difficult, even intractable problem of the relationship between ethics and politics, a problem coextensive with political thought. Aron refused to collapse politics and ethics. Ancient philosophers regarded prudence as the root of virtue, and prudence in politics requires sensitivity to context, to the historical, personal, and social setting of the moral act. Aron distanced himself from Max Weber (whose influence on him was otherwise so profound) by rejecting the distinction between the ethics of conviction and the ethics of responsibility.[36] In the ethics of conviction, the ethical actor, whether revolutionary or pacifist, does what he will *regardless* of the consequences. In the ethics of responsibility, on the other hand, the actor recognizes that consequences must be taken into account, whether by citizen or by statesman. Weber gave us no means of preferring one to the other in the political domain. All values are for Weber a matter of irrational choice: the revolutionary madman chooses his demon, the Churchillian Prince his, and never the twain shall meet. Aron could not accept this, although his study of Weber often pressured him to do so, particularly in his earliest writings on the philosophy of history. As we later see, Aron came to the conclusion that while Weber was correct in seeing the radical plurality of values on the level of sociological observation, he was wrong to turn this into a nihilistic political philosophy. The ethics of responsibility, and the political moderation it carries, describe the day-to-day hopes and conflicts of men better than do the ethics of conviction.

Aron's prudence was not that of St. Thomas Aquinas, however. Aron was critical, for example, of Jacques Maritain's Thomistic (or better, Thomas inspired) understanding of the common good as the appropriate benchmark for the conduct of the statesman, rejecting it as too unrealistic, too destructively naive for the time of Hitler and Stalin.[37] Aron believed that there was finally an antinomy between justice and success, and that the lessons of Machiavelli could not be dismissed easily by the prudent statesman. Maritain's politics of the common good, Aron argued, depended on the primacy of domestic over foreign policy. But the political was not ruled by the domestic. There were, are, and indeed will be extreme situations in which statesmen, haunted by the clash between principle and necessity, must justify the means by virtue of the ends in order to preserve the existence of the regime. While Aron did not begin, as did Machiavelli, from those extreme situations, he was convinced that political thought had to be aware of their possibility. Any viable political ethics would thus have to be attentive to the possible consequences of political choice. Aron is honest enough to admit, however, that there is no theoretical solution to the problem of the relation between politics and ethics. Maritain's accusations of immorality, rooted in natural law, remain relevant. Our fourth chapter will examine these problems at greater length.

We have pursued in this introductory discussion the various aspects of Aron's defense of political reason. As we have seen, the conditions of political reason and their implications form the nucleus of Aron's political thought. These themes will remain present throughout the detailed textual exploration of Aron's major works that follows. Before we begin that exploration, however, it is appropriate to present an outline of the remaining chapters.

Our effort to grasp the essence of Aron's political thought in light of the above considerations will begin with chapter 2, "From the Philosophy of History to Political Reason," in an investigation of Aron's *Introduction to the Philosophy of History* and other writings on historical epistemology. Aron's first major work is designed as a methodological primer for political thought, and we will assess the strengths and weaknesses of Aron's epistemological position. The interpretation will reveal that Aron does not completely succeed in the *Introduction* in avoiding the Nietzschean threat to historical objectivity and thus the threat to political reason. The chapter will conclude with a critical examination of the various strategies later adopted by Aron in order to overcome the relativist impasse.

The third chapter, "The Critique of Ideology," presents a lengthy treatment of Aron's writings on Marxist and radical leftist ideology, opening with a discussion of Aron's concept of "secular religion," moving through reconstructions of Aron's understanding of the "Marxism of Marx" and twentieth-century Marxism-Leninism, and concluding with Aron's encounter with the Marxist existentialism of Sartre and Merleau-Ponty. Much of Aron's work was critical in nature, and he often defined what it meant to think politically *negatively*, by showing what it meant *not* to act so. Besides offering a thorough presentation of Aron's thought on one of the twentieth century's most destructive ideological movements, Chapter 3 will provide, as though in a set of negative images, the outline of a nonideological approach—what I have called Aron's defense of political reason—to theorizing the political world.

Chapter 4, "Antinomic Prudence," will look at Aron's writings on the life of nations, particularly his magisterial work *Peace and War*, and argue for the superiority of Aron's prudence over either a naive cosmopolitanism or a cynical philosophy of power politics. The study of international relations particularly has been marked by efforts by both realists and idealists to excise or abstract away from politics, so Aron's example is perhaps more convincing here than anywhere else for its political relevance and adequacy. We will also place Aron's antinomic prudence against the backdrop of an older "prudence tradition," revealing what differentiates his prudence from that of his predecessors.

Finally, in our concluding chapter, "Raymond Aron and Contemporary Political Theory," we will situate Aron's disenchanted conservative liberalism within certain currents of contemporary political theory. Drawing on the critique of John Gray, we will discuss *why* recent political thought, particularly Anglo-American liberal theory, is so far removed from the reality of political life, and offer Aron's work as a powerful corrective to that apoliticism. In addition, this discussion will allow us to get a better grip on the distinctiveness of Aron's liberalism, which rests in its deeply political nature. In pursuit of this aim, Aron's thought will be brought into dialogue with that of three other liberal theorists, representing very different perspectives: Friedrich Hayek, Isaiah Berlin, and Francis Fukuyama. First, Aron's critique of Hayek will be developed in order to distinguish the former's political liberalism from the return to classical liberalism of the latter. Second, Aron's conception of the antinomic structure of the political world will be contrasted with Berlin's value-pluralism. Finally, Fukuyama's "end of history" thesis will be criticized from the standpoint of Aron's philosophy of history. In concluding our conclusion, we will briefly ask what Aron understands to be the political responsibility of the intellectual in the post-Marxist era opening before us.

My interpretation will remain, as it has been in this chapter, thematic and not temporal. This poses few problems, for Aron's thought was, as we observed earlier, remarkably consistent over the four decades he served as a "committed observer" of the twentieth century. There were shadings, and occasional self-criticisms, and these will be raised when appropriate, but on the whole the vision that was in place in

Aron's earliest essays was the same in his final writings. In order to keep this work at a reasonable length, certain of Aron's writings will form the basis of the exposition: *Introduction to the Philosophy of History*; *Marxism and the Existentialists*; *Main Currents of Sociological Thought*; *Peace and War*; *An Essay on Freedom*; *Progress and Disillusion*; and *In Defense of Decadent Europe*. We will also consult several books in which Aron's numerous essays have been anthologized, particularly *In Defense of Political Reason* and *Politics and History*. References to other works will be made when necessary.

This book, therefore, can be seen as pursuing three tasks: 1) presenting a reconstruction and overview of Aron's conservative liberalism as a whole; 2) offering an interpretation of the major writings of Aron that ties together his various efforts using the idea of political reason; and 3) furnishing a critique of dominant currents of contemporary political theory for which Aron's thought can be seen as a corrective. I believe that Aron presents one of the most rigorous ways of gaining, in J. A. Hall's phrase, a political "diagnosis" of our time.[38] It has been a time threatened with the horror of totalitarianism and the withering away of the instinct for political existence in the liberal democratic world through relativism and social pathology.

While Aron is probably not, as Bloom feared, "the last liberal," his conservative and deeply political liberalism has lessons to teach anyone interested in the fate of the liberal democratic regime, human freedom, and reason in the modern world. Liberal society is imperfect, as every human society must be.[39] That it is indefensible is something Aron would never admit. Although there is no Aronian "school," a number of thinkers have sprung up around the Centre de recherches politique Raymond Aron and the important journals *Commentaire*, *Le Débat*, and, most recently, *La Pensée politique*. These thinkers, whatever their differences (and some of them are decisive), have begun to explore the paradoxes, imperfections, and possibilities of liberal society in ways inspired by Aron.

Most of all, however, Aron enlightens the universe of the political, a world often forgotten or covered over in recent intellectual endeavor. When much of the contemporary world is struggling to come to terms with the workings of liberal democracy and the paradoxes of liberal civilization and with the dramatic failure of the Marxist project (an off-shoot of the Enlightenment that has run its course with great cost in human suffering), Aron's disenchanted, deeply *political* liberalism offers us a pathway to rethinking our political condition. Aron's recovery of the political offers us a renewal of political thought, and we now turn to measuring the extent of that renewal.

## NOTES

1. Part of this introduction has been adapted from my review essay "The Aronian Renewal" in the journal *First Things*, March 1995, pp. 61–64. I reproduce it here with permission.

2. On Aron's influence on the "New French Thought," as it has been coined, see editor Mark Lilla's inaugural volume to the series sharing that name, *New French Thought: Political Philosophy* (Princeton: Princeton University Press, 1994), particularly his fine introduction, "The Legitimacy of the Liberal Age," pp. 3–34. Suffice to say, the differences among these thinkers are pronounced, and, in the post-Marxist period, they are sure to grow.

3. Stanley Hoffmann, "Raymond Aron and the Theory of International Relations," *International Studies Quarterly*, No. 29, 1985, p. 13.

4. For Aron's hardest-hitting critique of what he called Jean-Paul Sartre's failure to think politically, see the essay "Alexander Solzhenitsyn and European 'Leftism'," in Raymond Aron, *In Defense of Political Reason*, ed. by Daniel J. Mahoney (Lanham, MD: Rowman & Littlefield, 1994), pp. 115–24.

5. Roger Scruton, drawing on the phenomenological tradition, refers to this common understanding as "the human world," a term I will use throughout, along with the "political world," the specifically political dimension to the human world. See *Modern Philosophy: An Introduction and Survey* (London: Sinclair-Stevenson, 1994), pp. 237–50.

6. As political philosopher Blandine Kriegel recently observed, this disappearance of the political was also characteristic, with the notable exception of Aron, of the French intellectual milieu: "Let us be clear: previously there had been no political philosophy . . . politics had been reduced to morality or science. To morality: political discourse took up the engagement against colonialism or class exploitation (Sartre), it taught a doctrine of the person (Mounier), or even, a version for the *happy few*, a metaphysics of dereliction and an anthropology of finitude (Heidegger). . . . Or else it gave itself up to science. . . . The program of the great Cavailles . . . would find its realization in the works of Althusser, of Foucault, of Levi-Strauss, who would dissolve the political problem into an epistemological problem." Kriegel singles out Aron for his resistance to this tendency: "Everything which exists, exists, and politics is a moment both indispensable and unpassable which cannot be avoided. As a moment where

contraries are conciliated, it is anterior to democracy. This pragmatism, reinforced by the quarrels of the Cold War, led Raymond Aron to remind us ceaselessly, invoking the lessons of Machiavelli and Max Weber, that politics is the foundation of pluralism and liberty . . ." Blandine Kriegel, "De la philosophie politique," *magazine litteraire*, No. 339, Jan. 1996, p. 51. (My translation.)

7. See Raymond Aron, *Thinking Politically: A Liberal in the Age of Ideology*, with an introduction by Daniel J. Mahoney and Brian C. Anderson (New Brunswick, NJ: Transaction Publishers, 1997), pp. 154–55.

8. Raymond Aron, *Politics and History*, trans. by M. Conant, with an introduction by Michael Ledeen (New Brunswick, NJ: Transaction Publishers, 1984), p. 65.

9. Aron, *Thinking Politically*, pp. 154–55.

10. See Raymond Aron, *Opium of the Intellectuals*, trans. by T. Kilmartin (New York: Doubleday, 1957). See also Daniel J. Mahoney, *The Liberal Political Science of Raymond Aron* (Lanham, MD: Rowman & Littlefield, 1992), pp. 13–16, 109–10.

11. For a commentary on Sartre, Merleau-Ponty, and other French philosophers during the postwar period, see Tony Judt's *Past Imperfect: French Intellectuals, 1944–1956* (Berkeley: University of California Press, 1993). Judt's book notes correctly that Aron was virtually alone in defending political sanity in French intellectual life and was largely responsible for the recent resurgence of serious French political theory. See also Thomas Pangle, "Political Theory in Contemporary France: Towards a Renaissance of Liberal Political Philosophy?" *PS*, Fall, 1987, p. 1002.

12. See Pierre Manent, "Raymond Aron—Political Educator," introduction to Raymond Aron, *In Defense of Political Reason*, p. 16.

13. Ibid., p. 16.

14. Allan Bloom, *Giants and Dwarfs: Essays 1960–1990* (New York: Simon & Schuster, 1990), p. 262.

15. For a useful collection exploring Shklar's notion, see Bernard Yack, ed., *Liberalism Without Illusions: Essays on Liberal Theory and the Political Vision of Judith N. Shklar* (Chicago: University of Chicago Press, 1996). See as well "The Derelict Utopia" by John Gray in *TLS*, May 24, 1996, p. 29. As I will suggest several times in what follows, there is a view of human nature suggested, but not articulated fully, in Aron's thought.

16. Kenneth Minogue, *Politics: A Very Short Introduction* (Oxford: Oxford University Press, 1996), p. vii.

17. For Strauss's reading of the historicist and relativist drift of modern thought, see his classic *Natural Right and History* (Chicago: University of Chicago Press, 1953). Strauss has not been alone in this reading of modernity. See Alasdair MacIntyre's *After Virtue* (Notre Dame: University of Notre Dame Press, 1984), particularly pp. 121–130.

18. Aron's sympathies with the Straussian critique are evident in the essay "Fanaticism, Prudence, and Faith" in *Marxism and the Existentialists* (New York: Praeger, 1969), pp. 81–108. On Aron's rejection of positivistic social science, which he saw as finally succumbing to a cynical philosophy of man, see *Democracy and Totalitarianism: A Theory of Political Systems*, ed. by R. Pierce (Ann Arbor: University of Michigan Press, 1990), where he writes: "The sociologist does not appear to me to be doomed either to cynicism or to dogmatism. He does not necessarily become a cynic because the political or moral ideas which he calls upon in judging political regimes are part of reality itself. The great illusion of cynical thought, obsessed by the struggle for power, consists in neglecting another aspect of reality: the search for *legitimate* power, for recognized authority, for the *best* regime. Men have never thought of politics as exclusively defined by the struggle for power. Anyone who does not see that there is a 'struggle for power' element is naive; anyone who sees nothing but this aspect is a false realist. The reality which we study is a human one. Part of this human reality is the question relating to the legitimacy of authority." ( p. 24)

19. Bloom, *Giants and Dwarfs*, p. 260.

20. This line of thought was suggested to me by Pierre Manent. See his "Aurel Kolnai: A Political Philosopher Confronts the Scourge of Our Epoch," the introduction to Aurel Kolnai, *The Utopian Mind and Other Papers*, ed. by Francis Dunlop (London: Athlone Press, 1995), pp. xxi–xxiii.

21. Aron, *The Opium of the Intellectuals*, p. 21.

22. For Aron's most extended discussion of Prometheanism, see *An Essay on Freedom* (New York: NAL, 1970). We will return to the idea in our discussion of secular religion in chapter 3.

23. For Berlin's formulation of this thesis, see *The Crooked Timber of Humanity* (New York: Knopf, 1991). John Gray's *Isaiah Berlin* (New York: HarperCollins, 1996), while radicalizing Berlin's construal of value pluralism beyond the point where I believe Berlin would accept it, is an excellent introduction to the range of problems opened up by Berlin and at the same time plaguing his thought.

24. Aron, *Marxism and the Existentialists*, p. 108.

25. For Aron's criticisms of Althusser's abstraction from political economy, see *D'une sainte famille à l'autre: Essais sur les marxismes imaginaires* (Paris: Gallimard, 1969), pp. 69–276. (*Marxism and the Existentialists* is a significantly abridged translation of this book.)

26. See Manent, "Raymond Aron—Political Educator," p. 17. Aron's most sustained treatment of industrial society can be found in *18 Lectures on Industrial Society* (London: Weidenfeld, 1967).

27. I use the term "The Prince" in the traditional sense: to refer to the ultimate source of decision in the political community. Although the advent of

modern democracy has attenuated the Prince's sovereignty, it has not eliminated it. I shall use the term interchangeably with "statesman" throughout.

28. There is more than a passing resemblance between this imperative or condition and Max Weber's "ethics of responsibility," the principal difference being that Weber provided no means of preferring responsibility to conviction—whatever conviction—in political morality, a nihilistic philosophy Aron refused to accept. See his "History and Truth" in *Introduction to the Philosophy of History* (Boston: Beacon Press, 1961), as well as later in this chapter and the next.

29. Raymond Aron, *Memoirs: Fifty Years of Political Reflection*, forward by Henry Kissinger, trans. by G. Holoch (New York: Holmes & Meier, 1990), p. 42.

30. Bloom, *Giants and Dwarfs*, p. 261.

31. Aron, *Memoirs*, p. 58.

32. Manent, "Raymond Aron—Political Educator," p. 14.

33. Ibid., p. 14. Mahoney has explored in detail the relationship of Aron's thought to Aristotle's political science. See *The Liberal Political Science of Raymond Aron*, pp. 137–147.

34. J. A. Hall, *Diagnoses of Our Time* (London: Blackwell, 1981), p. 175.

35. Isaiah Berlin and Ramin Jahanbegloo, *Conversations with Isaiah Berlin* (New York: Scribner's, 1991), p. 189.

36. See the essay "Max Weber and Power Politics" in Aron, *In Defense of Political Reason*, pp. 31–48.

37. See "French Thought in Exile: Jacques Maritain and the Quarrel Over Machiavellianism" in Aron, *In Defense of Political Reason*, pp. 53–63. Maritain's original essay, "The End of Machiavellianism," first appeared in the *Review of Politics*, January 1942.

38. See Hall, *Diagnoses of Our Time*.

39. Bloom's testimony to Aron's greatness is worth recalling: "He worked perpetually with a truly remarkable focus of energy, and his personality was a seamless unity. He must be judged not by any single part of his product but by his whole life—his scholarship, his teaching, his journalism, and his presence itself. One sees in it none of the spectacular metamorphoses so characteristic of intellectuals. He was what he was and, as such, achieved what others talked about all the time, authenticity. He was the living example of the possibility of the democratic personality. Finally all those who cared about freedom were forced to drink at this trough. He was the man who had lived liberal democracy in its best and most comprehensive sense, and to refer to him is to touch ground." *Giants and Dwarfs*, pp. 266–67.

# 2

# FROM THE PHILOSOPHY OF
# HISTORY TO POLITICAL REASON

R aymond Aron's thought, in all of its richness, finds its unity in
the defense of political reason. The imperatives of political reason
enjoin the political thinker to begin, as Aristotle did, from within political life, from the perspective of the citizen or Prince, before moving
beyond, broadening, or balancing those perspectives, just as they demand an attentiveness to questions of feasibility too often ignored by
political theorists. The political thinker must, in Allan Bloom's words,
"always begin from the real situation and goals of the political actors—
how one gets from here to there."[1] The various enemies of political
reason—historicism, radical relativism, models of human nature or the
best regime void of any coherent philosophical anthropology or social
theory—have dominated modern reflection on politics, from Marxism
to the abstractions of the contemporary "liberal versus communitarian"
debate, often at great cost to the cogency of political thought. Aron's
approach to theorizing political life avoids these various difficulties from
the outset by grounding itself in a wide-ranging and philosophically
complex analysis of the nature of historical knowledge, articulated most
explicitly in his earliest writings but present throughout his *oeuvre*.

Aron's exploration of the "conditions of historical objectivity,"
densely argued in his pre-World War II dissertation, *Introduction to the
Philosophy of History*, will be our main focus in this chapter.[2] Central to
grasping the import of the *Introduction* for Aron's later work, and for our
theme of Aron's recovery of the political, is discerning the structural
affinity it establishes between the observer *of* history and the political
actor *in* history. Looking back at the *Introduction* nearly a half-century
later, Aron accentuates exactly this point: "Since I had devoted myself

to the role of committed observer, I owed it to myself to bring into the open the relationship between the historian and the man of action, between the knowledge of history-in-the-making and the decisions that a historical being is condemned to make."[3]

The *Introduction*, Aron's first major work and one of his philosophically most difficult, is, then, best seen as probing from within the often tragic situation of the political actor caught in the grip of history. As we noted in our first chapter, Aron, spurred by the failure of his teachers to adequately grasp the meaning of the frightening events taking place in Germany during the 1930s, would look elsewhere for insight into the tragic nature of politics and history.[4] The cataclysmic events of the Russian Revolution and Adolph Hitler's ascent to power in Germany should have made abundantly clear to any serious observer that, in the war-torn twentieth century, "man's fate" was often determined by politics. Yet the philosophical and sociological thought of Aron's intellectual milieu, a kind of naive liberal progressivism, neglected the political and thus was without the necessary tools to comprehend the major events of the age (just as the leading variants of more contemporary liberal theory have ignored the world-historical events of our time). Aron turned to the more historically minded German sociologists Wilhelm Dilthey and Max Weber as a response to this neglect. These theorists asked questions the French ignored: What is the relationship between actor and observer in history? How does one achieve objectivity, or *can* one achieve objectivity, about the past? What method is most suitable for understanding politics and history? Behind these various questions for Aron was the dilemma faced by citizen and statesman: *what must be done?* Is reasonable political action possible? The political and historical upheavals of the time made such questions unavoidable for the citizen and statesman; if the political thinker was to be faithful to his vocation, he, too, would need to ask them. Two enemies stood in Aron's way: evolutionary determinism and historical relativism.

As Aron often remarked, a theoretical encounter with Marxism (particularly in its Hegelian form) provided the starting point for his reflection:

In Germany, after 1930, I began my intellectual career with a reflection on Marxism. An "advanced thinker" like most of the intellectuals who came out of the Jewish bourgeoisie, I wanted to make a philosophical critique of my political convictions, which I felt to be naive, dictated by the milieu, with no other foundation than spontaneous preferences or antipathies. This critique consisted, and still consists, of two elements: a comparison of the historical perspectives opened by the Marxism of Marx with the actual development of modern society; and an exploration of the relation between history and the one who interprets it, between the historicity of collective institutions and that of the individual.[5]

Aron's response to the problems raised by his critique of Marxism (a critique examined in the next chapter) can be swiftly summarized: If political action is to be reasonable, it is essential to recognize *the limits of our historical and political knowledge* in order to apply that knowledge to our circumstances more effectively, moderately, and humanely.

What Hegelian Marxism brought with it, as the French philosopher Luc Ferry has argued, was the extension of the principle of reason to the whole of the historically real. History is viewed as a continuous process, with each event *necessarily* connected to what proceeds from it by a causal nexus, culminating in a preordained "end of history."[6] The autonomy of political phenomena is then denied, as they are seen as mere "products" of historical development. Freedom, on the Marxist model, can only be the recognition of necessity. Political reason, which requires more of freedom, is thus made impossible and replaced by a "revolutionary science," either eliminating the importance of political judgment entirely, or stipulating the "correct" decision to the political actor. [7] The danger of Marxism lies in conceiving humanity as, in Pierre Manent's evocative formulation, the "Lord of Time," paradoxically bringing together in an unholy alliance the extension of the principle of reason to the totality of history with the idea of controlling and "accelerating" history in order to meet its determined end ahead of schedule.[8] This is the nightmare of Stalinism, finding its germ in the thought of Marx himself.

In what follows, we will see that Aron's stance toward the relationship between the historical observer and the social, political, and historical experience he seeks to grasp, while acknowledging the dangers of extending the principle of reason beyond its legitimate boundaries, does not go as far as to completely dismiss the claims of reason and the prospect of objective knowledge of historical tendencies. The fundamental question is this: Does the rejection of Marxian "revolutionary science" entail the complete abandonment of the principle of reason as it applies to historical or social phenomena? If we were to surrender completely the principle of reason, would we not then become, to borrow Manent's terminology again, the "plaything of Time?"[9] No knowledge of history would be possible, only aesthetic interpretation: history and the social sciences would be nothing more than peculiar forms of literature, reasonable political action left without foundation.

Luc Ferry, in the study referred to above, calls this approach to history the *destruction* of historical reason, and associates it with the thought of Martin Heidegger. In its Heideggerian version, history is seen as a "miracle of Being," in essence inexplicable and beyond control.[10] The historical event cannot be explained in a scientific sense because historical reality is not subject to the principle of reason. History is instead marked by difference and mystery, and the observer's role is contemplative. Hannah Arendt, deeply influenced by Heidegger on this understanding of the principle of reason in history, expresses it clearly:

> Newness is the real of the historian who, unlike the natural scientist concerned with ever-recurring happenings, deals with events which always occur only once. This newness can be manipulated if the historian insists on causality and pretends to be able to explain events by a chain of causes which eventually led up to it. . . . Causality, however, is an altogether alien and falsifying category in the historical sciences.[11]

There is another side to the abandonment of reason in history. In the more activist, Nietzschean version of the renunciation of reason, history is the raw material out of which the creative artist sculpts his work.[12] The historian or social "scientist" becomes an artist. This kind of thinking about reason and history reaches its culmination in the work of the theorist Michel Foucault, who was unafraid to call his historical studies "fictions," however useful they might be as political "interventions."[13] What we see in *this* form of historical relativism is the apotheosis of the *will*: the "plaything of Time," constrained by no truth, turns the tables and plays *with* time, thus becoming the uninhibited, polymorphously perverse "master" of all he surveys.

Whether in its more contemplative Heideggerian guise or in its Nietzschean activist form, we are confronted with the impossibility of political reason. But Aron did not think that this relativist conclusion necessarily followed from the critique of Marxism. The *Introduction to the Philosophy of History* offers the philosophical justification for Aron's position, although Aron's book was haunted by the Nietzschean epistemological relativism it attempted to overcome. It was not until revisiting the subject years later, and moving his thought in a more explicitly Aristotelian direction, that Aron was finally able to exorcise the ghost.

What *means* did Aron employ to ward off these twin threats of historical or evolutionary determinism and historical relativism? How successful were they? What are the implications of Aron's epistemological meditations for political thought? We will address these important questions in what follows, but not before reconstructing Aron's own philosophy of history, which can be called *aleatory* or *probabilistic* determinism.[14] The basic arguments of the *Introduction* rest on an analysis of the two modes of knowing in the social and historical sciences: understanding, or *verstehen*, as it is called in the German historicist tradition, and causal explanation. While the language of Aron's first major work is unfortunately hermetic in a way that might be surprising to those familiar with the clarity of his later writings, it is possible to translate Aron's insights into less arcane formulations. In doing so, we shall first consider Aron's analysis of historical understanding, then take up his critical examination of causal explanation in the study of history and society.

## 1. THE LIMITS OF HISTORICAL OBJECTIVITY: UNDERSTANDING

Advocates of the *verstehen* school hold that knowledge of human phenomena must include consideration of specific characteristics of human beings that separate them from the objects typically studied by the natural sciences. Chief among these characteristics is human consciousness: Human beings are not inert matter, subject only to natural or social forces, but acting, thinking beings. While causal explanation would see man as determined by forces both external and internal, understanding pursues the immanent intelligibility of human action. *Verstehen* views the actions and creations of human beings as meaningful and seeks to communicate with them across time and space. When we read Homer, we try to imagine the world, the very universe, that Odysseus inhabited. Doing so helps us to understand Odysseus, which means, ultimately, recognizing him *as* human, as a member of the human species. Aron, in the following passage from his *Memoirs*, returns to the conception of understanding at work in the *Introduction*:

> Understandings of an action, a work, an institution, share the characteristic of looking for a meaning, and intelligible connections, immanent to the object. I would have accepted the enumerations I find in a working paper by a Norwegian philosopher: objects of understanding are people, their acts and their words, certain products of their acts and their speech, generally the manifestations of the human spirit (painting, sculpture, and the like), finally some objects that are called meaningful, like instruments, tools, and the like. The theory I set forth at the beginning was at the opposite pole from the presumably irrationalist conception of understanding, namely the affective participation of the consciousness in the consciousness of others. I designated understanding as the knowledge of meaning that, immanent in reality, was or could have been thought by those who experienced it or brought it into being.[15]

For Aron, the objects of understanding—the actions and creations of human beings—have an essential historical component. Human consciousness of the past becomes part of the past itself, intertwining the past and present. The implications are considerable: the meaning of an event or a work may take on different aspects from era to era as we ask different questions of it. There is nothing comparable to this interweaving in the natural sciences. A mathematical law, once discovered, is free from the corruption of history; it is outside history and is universal. The central question raised by the *verstehen* school is thus: Does the unique nature of the objects of understanding, their openness to the influence of history, make objectivity difficult or even impossible to establish? Or, put differently, can we understand the meaning of an event or work exactly as understood by the actor or creator?

Aron's analysis of historical understanding proceeds by way of a phenomenological investigation of the various dimensions of historical existence. Manent has captured Aron's intent perfectly: "He describes, classifies and articulates the various fields of human existence in which man finds himself by his essence in direct or indirect relation with Time; so he surveys the several modes by which Time is experienced and known: from the knowledge of oneself to knowledge of others, from the various spiritual universes in which the individual has his place to the plurality of perspectives which are offered to him, as actor and as spectator, as private man, citizen, or historian."[16]

The three dimensions of historical existence in Aron's schema are, then, the following: the past of one's own consciousness; the awareness we can reach of the intentions and motives of other subjects; and the knowledge we can attain of the spiritual universe of society and its institutions and creations. In each case, Aron believes, there is a gap between the lived experience and the way it is apprehended.[17] We will look more closely at each of these dimensions as described by Aron, and add supplemental illustrations of our own, in an effort to make his analysis as clear as possible.

What can the self understand of its own past? If I strive to attain objective knowledge of my own past experience, to what extent is this possible? *Prima facie*, self-knowledge of my past seems unexceptionable. I am usually aware of myself as forming a continuity across time; my past is, after all, my own. On closer examination, however, this identity is not so self-evident. While Aron resists the extremes of Humean skepticism, he recognizes that a complete fusion of consciousness with the past self is impossible: memory is inevitably imperfect, and more important, we can never fully be certain that our past actions are not being perceived, and distorted, on the basis of present circumstances. We are thus led to treat our past selves as objects, partially inaccessible, always retreating from the reflecting self-consciousness in the present. What *can* be done as a way of countering this flight of the self, Aron stresses, is to *reconstruct rationally* what one's past *might* have been. But this reconstruction will depend in part on our view of the future as well as the events of the past. A concrete example will help illustrate Aron's argument.

Let us say that I have led a dissolute life, characterized by alcoholism, debauchery, and mendaciousness. But recently I have made a conversion, leaving behind my many vices. I now live a life far removed from my former bad habits, marked by sobriety, self-possession, and honesty. In short, I have improved my *character*. My perception and judgment of, indeed the meaning *itself* of, the debauched period of my life will inevitably be affected by who I am *now*. Had my conversion not taken place, in other words, I might have endlessly rationalized my behavior, justifying what I felt could be justified, ignoring what I felt could not. With the drama of conversion having taken place, however, my past life takes on new meaning. I might resolutely condemn it, or see it as a necessary preparation for my recent self-transformation; either way, the meaning of my past is transformed. It may even be difficult to recognize my past self as the same person. Aron captures perfectly this dialectic between past and future in the following passage from the *Introduction*:

> It is not granted to us to know ourselves completely, as long as we seek the inaccessible goal of exhausting the exploration of an incomplete being. The self, a sum of our ways of life, always escapes us partially because it is not yet fixed. It continues to live and change. But we are always capable of possessing ourselves because we can determine ourselves. And, as a matter of fact, any grasp of consciousness is efficacious, our judgment of our past behaviour is part of ourselves and influences our future. Knowledge of self does not aim at an ideal of pure contemplation: to know oneself is to define what one wants to be and to strive to attain one's concept of oneself.[18]

Self-knowledge, then, develops on the basis of a never-finished renewal of the past and a never completely free decision regarding the future. The individual, on Aron's view, is defined by this double effort at "lucidity and creation." But beyond that double effort, the past *itself* changes its meaning as time progresses. There is a danger of radical skepticism afoot here that Aron, at least in the *Introduction*, would have difficulty avoiding. If there is no "end point," can we ever be sure that lucidity has been achieved? Could not my present self be rationalizing as well? As we will see later in this chapter, Aron was to draw back from the more relativistic implications of his early work in epistemology. He did so by recognizing a certain natural pre-articulation of the historical world (what we have elsewhere referred to as the human world) that rendered these skeptical analyses too abstractly philosophical, too removed from what can be called common sense. But we shall return to this.

We have just seen that, for Aron, the understanding of the past of one's own consciousness is limited by an irreducible temporality and an inevitable reconstructive dimension. Any complete autobiography of a life, in other words, is impossible. But what about understanding the meanings associated with other individuals? What can one know of the intentions and consciousness of the *other*? Is complete understanding between two individuals possible in a way that it is not with one's own past?

In Aron's view, understanding is also marked by uncertainties in this dimension of historic existence. While we can seek to understand partially our own past with the help of memory, this tool is obviously not available when we attempt to understand the other, whether in the past or present. We know the experiences of others only through various objectifications. Let us return for a moment to my imagined past self, as discussed above, and picture that, during a particularly self-destructive binge, a good friend confronts me with what appears to be great anger, heaping scorn and abuse on me and perhaps even striking my face. This harsh treatment from a good friend is enough to break the self-destructive pattern into which I had fallen; it is, in fact, the beginning of the conversion that changed the meaning of my life.

But perhaps I meet this friend, a few years later, and he explains to me that his anger on the earlier occasion was feigned, that the entire incident was designed to do exactly what it did, shake me out of my complacent, self-destructive spiral. What, then, was the objective meaning of my friend's angry behavior? Was it the meaning I originally gave it, derived from my observation of angry speech, the experience of stinging pain from a slapped face? Or was it, rather, the account later given by my friend, where his retrospective elucidation serves as the objectification? Perhaps the answer is somewhere in between: his solicitous deception may have also contained real elements of malice, either conscious or unconscious to my friend. It should be clear from this example that intersubjective understanding (and communication) is at least opaque; when the other we seek to understand exists in the past, the problem is exacerbated. Without laying bare the system of symbols, the knowledge, and conceptions of good and evil that structure the mind of the other, perfect understanding remains impossible. Given that such a laying bare is a potentially endless task, understanding the other will never be free from opacity and possible misunderstanding.[19] This is even more powerfully the case when the other belongs to a cultural world far removed from that of the observer.

Yet there always exists, Aron believes, at least a minimum of community between self and other that makes *some* kind of understanding possible. Earlier, in our opening chapter, we briefly touched upon the tension in Aron's thought between the universal and particular; we see another example of that tension here, in the earliest of his writings, with the positing of a common human nature underlying the cultural and temporal plurality confronted by the interpreter. This minimal universal is what makes possible our ability to recognize the purpose of an ancient artifact—for example, a bowl from a prehistoric epoch—as a meaningful human creation. It is what enables us to read Homer and understand Odysseus's thirst for revenge as a typically human reaction, not the deportment of a different species. But, as Aron writes in the *Introduction*, the unity of human nature manifests itself in many different historically and culturally mediated ways.

We encounter a form of understanding, for example, in *affective communication*. When I am in a crowd at an exciting sports event or at a moving performance of Mahler's Fourth Symphony, I can feel myself being swept away with the other spectators or listeners. This is a relatively benign form of affective communication. A much darker version would be the contagion that grips a mob whipped into a frenzy by a demagogue, a form of affective communication that, in the case of Germany, swept away an entire nation (an example not far from Aron's concerns while he wrote the *Introduction*). At the other extreme, Aron argues, we can also find understanding in *intellectual communication* through the use of *language*. Even if the other is far distant in time and forbidding in cultural difference, language can serve to reduce the distance and bring the other closer to the same. When the other is present, the sharing of meaning becomes less difficult since questions can be asked and answers hopefully received.

A third source of community exists in the *shared practices* that constitute what Aron calls *"active collaboration."* As a familiar example of active collaboration, we can call to mind a policeman's raised hand in busy traffic: we understand this gesture as a signal to stop. Such participation in a web of shared intentionality, and we could think of a thousand other examples from daily life, allows a *tendency* toward understanding the other. We share a prereflective way of life, a human world, that makes such practical interpretations commonplace. All of these sources point for Aron to a shared human nature: we use language, exist prereflectively through shared practices, and experience shared emotional responses to the world. Any fully human being will exhibit, at one time or another, familiarity with these phenomena. They all serve to limit the relativity of historical understanding.

But in spite of the universality represented by these various sources, Aron's argument in the *Introduction* rests on the conviction that there is ultimately no fusion of consciousness with the other that allows a completely transparent transfer of meaning. Beyond the fields of active, intellectual, and affective communication, one runs up against the wall of the psychological. In the quest to understand fully the actions of another, we encounter the possibility of an infinite regression: How could all of the psychological antecedents of an act be traced? Any understanding of the other that requires the introduction of the psychological dimension for full comprehension must be the result, at least in part, of the rational reconstruction of character. Any such rational reconstruction, however, inevitably implies something lost or transfigured. As Aron somewhat grimly puts it:

> We know the essential character of an individual no more than we understand the ultimate intention of an act. The only construct that can be called universally valid according to a given theory is the psychologist's: it conforms to both the facts and the established generalities. Beyond this essentially limited interpretation no truth is even conceivable. God alone could weigh the value of all our deeds, put contradictory episodes in their places, unify character and behavior. The idea of this absolute truth must vanish along with theology. It is not a question of denying the capability of the mind, but of discarding a fiction in order to describe the conflict of perspectives and the dispute between the self and others. The knowledge of others is neither more nor less privileged than is self-knowledge; it moves towards a goal situated at infinity, but in contrast with the positive sciences it is always open to question. Just as every individual transfigures his own past, so does the painter transfigure his model, and the biographer his hero.[20]

For Aron, then, understanding the other is as full of epistemological uncertainty as is the self's understanding of its own past. The possibility of universally valid knowledge in these two areas—a complete transparency of meaning—is limited by an irreducible dimension of mystery; some degree of interpretation, invariably influenced by the subjectivity of the interpreter, is unavoidable.

Thus far, we have considered Aron's views on self-understanding and understanding the other's consciousness. But removing these two dimensions of historical experience from their embeddedness in a social and cultural matrix can seem unnecessarily abstract. Preceding both the individual and the other, there is, Aron argues, a *collective* reality (an "objective spirit") made up of the institutions and identifications of the community.[21] This collective reality is transcendent to and immanent within individuals; it consists of the various representations that form the fabric of a culture, a "way of life." It is transcendent to the individual in that, while he is part of it, its full reality goes far beyond what he can know of it or participate in; it is immanent in that the community provides the interpretive categories through which he discovers who he is and from which he draws in seeking to answer questions about the meaning of existence. While the historical observer can perceive patterns in this fabric, or even achieve a sense of the whole garment, the fabric remains inexhaustible and elusive, at the limit exceeding the powers of human comprehension. As Aron describes it, this collective reality is "multiple, incoherent, without definitive unity or certain limits."[22]

But to fully understand one's own past, or that of the other, past or present, we must refer to common representations and explore the spiritual universes that give meaning to human activities. Returning to the example used earlier, if, following my "conversion," I want to grasp the meaning of my past history, I am of necessity led to my upbringing. Perhaps my self-destructive behavior had its roots in a sense of emotional distance from my parents and my (possibly confused) impression that they loved my older brother more than me. But familial history does not occur in a void: The family is in part a cultural artifact. Economic difficulties may have constrained the time my parents could spend with me as a child; or, alternatively, maybe there had been within my extended family a tradition of emotional reserve still present in the attitudes and predispositions of my parents. All this is to say that in seeking to understand our own past, we are inexorably led to numerous factors of a psychological, political, economic, or sociological type—to the historical experience of collective reality. Where the line should be drawn in reaching a satisfactory understanding of one's own behavior is difficult, but not impossible, to determine. (In many cases, we can stop far short of a complete account and understand our own behavior, or the behavior of another, with sufficient probability as to view the discernment as more or less determinate, with a *complete* account opening onto a potentially interminable investigation.)

When I strive to understand my friend's behavior I am similarly confronted (depending, of course, on what I seek to understand), with the plurality of historical existence. In order to grasp the meaning of a single action, whether the action of my friend or the decision of a statesman, it is necessary to place it within a larger context, where, in certain cases, there is no *a priori* limit to the enlargement of that context. It is important to stress that Aron's analysis remains on the transcendental level of ascertaining the *conditions of possibility* of historical knowledge; there is an obvious, and natural, gap between the transcendental analysis of understanding and its *practice*. As Sylvie Mesure has emphasized, the latter remains far short, and rightly so, of what the transcendental idea requires. In general, an action is considered understood when meaning is recognized. But the *potential* meaning of an action is not, at least on the level of transcendental analysis, exhausted by this initial recognition.[23] Historical reality possesses a multiplicity and richness for the historical observer that is virtually limitless.

The task of interpreting collective reality must not, Aron warns, give rise to metaphysical notions of "national souls" or collective consciousness. These organic metaphors, when viewed as in some way substantial—extended from the descriptive to the ontological—have resulted in atrocities our century is all too familiar with. Understanding an individual action refers the observer to collective reality; interpreting collective reality refers the observer to the acts and creations of individuals.

This problem of the *hermeneutic circle* is seen as a difficulty by Aron, but not an insoluble one, since the circle is not vicious. The "coming and going" between individual and society as terms of reference in the quest for understanding is unavoidable, but it is a far from empty exercise; indeed, it is the historic condition of humanity. The existence of a certain shared human nature makes understanding a promise, sometimes partially fulfilled, sometimes broken, but always possible. Aron would later, in his study of the thought of Clausewitz, moderate the pathos of his description of the hermeneutic circle in the *Introduction*, although the underlying argument remains the same:

> There are some people who retort that the historian loses himself in a
> vicious circle between the age and the work. He construes the age

through which he then explains the work, without taking heed of the fact that he only knows the age through the works, and these reveal to him what he claims to explain. This real but not insurmountable difficulty marks the limits of the historical method of explanation, it does not entitle us to exclude it. Clausewitz's experiences of the years from 1792 to 1815 do not explain what places the *Treatise* above all other books by military writers, nor do they explain why we passionately take sides for or against *The Prince* or *Capital*. But every interpretation which respects and honors its subject cannot and should not avoid diversion through the age, the environment or any other expression that might be chosen to define the historical field. Of course there is a coming and going between the work and its age, between the works and the events of the age which might perhaps be called the hermeneutic circle—a circle which is not vicious.[24]

What conclusions can we forward at this stage of our analysis of Aron's theory of historical knowledge? First, we can now see that, according to Aron, there is, in each dimension of historical existence, an irreducible hiatus between lived experience and the retrospective grasp of that experience. This was the case with self-understanding, just as it is true of understanding the other and, more broadly, the collective reality in which we find both the other and ourselves. Historical understanding, on Aron's view, is thus never a resurrection but always a reconstruction.

The second conclusion we reach, therefore, is the following: conceptual reconstruction, because of its very nature, will never completely escape the intrusion of the observer's subjectivity. To escape it would imply both coincidence with the historical totality and the ability to penetrate the ultimate depths of psychological motivation. But to coincide with the historical totality would place the observer outside history, in the position of God. The historical observer is, however, situated firmly within history. The finitude of the human subject logically excludes access to any complete understanding of the historical totality. From his first writings, Aron was deeply suspicious of any attempt to deify the human, seeing harbored within such attempts many of the evils of the modern age.

To plumb the depths of psychological motivation would similarly entail an impossible coincidence: psychic reality is equivocal and inexhaustible. Attempting to trace all the psychological antecedents of a given action or decision would also run the observer headlong into the wall of human finitude. Aron calls this flight of the phenomena the *dissolution of the object* (a formulation he would later reject as excessive). When the object of understanding is either reduced to its component parts (e.g., the unconscious motivations of a particular act or decision) or extended to the totality of an entire civilization, it "dissolves." In the *Introduction*, the space of truth exists between these twin dissolutions. Reality is so rich, so complex, and human understanding so invariably affected by the historical situation of the observer, Aron argues, that an *interpretive pluralism* implying the partiality and irreducibility of interpretation is the method best suited to the comprehension of the equivocal nature of the historical fact in the historically real.[25] The search for totality becomes the never achieved *ideal* of historical observation. Total coincidence in understanding is never realized, but the search for such coincidence retains its significance on the methodological level.

What implications does Aron's critical analysis of historical understanding have for the defense of political reason? In order to *think politically* it is fundamental, as we have seen, to place oneself within political life, to inform political judgment by recreating the range of choices, the intellectual world, and the historical context of the political actor. Aron's theory of understanding secures this horizon of meaning, leading him to concrete men and women and existing societies, subject to varying, often contradictory motivations and beliefs but still open to the possibility of communication. The limits to understanding should, in addition, direct the political thinker to moderation. The recognition of the partiality of historical perspectives entailed by the limits to understanding implies that any politics which presumes a total knowledge of the meaning of history is intrinsically confused and potentially dangerous. At the same time, however, abandoning the *search* for understanding denies the very real commonality and meaning we *can* reach through patient effort and distorts the nature of the human world. The interpretation of the meaningful reality of actually existing human beings, immersed in their communities and histories, while limited by human finitude, is a necessary task for the political thinker if he wants to cleave close to the grain of political life, to the structure and possibilities of the human world, in all of its tragic complexity.

## 2. THE LIMITS OF HISTORICAL OBJECTIVITY: CAUSAL EXPLANATION

Thus far, we have considered Aron's theory of understanding. The *Introduction* also has much to say about *causal explanation* in the historical and social sciences, to which we now turn. Can the principle of reason be extended to include human phenomena? If so, how far does it extend, and what can we know about the phenomena in question? As we noted earlier, thinkers such as Hannah Arendt either rejected entirely the application of causal explanation in the fields of history and society, or drew very tightly the boundaries within which it is deemed useful. Aron does not go as far as these critics of rationalism in abandoning the principle of reason in the study of history and society. As we will see in what follows, Aron holds that recourse to causal explanation, if informed by the limitations of human finitude, the complexity of historical phenomena, and a respect for an essential margin of human liberty, is essential to the task of thinking politically.

To lay hold of Aron's conception of historical and social causality, we can place ourselves in the position of the historian seeking the causes of a particular human event. The event in question can be something as localized as the outcome of a specific battle during the course of a protracted war or as extensive as the historical development of capitalism and the fall of communism. The historical observer seeks the cause of an event just as the expert is asked to determine the cause of a railway accident. Aron elaborates:

> The expert studying the cause of a railway accident tries to specify the particular circumstances immediately preceding the accident (lack of prudence, bad visibility, etc.) and the relatively constant facts (condition of the track, signal system, etc.) more or less favorable to the catastrophe (which increases the number of variable causes possessing the nature to provoke it). Both expert and historian deal with the question of responsibilities.[26]

The historian is concerned with determining the antecedents of an event as well as which of those antecedents are necessary and which sufficient for bringing the event about. (The actual practice of historians, of course, will not be so tidy: it is important to remind ourselves, once again, that Aron is performing a transcendental analysis of the *conditions* of historical knowledge, *not* describing its actual practice.) There are difficult questions inseparable from such an inquiry: How does one weigh the influence of the various antecedents? Is there *responsibility* to be established, someone to blame? If so, to what degree? In order to provide answers to these questions, the historian must do what common sense dictates and ask a further question: What *might* have happened?

There are two types of causality Aron addresses in the *Introduction*. The first involves measuring (or, more accurately, attempting to measure) the respective causality, the *weight* of the various causal agents, through retrospective calculations of probability. This is *historical causality*, and it concerns events in their singularity. The second type of causality Aron explores as theoretically useful is *sociological*. Sociological causality requires the explanation of an event by means of a rule or a law. As Aron was later to express in a more analytic idiom, "the law establishes that event x occurs in circumstances a, b, c; if we observe that a, b, c were given, we consider event x explained."[27]

There are, Aron argues, four separate stages in determining the role of causality in the historically singular event. As is the case with understanding, however, causal explanation also comprises an irreducible element of subjectivity, and is hence partial in its explanatory power. The first stage is to isolate the "phenomenon effect" for which one seeks an explanation. This isolation inevitably involves an active role for the historical observer in *constructing* the phenomenon. As we saw earlier, the event under explanation can be as vast in scale as the emergence of capitalism or as localized as the outcome of a particular battle in a war. The first methodological rule, then, is to define precisely the object of analysis, and this necessitates an active role for the observer.[28]

The second stage elaborated by Aron is the "discrimination of the antecedents and isolation of one antecedent, the efficiency of which it is desired to measure."[29] A specific antecedent must be separated out, with a determination then made to see if its absence affects the phenomenon one is trying to explain. Borrowing an example from Max Weber, Aron asks the following *counterfactual* question: If the Greeks had lost the battle of Marathon, would the development of Western civilization have been the same? We can ask a more contemporary question: If the United Nations, led by the United States, had not gone to war in the effort to stop Iraq's Middle East power grab in 1991, would the subsequent breakthrough we have witnessed over the past half-decade in the Israel-Palestinian conflict (however tenuous) have occurred?

In order to respond to a counterfactual query, Aron believes, it is necessary to move to a third stage, which Aron calls the "construction of unreal developments."[30] This stage requires imaginative thought on the part of the observer. If the Greeks had indeed fallen under Persian rule as a result of losing the battle of Marathon, one of the objectively possible outcomes would have been the emergence of a theocratic regime instead of a democracy. Or, in our example, if the U.N. had avoided military action, Saddam Hussein would have been in the possession of a large percentage of the world's oil supplies, well on his way to acquiring or developing nuclear weaponry, and possibly in a war with Israel.

The fourth stage of causal analysis is to make comparisons between unreal constructions and actual events, thus enabling the historical observer to conclude that the antecedent modified by thought was one of the causes of the event under explanation. But, as Aron goes to lengths to stress, the openness of history makes any determinative judgment impossible:

> The circumstances making that (unrealized) regime objectively possible, would in any case have combined with other events which would have been favorable or unfavorable to that evolution. The correct formula, then, will be one of probability: a Persian victory will be called an adequate cause of a theocratic regime; it would have produced it in a very large number of cases, or, more exactly, in a comparably larger number than the cases in which it would not have done so. An effect is called accidental with reference to a certain group of antecedents if the group leads to the effect only in a small number of cases (a number small in contrast with the number of those in which it would not lead to it).[31]

If Aron's argument is correct, then the Greek victory would have to be seen as an adequate cause of democracy; thus, the Greek victory was decisive in the history of Western civilization. In the case of the Gulf War, Iraq's defeat can be viewed as an adequate cause of the breakthrough in Israeli-Palestinian relations. Without it, Israel's legitimate security needs would have precluded taking the tremendous risks initiated by the late Yitzhak Rabin. We are not in the realm of strict determinism in Aron's scheme, however, but rather that of *probability*. Such retrospective calculation of probability never reaches exact determination and leaves open the chance that events could have been different through the application of human freedom. The U.N. coalition, a remarkable feat of statesmanship by United States Secretary of State James Baker and President George Bush that brought together both Western and Arab powers, could have easily unravelled, turning the conflict into a struggle between the Western and Arab worlds. President Bush might have avoided the decision to go to war, seeking negotiated settlement with Iraq. Given this openness of history to a margin of human freedom, what is thus excluded from Aron's theory of historical causality is the kind of Marxist theoretical ontology which eliminates probability (and hence the space for political reason) in favor of the unlimited extension of the principle of reason to the totality of historical reality. But Aron does not go to the opposite extreme of completely jettisoning the principle of reason in the study of history, and refusing the calculation of probability.

In terms of sociological causality, the observer searches for the constant antecedent and tries to discern the presence of regularities. Rather than attempting to determine the causes of a particular war, for example, the antecedents of war in general are sought. Once military forces oppose one another, the side with the preponderance of force or the technological advantage will usually succeed. Sociological analysis is also limited to probabilistic explanation. Regularities appear only at the macro-sociological level; when events are approached on the micro-sociological level, determinism is relativised and the efficacy of individual decisions and the play of chance are immediately apparent. There is, in Aron's terminology, a *probabilistic* or *aleatory determinism* that leaves open the margin of human freedom essential to political reason. As Aron expresses this idea in the 1972 essay "Three Forms of Historical Intelligibility":

> Given a historical situation, no one can prove theoretically and without exception that the act of an individual or a decision taker was inevitable, leaving aside the psychology of the actor; that this psychology was completely determined by economic, social, or intellectual factors in the environment, or finally that the consequences of individual choice do not go beyond a certain point, so that in the end, "it would have all been the same."[32]

Thus, when Marxists argue that relations of production determine society in its totality, they assert the unprovable. It could perhaps be shown that a certain state of productive relations regularly leads to a certain type of political regime or ideological formation, and Aron was supportive of a probabilistic use of Marxist categories in this fashion. When the evidence is assessed in an even-handed manner, however, even the probabilistic demonstration is clearly limited in scope for political constitutions very dramatically from one capitalist economy to another. The best we can expect from the quest for sociological causality are various negative conclusions (e.g., a totally planned economy excludes representative democracy, as the sociologist Peter Berger has shown[33]) or the gleaning of broad historical tendencies which fundamentally affect the range of choices available to the historical actor.[34] Although he accepted that these broad tendencies (technological, economic, sociological, etc.) influence the *conditions* of political choice, Aron refused to collapse the political into such subpolitical forces. As we have seen throughout, political reason requires a degree of political autonomy and freedom which cannot be explained away by economic or social determinations.

The Marxist, on the other hand (and this holds for sophisticated contemporary Marxist theorists such as G. A. Cohen or Perry Anderson as well as more "vulgar" Marxists[35]) carries out an historical demonstration that starts with a given event and establishes a causal regress that invariably culminates with economic phenomena. As Aron argues, performing a causal regress of this type is unexceptionable. Where the Marxist errs is in arbitrarily stopping the causal regress: by what right does the Marxist suspend the causal regress at all? Why should the economic antecedent always be seen as the ultimate cause? Without a *metaphysical* presumption in favor of their conception of historical and social causality, without, in other words, extending their concept *into the real*, the Marxist's ship runs aground. As Aron puts it in the *Introduction*:

> Beyond the economic antecedent other, non-economic, antecedents would show up. How can we give a meaning to the expression *"in the last analysis"*? How can it be proven that it is always the situation which is the *authentic cause* of an event, and that this situation itself is the effect of the method?[36]

This is not, of course, to say that economic analysis is unimportant in explaining historical events. No one can seriously doubt that economic forces influence the events and transformations of history. Aron is arguing, rather, that seeking an overriding cause at work in history is *undialectical*. An appropriately dialectical approach to historical and social causality, Aron believes, insists on the *interrelatedness* of the various spheres or levels of historical reality. Aron's former student Jon Elster calls this interrelatedness *reciprocal causality*, where the various spheres (political, economic, psychological, social, and so on) of the historical and social field are in mutual influence.[37] It is an extremely fruitful recognition for the social sciences to make, and one we shall continue to explore in the next chapter.

Earlier, during our investigation of the theory of understanding, we briefly addressed the salience of Aron's notion of interpretive pluralism as a response to the complexity of historical meaning and the finitude of the knowing subject; here, too, the necessity of interpretive pluralism emerges, now applied to the theory of causal explanation. On this view, a cause at the same time could be an effect and vice versa, since historical forces act on each other in a reciprocal manner. An appropriately complex theory of causal explanation would thus have to bring to bear on the phenomenon under explanation sociological, economic, and political factors (among others) in a way that would not dogmatically misrepresent the plurality and complexity of historical and social reality. This methodological approach to causal explanation is peculiar to human or social phenomena, because such phenomena are inseparable from human liberty, thus adding a dimension that never can be explained adequately in terms of strict causality. Again, as we saw with the pursuit of totality in the theory of understanding, one must recognize the irreducibility of the conceptual in Aron's thought *as a response to the complexity and richness of the historically real and to the finitude of man*. Similar in this regard to Max Weber, whose influence on the *Introduction* is considerable, Aron returned to concepts their status as methods and refused to eliminate from the methodological equation a strong awareness of the presence of freedom and human action in the midst of causal forces operating "behind the backs" of men and their historic communities. This means, however, that any successful interpretation of an historical phenomenon involves a reference to both understanding and causal explanation, as Aron was later to recall in the *Memoirs*:

all narratives, all interpretations, simultaneously use comprehensive understanding and causal analysis; fragmentary determinism hangs on a construction of facts and groups of facts; causal relations are accompanied and illumined by intelligible connections. The understanding of causality and the understanding of meaning, according to the formulation of Max Weber and the practice of all sociologists and historians, strengthen and confirm one another, even though each of the procedures has its own meaning.[38]

To return to the earlier example of the Persian Gulf War, a full account of the war, the factors leading up to it, and the consequences resulting from its being waged, would involve recourse to both comprehensive understanding (what were the stakes of the war as conceived by its participants, or their psychological, political, and moral motives before and during the conflict?) and causal explanation (what were the military, economic, and social configuration of forces and how did they affect the outcome)? While understanding begins with the immanent meanings of individual lives and is led to the never-completed project of embracing a total system of meaning making up the texture of those lives, causal explanation moves in the other direction, isolating broad historical tendencies and determining probabilities but failing in its search for a uniquely causal science of human affairs. A crucial margin of liberty remains open. There is, although Aron did not read him until much later, more than an echo in the *Interpretation* of the sober voice of Alexis de Tocqueville, who concluded *Democracy in America* with the following lines:

> Providence did not make mankind either entirely free or completely enslaved. Providence has, in truth, drawn a predestined circle around each man beyond which he cannot pass; but within those vast limits man is strong and free, and so are peoples.[39]

Historical intelligibility necessitates reference both to the actors within history and to the forces that resist, enhance, or transform their intentions. It is, in Aron's view, through the *narration* of history that these two methods are brought together. It is for this reason, we can surmise, that Thucydides's *History of the Peloponnesian War* held such a fascination for Aron: it combined an analysis of the broad forces of history and the lived experiences of the actors in its dramatic narrative of Athens meeting its destiny.[40] While Thucydides describes in meticulous detail the economic, political, and military forces influencing the onset of war and its subsequent development, he never loses sight of the contributions of historical actors that finally determined the denouement of the conflict. Aron's own historical narratives—from *The Century of Total War* to *The Imperial Republic*—are modeled on the Thucydidian example. It is the measured observer of politics and history who bridges the divide between the causal weight of social and historical forces and the dignity of human liberty.

Before we conclude this chapter with a closer look at the parallels suggested by Aron's transcendental analysis of the conditions of historical objectivity and the epistemological and moral position of the political actor in history, we must examine the threat of epistemological relativism that endangers Aron's philosophy of history. If this threat cannot be avoided, then the defense of political reason, which rests on the *prospect* of truth in history, will fall prey to the Heideggerian or Nietzschean abandonment of reason. Indeed, if this threat cannot be avoided, a politics may be conceivable, but it will not be reasonable.

## 3. THE RELATIVIST THREAT

It should now be clear that Aron's theory of causal explanation in the historical and social fields is as marked by the intrusion of subjectivity, as is his theory of understanding. Aron cannot avoid the Weberian problem of *selection*, and it is here that epistemological relativism intrudes. The role of the observer, the questions asked, are unavoidable elements of historical knowledge, both in attempting to understand the immanent meaning of events and creations for those who lived them, and in seeking to explain what goes beyond the intentions of men and women.

As Aron explains in the *Introduction*, the past is as indeterminate as the future: the historian or social scientist has to choose which facts are worthy of consideration. For Weber, on Aron's view, the choice rests ultimately on a concealed metaphysics, on the "values" held by the observer. Reality is, on the Weberian account, a meaningless, chaotic sequence of events (he was heavily influenced by the neo-Kantian philosophy of his time) upon which the interpreter imposes organization and meaning through the construction and application of "ideal types."

As Leo Strauss has underscored, for Weber "all meaning, all articulation, originates in the activity of the knowing and evaluating subject."[41] Since Weber believed that world views were plural and contradictory, and that there was subsequently no way to prove that one was morally superior to another, Weber's own defense of the universal truth of science, exemplified by his thorough and meticulous historical studies, seems ungrounded. Nietzsche's idea of the world as completely aestheticized, subject to endlessly renewed interpretations, is as plausible a response to Weber's epistemological and moral stance as the scientific attitude he actually adopted.

Aron was dissatisfied by the appearance of relativism, both moral and epistemological, in the *Introduction*. As he was later to regret in the *Memoirs*, were he to directly broach the themes of the *Introduction* again, he would "make a sharper distinction between social values and moral virtues, I would strengthen the foundations of scientific truth and human universalism."[42] While the Weberian influence was salutary and helped Aron overcome the inadequacies of Marxist ideology, he believed that Weber's irrationalist philosophy—a kind of radical value pluralism—was ultimately unlivable. While the various goods of the human world were not fully compatible, and could often conflict, to assume that conflict was inevitable, or that reason and prudential judgment were powerless in the face of such conflicts, was to make an unwarranted inference. In fact, Aron's political reflection took as its inspiration the Aristotelian duty of moderating the agonistically contending commitments of the various parties in society—to *tame* pluralism rather than exacerbate it.[43] In our concluding chapter we will return to this theme by comparing Aron's understanding of the antinomies of political life to the value pluralism of another great twentieth-century liberal, Isaiah Berlin.

Weber's methodology also raised a host of questions: If the social scientist had unlimited liberty to impose his own ideal constructions on reality, why call it social "science" at all? Could not his ideal constructions dramatically alter the nature of social, historical, and political phenomena? As Aron came to rethink the way he framed the relationship of the observer to the real, the latter, as we shall see, took on more and more "intrinsic coherence."[44] Weber's *practice* as a sociologist was sharply at odds with the flexibility he granted the observer on the level of methodology. Finding a way of getting beyond Weber's influence and rescuing the possibility for historical and social objectivity, as well as a more moral and humane politics, led Aron down several different paths, some more fruitful than others. We will now proceed to examine and assess several of these strategies, one of the most significant being a later development that emerged from a debate with Leo Strauss on the Weberian legacy.

Aron's least successful attempt to ward off the relativist threat rests on the idea of *commitment*. Weber's critique of historical determinism was appealing for Aron for the very important reason that it returned human freedom and moral choice to the center of political reflection. Without such freedom and moral choice, political reason is unthinkable. But Weber's ethical relativism, his idea that all values were ultimately without objective ground, threatened to undermine the foundations of his social science. If all values are equivalent, if there is no way to reasonably choose among them, then the choice of values rests on an arbitrary *decision*, an act of *will*. Nor was any synthesizing vision possible, for Weber held values not only to be ungrounded in reason but also contradictory. Ideals are bound to conflict, and humanity was condemned to an inexpiable "war of the gods."[45] Given the fact that the observer interprets his object on the basis of a reference to his values, and values are without reasonable ground and bound to conflict, the impulse to objectivity found in Weber's own work is, as Strauss has noted, robbed of its foundations. The choice for science and objectivity was worth no more than an alternate choice which rewrote history with complete arbitrariness. The Weberian dedication to science is ultimately, despite Weber's intention, irrational.

In order to avoid Weber's relativism, Aron asserts in the *Introduction* that historic relativity can be overcome through the *absoluteness* of decision. What does Aron mean by this? Let us attend to an important passage, which appears late in the book where, without naming him directly, it is clearly Weber that Aron is attempting to distance himself from:

> So, without yielding to a pathetic mode of philosophy, and without taking the anguish of a disordered era as an eternal datum, nor yet allowing oneself to sink into nihilism, one can recall that man determines both himself, and his mission, by measuring himself against nothingness. This is, indeed, only to affirm the power of man, who creates himself by judging his environment, and by choosing himself.

> Only in this way does the individual overcome the relativity of history
> by the absolute of decision, and make the history he bears within, and
> which becomes his history, truly part of himself.[46]

Aron is arguing that historical relativity is to be overcome by taking up
one's own history and affirming it. Beyond the existentialist language,
which marked Aron's intellectual milieu, we can see, in the respect for
human freedom, the barest outline of a philosophical anthropology. But
it is more to the point that Daniel J. Mahoney is correct when he concludes that, with regard to *this* tactic for overcoming relativity, "the
emperor still has no clothes."[47] What makes the "absoluteness" of decision somehow more objective than Weber's initial decision? Other than
its greater finality, nothing seems to separate Aron's decision from Weber's version. Could we not embrace an irrationalist position in an absolute way just as readily as a scientific position? What does the quality of
absoluteness add to the argument? Aron's absolute decision is ultimately
as irrational and groundless as Weber's. Both are based in a free human
choice, but relativity has not been overcome. The Aronian argument
from commitment fails.

Another strategy for avoiding epistemological relativism advanced
in the *Introduction* is *interpretive pluralism*, which we have discussed above
in reconstructing Aron's theories of interpretive understanding and
causal explanation. The basic idea of interpretive pluralism can be presented in concise terms: given the complexity of historical and social
reality and the intrinsic limits of human cognition, a methodological
approach that takes into account several dimensions of analysis or several
interpretive frameworks will be more objective than a reductive, monistic approach. If we seek to make intelligible a particular historical or
social phenomenon, an account that combines reference to the intentions and the self-understandings of the major participants with granting
causal factors their appropriate efficacity will be more successful than
an account which, for example, explains the phenomenon in terms of
economics, or which abandons causal explanation entirely (as, if we are
to take them at face value, the Heideggerian tradition recommends).[48] It
mirrors the structure of reality, taking into account the human element
in all of its indeterminacy.

Thus, the objectivity of the historian or social scientist on this view
can be gauged by his capacity to enlarge his perspective to include vari-

ous frameworks of interpretation. There is unquestionably something appealing and sound about this argument. An analysis of an event —World War II, say —which tried to reduce it to a predetermined result of economic factors, which banished the political stakes, the psychological dynamic, the difficult moral choices, and myriad other considerations from play, would be absurdly narrow. Interpretive pluralism has the powerful strength of granting to the historical and social world its manifest complexity. That said, however, it leaves the problem of relativism partially intact. This is the case for two reasons: there may be instances when more is too much, and there is the related difficulty of deciding between two differing interpretations.

An account of World War II which focused in part on the characters of Hitler and Stalin might have a great deal of relevance, given the dominant role their personalities played in the unfolding of events. But what of an account that included character studies not only of Hitler and Stalin but of every participant in a position of influence, however minor, in the conflict? We would soon find ourselves lost in an interminable maze while losing the real impact character had during the war. Other examples could readily be offered. In addition, while we may agree that there is an intuitive plausibility that a pluralist account is more satisfactory than a reductive account, how do we decide between different interpretations, if both happen to be pluralist in inspiration? Something more is needed by Aron if this strategy is to be concretized and relativism escaped. Interpretive pluralism cannot stand on its own.

A more successful strategy for overcoming relativism, which can successfully incorporate what is salutary about interpretive pluralism, is developed in Aron's later work, as a response, it can be surmised, to his sense of the insufficiencies of the first two efforts we have examined. This later attempt is based on the notion of *equity* as the exemplary disposition of the observer of history and society. It is an ideal both moral and epistemological, and it marks Aron's definitive bid to distance himself from Weber's influence. Weber was above all concerned with making science value-free and neutral. He thought he could succeed in doing so by prohibiting political and moral judgments from intruding on the object of analysis; by, in other words, separating facts from values. But, as Strauss has shown, Weber himself does not live up to this ascetic ideal:

His work would not be merely dull but absolutely meaningless if he did not speak almost constantly of practically all intellectual and moral virtues and vices in the appropriate language, i.e., in the language of praise and blame. I have in mind expressions like these: "grand figures," "incomparable grandeur," "perfection that is nowhere surpassed," "pseudo-systematics," "this laxity was undoubtedly a product of decline," "absolutely unartistic."[49]

Aron agreed with Strauss's line of argument in this passage fully, and in an important later essay, "Science and Consciousness of Society," developed the notion of equity as an alternative to Weberian value neutrality, seen as an impossible ideal which in fact distorts the phenomena of the human world.

What does equity consist in as a scientific and moral ideal? It involves, as an attentive reading of the essay will reveal, a push to *reduce bias* in the exploration of historical and social reality rather than pursuing an illusory ideal of neutrality. There are, Aron explains, five principal types of bias encountered in the study of things human. The first of these biases is the arbitrary selection of facts. As Aron puts it, "Science implies, above all, the will to see the facts as they are and not as they ought to be according to official doctrine."[50] Perhaps the most devastating of Marxism's theoretical errors (with immense practical implications) is the failure to distinguish real and ideal—to project, as Marxism did, wishes and hopes into the structure of reality itself. But Weber, at least on the methodological level, denied that reality had *any* pregiven structure.

Second, there can be a "confusion, at the theoretical level, between conventional definition and definitions that express the results of research."[51] This, too, must be resisted. As he did in the concluding pages of the *Introduction,* Aron insists that the observer of science and history must actually carry out empirical research before conclusions are reached. Too often, stipulative definitions distort the proceedings through establishing by fiat what should be the outcome of patient study. The third form of bias that equity works against consists in claiming certitude where the nature of phenomena are themselves equivocal. As we have seen, attributing motives to historical actors is an inexact procedure at best, particularly when there is a cultural or temporal distance of any magnitude between the observer and the object of study. Determining which cause is most important in a given context is also very difficult. To ignore these difficulties is to ignore both the real limitations of human knowledge and the complexity of reality. This suggestion of Aron's links up closely with his support for interpretive pluralism.

Fourth, Aron underscores the banal but important point that historical and sociological thought can fall prey to an arbitrary determination of what is essential or of importance. While a Marxist may feel that the most important question concerns ownership of the means of production, that decision must receive justification. When such a question is hypostatized as the *only* one of import, we are no longer in the realm of science but have entered speculative metaphysics. Finally, fairness requires the observer to avoid *projecting onto reality* his own beliefs in the merits or defects of the social order. Such a judgment can obviously be made, but it is "not inscribed in fact."[52]

This conception of equity, as should now be clear, carries with it an Aristotelian recognition that social and historical phenomena are not, as Weber would have it, a chaotic jumble of facts. Aron is, rather, following Strauss when the latter writes that there is "an articulation of reality that precedes all scientific articulation: that articulation, that wealth of meaning, which we have in mind when speaking of the world of common experience or of the natural understanding of the world."[53] This commonsense "articulation" can be seen in the following phenomena: in order to study Matisse, an art historian must be able to distinguish between the master and his imitators; great statesmen such as de Gaulle or Churchill cannot be spoken of in the same breath as despotic tyrants such as Hitler and Stalin. While there may be disagreements in this pretheoretical world, there is also a strong sense of human commonality, a sense of shared, natural meanings relating to lived experiences. Thus, to strive to avoid the prescientific articulation of meaning of "social reality as it is known in social life,"[54] as Weber tried but failed to do, is to misunderstand the nature of historical and political life fundamentally, and, more broadly, the nature of the human world itself. It is a misunderstanding which, if it were fully pursued, would rob the human sciences of what worth they can achieve. Social and historical reality is not *constructed* by the observer, but *developed* and *clarified*.[55]

Weber's fact-value distinction is, in other words, a misleading distinction, and it is rightly renounced by Aron. To summarize what we can call the argument from equity, then, it calls for an Aristotelian effort to recognize the specificity of human phenomena in the attempt to overcome relativism. Any science concerning itself with human action is going to be imprecise necessarily; admitting that fact and seeking the appropriate level of exactitude would help make the study of human things both more relevant and more objective.

Before Aron's reliance on equity can be viewed as part of a satisfactory response to relativism, however, it has to be wedded to another ethical imperative, an imperative more Kantian than Aristotelian in nature. We can call this an ethic of universality, and it is based on the *intention* toward universality rather than a presumption of its achievement. Aron believes that this intention can be discovered in the pages of Weber himself. Weber's "choice," the choice that oriented his work, was that of scientific truth. Weber made the choice for science because of the universality of scientific truth; because, as Aron says, such universality "constituted the proper grounds and domicile of a community of minds, across political boundaries and through the centuries."[56]

While Aron accepted Weber's claim that it was impossible to scientifically validate a value judgment, he refused to conclude from this that all valorizations are thereby rendered equivalent. Although, for example, the ethical imperative "thou should not kill" is not of the same order of truth as $2 + 2 = 4$, the taboo against killing, Aron believes, is "pertinent to all men" and thus partakes of universality.[57] What Aron is getting at can be clarified by focusing on this passage from the essay "Max Weber and Modern Social Science":

> What is more, the formal rules of the rationalistic ethic—rooted in Christianity but reaching their full expression in the philosophy of Kant—are not a simple matter of taste like that of color preference. They are, instead, the logical development of the notion of humanity, of the universal society of man, an idea inseparable from the profound significance of scientific truth. These rules are formal because the institutions which, from century to century, embody them cannot resist change as a function of material and social technology.[58]

Aron's argument can be parsed as follows: if epistemological relativism in the study of history and society is to be overcome, it is necessary to find grounds for the scientific ethic; such grounds can be found in the recognition of the "profound significance of scientific truth" (by which Aron means the remarkable achievements of the natural sciences) and ultimately in a philosophical conception of human nature, with theoretical and practical significance, as at least minimally rational.

While the facts unique to historical and social knowledge that we have canvassed in some detail above make the achievement of universal truth as understood in the natural sciences impossible in the human sciences, Aron holds that the *intention* to universal truth itself, rooted in certain shared traits of human nature, minimizes the danger of relativism. Motivated by this ethic, grounded in a richer philosophical anthropology than was present in the *Introduction*, Aron's other strategies are strengthened: equity is interlaced with a desire for truth consubstantial with man; interpretive pluralism is directed by the imperative to universality in such a way that reasonable judgment between conflicting interpretations becomes conceivable; even commitment can appear in a clearer light as an affirmation of humanity's universal vocation toward freedom, rather than the desolate destiny of measuring oneself against the void.

How successful Aron is at finally overcoming the threat of epistemological relativism in the historical and social field remains open to question. The fully articulated and developed set of arguments we have reconstructed seem plausible, particularly when we take into account the sobriety and equanimity of Aron's post–World War II writings. Most of us refuse to walk down the dangerous Nietzschean path where truth is replaced by an aesthetic ideal, or, ultimately, by power. Aron's account rests on a conception of human nature that has a strong Kantian dimension, but it is moderated by a rich sense of historical diversity and by a classical, Aristotelian "feel" for the interconnectedness of the pre-reflective human world. Aron's Kantianism was, as Alain Renaut has perceptively observed, "post-Hegelian,"[59]—and hence fundamentally historical in its sensibility—but it was in some crucial sense pre-Kantian, and indeed Aristotelian as well. Aron's awareness of historical diversity makes his philosophy of history an act of suspension, a true high-wire act, between historicism and an acknowledgment of universal, trans-historical truth. Pierre Manent has followed this act of suspension in Aron's thought:

> One might perhaps state the following: Aron's thesis gives too much
> weight to historicism—to the idea that man is essentially an historic
> being who fashions himself and determines himself within history—to

admit as classical philosophy did a theory of man's nature and condition *sub specie aeternitatis*; on the other hand, it retains too much of the traditional conception of philosophy—as the elaboration of universal articulations of the human experience—to succumb to the seduction of either relativism or of the historic totality, Hegelian or Marxist. Aron, while refusing both a philosophy which would abolish history and a theory of history which would abolish philosophy, tries to delimit and mark the intermediary terrain defined by the insurmountable distance between philosophy and history. Herein lies that which one might call his Kantianism: indeed reason provides us with "regulatory ideas" to orient us within history and in one way to judge history; however, even if one is allowed to hope that humanity will in the future conform more readily to the requirements of reason, we cannot conceive of history as being the history of the triumph of reason.[60]

Manent has it exactly right: Aron's support for reason was an "as if" holding open the possibility that the world might not conform to our demands for intelligibility, and acknowledging the finitude of the historical observer, but still orienting the project of the political thinker.

Having now examined in detail the fundamental elements of Aron's philosophy of history, what does the complete picture look like? We have, first, the component of understanding, which insists on the effort to meet the actors of history on their own terrain, however much this effort is limited by the contingencies of history and human finitude. Second, we have the component of causal explanation, which seeks to render history and society intelligible by isolating the broad forces at work on humanity, without reducing the complexity of the real or the contribution made by human liberty. In both cases, an interpretive pluralism is necessary in recognition of the complexity of reality and the finitude of the knowing subject. And finally we have, completing the tableau, a twin ethic of universality and equity, aware of its limits and assuring a moderate faith in the capacities of human freedom and reason to limit the effects of relativism and hubris in the historical and social fields. We now turn, in the conclusion to this chapter, to drawing out the connections between Aron's philosophy of history and the defense of political reason.

## 4. POLITICS AND HISTORY

As we have observed above, there is a structural affinity between the historical observer and the political actor. Aron's epistemological investigations in the *Introduction* and elsewhere were undertaken with this affinity in mind. It would be appropriate to say a few more words about the relationship of politics and history in Aron's thought.

The Prince or citizen is confronted with the nature of political choice in such a way that steers him to the contemplation of history. If the political actor is to be reasonable, his decision must be rooted in an awareness of what alternatives are open, and the only way such an awareness is to be achieved is through the study of the historical and social world. The political thinker, if he is to be of any assistance to the political actor, must pursue the study of the historical and social world in order to enlighten the conditions of choice. But political choice does not occur in a void; it is a part of an on-going history, a history which both forces and constrains choice.

The *first* choice, unavoidable for all who truly want to think politically, is the choice for or against the existing regime. To be for the existing order is not to deny that it can be in need of reform—often dramatic—but it *is* to decide against the revolutionary upheaval of what exists, the effort to wipe the slate of society clean. (Nor is it to deny that, under certain conditions, the existing order may be so corrupt as to be beyond reform.) Aron's debate in the *Introduction* was with Marxism and Fascism, two choices against the existing regime forming the backdrop to Aron's reflection: the liberal democratic West. This choice, Aron writes in his *Memoirs*, has the following meaning:

> In the first place, and above all, it calls for the most rigorous possible study of reality and the possible regime that might replace the existing one. Rational choice in political history as I understand it does not result uniquely from moral principle or ideology, but from an analytical investigation, as scientific as possible. An investigation that will never be exempt from doubt, that will not impose a choice in the name of science, but that will protect against the traps of idealism or good will.[61]

His decision was for a disenchanted, but resolute support for the imperfect liberal democratic regime. The choice in question would not be free from doubt, however, because of the tragic nature of choice: every decision entails loss. This is so, first of all, because of the often antinomic criteria of evaluation: should we prefer liberty or equality? Which liberties? Should we seek power or wealth? As we will see in more detail later, Aron was profoundly sensitive to the antinomic structure of political life. Not all goods could be combined, and in many cases such goods were in profound conflict. Political *actors* experience such conflicts daily; political theorists too often conquer them in the empyrean of theory while failing to theorize their dominion in practice. There is, and it is one of the enduring lessons of Aron's thought, a permanent condition of *political scarcity* in the human world. The effects of political scarcity can be moderated through judicious application of the political art, but to seek to overcome permanently the condition is hubristic and risks unleashing the forces of political evil.

Second, doubt is unavoidable, too, as we have seen, because of the limitations of human knowledge. Yet to acknowledge the limits of historical objectivity is to acknowledge certain political actions as immoderate, as incompatible with what we *do* know and are capable of knowing, and to lay the groundwork for a more reasonable politics. The liberal democratic regimes of the West, flawed as they were, still preserved certain goods essential to human flourishing—liberty, security, equality under the rule of law—far better than any of the existent alternatives. They were more in tune with the limits to historical objectivity and the various goods of our human nature than were the "secular religions," proud with the knowledge of history's meaning or laws of development, which have exacted such a price in human suffering during our long and troubled century.[62] But to declare that the liberal democratic regimes are the culmination of history, as has Francis Fukuyama, would be to say more than we are warranted to say.[63] The future is open, and new and unforeseen dispensations may arise, as they have throughout history.

In the *Introduction,* Aron established a distinction that was to remain relevant to him for the rest of his life: the distinction between the *politics of Reason* and the *politics of understanding.* The politics of understanding has the function of conserving and protecting specific goods (i.e., moderation and liberty) in contexts that are always new and endlessly transforming. There are echoes here of Michael Oakeshott's idea of politics as navigating the sea of the particular. In Oakeshott's terms, political activity consists of men sailing "a boundless and bottomless sea; there is neither harbor for shelter nor floor for anchorage; neither starting-place nor appointed destination."[64] As Aron similarly put it in the *Introduction,* the politician of understanding "is like a pilot navigating without knowledge of the port; no present totality or predetermined future, each moment is new for him."[65]

The politics of Reason, on the other hand, finds its most fully realized expression in Marxism. Here, at least the next stage of the historical evolution is foreseen by the political actor: "The Marxist knows the disappearance of capitalism is inevitable and that the only problem is to adapt tactics to strategy, the accommodation to the present regime with preparation for the future regime."[66] Unlike Oakeshott, however, Aron's philosophy of history views both the politics of understanding and the politics of Reason as ideal types:

> These two types are, it goes without saying, ideal types; they mark two extreme attitudes. The latter risks degenerating into resignation, the former into blindness; the latter becomes powerless because of the force of trusting itself to history, the former by the power of forgetfulness; the latter is more wise, the former more heroic. This is to say as well that any politics is both one and the other. There is no immediate action that is not responsive to distant concerns; no confident in Providence who is not seeking out unique opportunities. The qualities of the Prophet and the empiricist should not be incompatible. Politics is both the art of irreversible choice and long-range plans.[67]

Aron believes, in other words, that the political thinker, if he wants to adequately conceptualize the political, must bring together the politics of understanding *and* the politics of Reason. We can find this point underscored in the *Memoirs*, where Aron stresses that "the interpretation of events is only valid to the extent that it grasps the originality of the event and its place in the whole, whether system or process."[68] Central to the defense of political reason is the determination of the *margin of freedom* available to the political actor.

What should now be apparent is that Aron's philosophy of history is oriented by a theory of action, that the *Introduction* is, in fact, an introduction to political reason. To think politically, as we have emphasized, it is first necessary to place oneself within politics, to recreate the world faced by the political actor. In order to enlighten the conditions of political choice, one must ascertain the possible. When the moralist rejects the inequities of market economics without asking what feasible alternative institutions for regulating economic life present themselves in the event of the suppression of the market, he is not thinking politically.[69] When a determinist view of history undergirds a political program in keeping with its view of the meaning of history, political reason has once again been lost: the indeterminacy of choice, the tragedy of politics, has been swept away by a pseudo-science of the political. On the other hand, when politics is reduced to power, when reason is seen as the enemy, when the political actor is seen as an artist, political reason has also been eclipsed.

Aron's philosophy of history avoids these various alternatives by exploring what it means to think politically. Just as the historical observer, aiming at objectivity, tries to detach himself from his historical determinations in order to reach the truth, so too the political actor in history strives to overcome his historical determination in order to make the right decision. Both unavoidably make reference to moral considerations; both seek transcendence in immanence; both run the risk of subjectivism and of confusing their hopes for reality.[70] Such is the lesson of Aron's *Introduction* for the political thinker.

Contemporary political theory, particularly in its analytic liberal variant, has largely left behind the terrain of politics, its abstractions of little interest or relevance to political actors, its theoretical distorting lens failing to adequately capture the most important events of our time: the Holocaust, the conflict between the East and the West, the failure of socialism, the continuing persistence of war, and the irreducibility of the nation.[71] Aron's philosophy of history, central to his defense of political reason, forced him to stay on this terrain and thus come to terms with these world-historical transformations. Thus has the argument run in this chapter. We now turn to an extended analysis of Aron's encounter with Marxism in all its disparate versions.

## NOTES

1. Bloom, *Giants and Dwarfs*, p. 260.

2. The *Introduction* had a companion book, never translated, where Aron offered analyses of Dilthey, Rickert, Simmel, and Weber. See Raymond Aron, *La Philosophie critique de l'histoire: Essai sur une théorie allemande de l'histoire* (Paris: Julliard, 1987).

3. Aron, *Memoirs*, p. 79.

4. Manent, "Raymond Aron—Political Educator," p. 1.

5. Aron, *Marxism and the Existentialists*, pp. 1–2.

6. The idea of an "end of history" has outlived the theoretical framework of Marxism. See Francis Fukuyama's *The End of History and the Last Man* (New York: Free Press, 1993).

7. See Luc Ferry, *The System of Philosophies of History: Political Philosophy*, Volume 2, trans. by F. Philip (Chicago: University of Chicago Press, 1992), pp. 1–60.

8. Manent, "Raymond Aron—Political Educator," p. 8.

9. Ibid., p. 8.

10. Ferry, *The System of Philosophies of History*, pp. 17–18, 61–74.

11. Hannah Arendt, "Understanding and Politics," *Partisan Review* 20, July–August 1953, p. 388. Aron was extremely critical of this aspect of Arendt's thought, as can be discerned from his careful reading of the latter's *The Origins of Totalitarianism* (New York: Harcourt Brace Jovanovich, 1951), "The Essence of Totalitarianism According to Hannah Arendt" in *In Defense of Political Reason*, pp. 97–112. As Aron puts it, "The totalitarian phenomenon . . . entails many interpretations because it has many causes. The method that aims at grasping its essence is legitimate, but on condition that it does not neglect complementary methods."

12. On this demiurgic aspect of Nietzsche's thought, see Peter Berkowitz, *Nietzsche: The Ethics of an Immoralist* (Cambridge: Harvard University Press, 1995), pp. 145–46, 149–75.

13. For a methodical analysis of Foucault's historical and sociological errors, see J. G. Merquior, *Foucault* (London: Twayne, 1985).

14. See Aron, *The Opium of the Intellectuals*, p. 163: "Political history, the history of wars and States, is neither intelligible nor accidental. It is no more difficult to understand a battle than to understand military institutions or methods of production. Historians have never attributed the grandeur and the decadence of peoples to chance alone. But military defeats do not always prove the decadence of empires: foreign invasion has destroyed some of the most flourishing civilizations. There is no correlation between the cause and the effect. The events reveal only an aleatory determinism, connected not so much with the imperfection of our knowledge as with the structure of the human world." For a similar critique of historical inevitability, see Isaiah Berlin, *Four Essays on Liberty* (Oxford: Oxford University Press, 1969), pp. 41–117.

15. Aron, *Memoirs*, p. 83. The Norwegian philosopher in question is, I believe, Aron's former student, Jon Elster.

16. Manent, "Raymond Aron—Political Educator," p. 8.

17. The key pages on this topic can be found in Aron, *Introduction*, pp. 45–155. For a reformulation, see the later work, posthumously published, *Leçons sur l'histoire*, ed. by S. Mesure (Paris: Fallois, 1989), pp. 174–216.

18. Aron, *Introduction*, p. 56.

19. See Aron's essay "Three Forms of Historical Intelligibility," in *Politics and History*, p. 49. On this basis, we can safely assume the incompatibility of Aron's approach with various efforts at forging a "communicative ethics," as found in the work of Jürgen Habermas.

20. Aron, *Introduction*, p. 68.

21. On the idea of "objective spirit" in Aron's thought, see Stephen Launay, *La pensée politique de Raymond Aron* (Paris: PUF, 1995), pp. 23–28.

22. Aron, *Introduction*, p. 76.

23. See Sylvie Mesure's discussion in *Raymond Aron et la raison historique* (Paris: Vrin, 1984), pp. 90–92.

24. Raymond Aron, *Clausewitz: Philosopher of War*, trans. by C. Booker and N. Stone (Englewood Cliffs, N.J.: Prentice-Hall, 1985), p. 3.

25. Ibid., pp. 86–120. See also Philippe Raynaud's comparison of Aron with Weber "Raymond Aron et Max Weber: Épistémologie des sciences social et rationalisme critique" in *Commentaire*: 28–29, 1985, pp. 213–21.

26. Aron, *Introduction*, p. 219.

27. Aron, *Memoirs*, p. 84.

28. Aron, *Introduction*, pp. 160–161. See Mesure's *Raymond Aron et la raison historique*, passim.

29. Aron, *Introduction*, p. 160.

30. Ibid., p. 161.

31. Ibid., p. 161.

32. Aron, *Politics and History*, p. 50.

33. See Peter L. Berger, *The Capitalist Revolution: Fifty Propositions About Prosperity, Equality, & Liberty* (New York: Basic Books, 1986).

34. This relationship between choice and necessity in Aron's thought is one of the central themes of Mahoney, *The Liberal Political Science of Raymond Aron*. See in particular, pp. 17–72.

35. On the "Marxist vulgate" see Raymond Aron, *In Defense of Decadent Europe*, with a new introduction by Daniel J. Mahoney and Brian C. Anderson (New Brunswick: Transaction Publishers, 1996), pp. 2, 27, 102–03, 211–12.

36. Aron, *Introduction*, p. 246.

37. For a recent presentation of this idea of reciprocal causality (focusing on the thought of Tocqueville), see Jon Elster, *Political Psychology* (Cambridge: Cambridge University Press, 1993), pp. 125–26. See also my review in *Perspectives on Political Science*, Fall 1994, p. 211.

38. Aron, *Memoirs*, p. 85.

39. Alexis de Tocqueville, *Democracy in America*, trans. by G. Lawrence (New York: Harper & Row, 1969), p. 705. This is a passage Aron loved to quote. See, e.g., Aron's *An Essay on Freedom* (New York: NAL, 1970), pp. 6–7.

On Aron's "elective affinity" with Tocqueville, see the acceptance speech upon receiving the first Tocqueville Prize in 1979: "On Tocqueville," included as an appendix to *In Defense of Political Reason*, pp. 175–78.

40. See "Thucydides and the Historical Narrative," in Aron, *Politics and History*, pp. 20–46; Aron's biographer Nicolas Baverez entitles the third section of his biography of Aron "Thucydide au XX siécle," *Raymond Aron: Un moraliste au temps des idéologies* (Paris: Flammarion, 1993), pp. 295–454.

41. Strauss, *Natural Right and History*, p. 77.

42. Aron, *Memoirs*, pp. 474–75.

43. For Aristotle's understanding of the civic role of the political philosopher, see Book III of *The Politics*, trans. by B. Jowett, (Cambridge: Cambridge University Press, 1988), pp. 51–80.

44. I borrow this phrase from Mahoney. See *The Liberal Political Science of Raymond Aron*, p. 3.

45. See Max Weber, "Science as a Vocation," in *From Max Weber: Essays in Sociology* (New York: Oxford, 1946), p. 148.

46. Aron, *Introduction*, p. 334. See also the essay "History and Politics" in Aron, *Politics and History*, pp. 237–48.

47. Mahoney, *The Liberal Political Science of Raymond Aron*, p. 2.

48. See Luc Ferry and Alain Renaut's discussion of Aron's interpretive pluralism in *French Philosophy of the Sixties: An Essay on Anti-Humanism*, trans. by M. Schnackenberg Cattani (Amherst: University of Massachusetts Press, 1990), pp. 59–63.

49. Strauss, *Natural Right and History*, p. 51. For a recent discussion of Strauss, Weber, and Aron, see Tzvetan Todorov, *The Morals of History*, trans. by A. Waters (Minnesota: University of Minnesota Press, 1995), pp. 197–208. Todorov overestimates Aron's Kantianism and underestimates his basic agreement with Strauss's Aristotelian critique of Weber.

50. See "Science and Consciousness of Society" in Raymond Aron, *History, Truth, Liberty: Selected Writings of Raymond Aron*, ed. by F. Draus (Chicago: University of Chicago Press, 1985), p. 217.

51. Ibid., p. 212.

52. Ibid., p. 214.

53. Strauss, *Natural Right and History*, p. 77.

54. Ibid., p. 77.

55. As Mahoney puts it, for Aron "science does not impose ideal types on 'incoherent facts' but instead develops concepts based on commonsensical or reasonable reflection about the order, however partial, of a given whole." *The Liberal Political Science of Raymond Aron*, p. 3.

56. See "Max Weber and Modern Social Science" in Aron, *History, Truth, and Liberty*, p. 362.

57. Ibid., p. 362. See also Sylvie Mesure, "Objectivité théorique et objectivité pratique chez Raymond Aron: De l'histoire à la politique" in *Cahiers de philosophie politique et juridique*, no. 15, 1989, pp. 13–23.

58. Aron, *History, Truth, and Liberty*, p. 362.

59. Alain Renaut, "Raymond Aron et la retour à Kant" in *magazine litteraire*, no. 293, 1992, pp. 62–63.

60. Manent, "Raymond Aron—Political Educator," p. 9.

61. Aron, *Memoirs*, p. 86; See also the *Introduction*, pp. 320–328.

62. Aron coined the phrase "secular religion" in 1944 as a way of describing Marxism and fascism in the famous, as of yet untranslated, essay "L'avenir des religions séculières." See *Commentaire*, Feb. 1985, Vol. 8/No. 28–29, pp. 369–83; and Raymond Aron, *Une histoire du vingtième siècle*, ed. by C. Bachelier (Paris: Plon, 1996), pp. 139–222. We will look more closely at this important concept in our next chapter.

63. Fukuyama's inspiration for the "End of History" thesis was the Russian émigré Alexandre Kojeve, an influence on an entire generation of French intellectuals through his lectures in the 1930s on Hegel's thought at the École Pratique des Hautes Études. But while Aron deeply respected Kojeve's intelligence, the end of history remained for him only a philosophical speculation. See Bryan-Paul Frost, "Raymond Aron's Peace and War, Thirty Years Later," *International Journal*, LI, Spring, 1996, p. 47; Aron, *Memoirs*, pp. 68–69. We will return to Fukuyama's hypothesis in the concluding chapter.

64. Michael Oakeshott, *Rationalism in Politics and Other Essays* (London: Methuen, 1962), p. 127.

65. Aron, *Introduction*, p. 327 (trans. modified).

66. Ibid., p. 327 (trans. modified).

67. Ibid., p. 327 (trans. modified).

68. Aron, *Memoirs*, p. 87. See also Launay, *La pensée politique de Raymond Aron*, p. 2.

69. The analytic philosopher N. Scott Arnold calls for an "alternative institutions" requirement for any serious social critique. See his *Marx's Radical Critique of Capitalist Society: A Reconstruction and Critique* (Oxford: Oxford University Press, 1990), pp. 290–91.

70. See Mesure, "Objetivité théorique et objectivité pratique chez Raymond Aron," p. 14.

71. See John Gray, "Notes Toward a Definition of the Political Thought of Tlon" in *Enlightenment's Wake: Politics and Culture at the Close of the Modern Age* (London: Routledge, 1995).

*3*

# THE CRITIQUE OF IDEOLOGY

A s the turbulent twentieth century reaches its conclusion, some argue that the great ideological forces which have scarred the political history of our time have been exhausted—fascism defeated on the battlefields of Europe during World War II, communism collapsing as a result of internal contradictions, Western resolve, and the clear superiority of free markets over centralized planning in efficiently allocating scarce resources—with the liberal democratic regime alone emerging victorious from the war of ideas and institutions, its sole remaining task the staving off of boredom.[1]

While there is a partial truth in this thesis—that liberal democracy is now recognized as the fullest or most adequate embodiment of the democratic principle of consent (although with qualifications from many quarters)—the argument ignores or downplays several important considerations: the emergence of Islamic fundamentalism and the resurgence of tribalist conceptions of national identity as serious threats to the future security of liberal democratic regimes; the open-ended nature of historical experience; and the persistence of the political impulse, inseparable from human nature. It is, as well, too sanguine about the stability and *virtu* (in Machiavelli's sense) of the liberal democratic regimes themselves, which increasingly lack what Pierre Manent has called the "instinct for political existence."[2] The argument is correct on one other point, however: the utter failure of Marxism both as a political ideology and as a theory of economic organization can no longer be ignored.

Raymond Aron has been vindicated in the remarkable decade since his death. For many years his was one of the few voices within the French intellectual milieu that dared to criticize Marxism and portray the Soviet Union for what it really was: one of the most destructive

61

tyrannies in human history, unprecedented in its systematic efforts to eliminate civil society and control every aspect of the daily lives of its citizens.[3] For this stubborn refusal to justify the unjustifiable, Aron was rewarded with the contempt and scorn of many of France's leading thinkers, most notably that of his former friend Jean-Paul Sartre. Since his death, however, Aron's influence has waxed while that of Sartre has waned; indeed, as noted earlier, a new generation of French intellectuals, including Luc Ferry, Pierre Manent, Marcel Gauchet, and Alain Renaut, has tried to reconstitute French philosophical support for the liberal democratic regime while explicitly following, often with very different rhythms, in Aron's footsteps.[4] Aron's tireless efforts to defend moderation in political thought in an atmosphere seldom conducive to it may have finally borne fruit with this resurgence of a sober French liberalism.

It is easy to forget, from our post-Marxist standpoint, the extent of Marxism's influence over an earlier generation of intellectuals. With the worldwide collapse of Marxist-inspired regimes and the general discredit into which Marxist theory has fallen, it would be difficult to deny that Marxism is theoretically and practically bankrupt. Only a handful of academics still categorize themselves as Marxists, and the remaining Marxist regimes totter precariously on the brink of ruin. In the case of "analytic" Marxist philosophers like Jon Elster and G. A. Cohen, it is increasingly unclear in what sense they can still be called Marxists. Indeed, in Elster's case, many of the central arguments of his work have been directed at the egregious errors of Marxist theory, and he has become more and more skeptical about the possibility of social science being anything more than partial and retrospective in explanatory power.[5] It is perhaps instructive to recall that Elster was Aron's student.

But Marxism was not always so discredited, and this was particularly the case in the Parisian intellectual milieu. It has only been a few short decades since Jean-Paul Sartre called Marxism the "unsurpassable philosophy of our time,"[6] Maurice Merleau-Ponty dialectically exculpated the worst excesses of Stalin's puppet-trials,[7] and large communist parties threatened the regimes of Europe (France included) with destabilization from within. Tony Judt, in his study of postwar French intellectual history, *Past Imperfect*, has adroitly characterized the appeal of Marxism for French intellectuals in the aftermath of World War II and the Occupation of France:

Of all the newly reemergent political parties, it was the Communists whose appearance mattered the most for the intellectual community. This is not because the Communist party could count on a significant membership among the *haute intelligentsia*—quite the contrary: the impermeable, deathless commitment of an Aragon ("My Party has restored to me the meaning of the times/ My Party has restored to me the colors of France") was only ever a minority taste. But for many younger intellectuals, not only had the party redeemed itself in action since 1941, but it represented in France, both symbolically and in the flesh, the transcendent power and glory of Stalin's Soviet Union, victorious in its titanic struggle with Nazi Germany, the unchallenged land power on the European continent and heir apparent to a prostrate Europe. A sense of having experienced the prelude to an apocalypse was widespread among those for whom the Occupation had been their formative political experience.[8]

It was against this backdrop that Aron carried out his critical engagement with Marxism, armed with his distaste for fanaticism and his sharp discernment of the realities of political life, weapons that would serve him well in the years ahead. The movement of Aron's thought and the nature of his defense of political reason cannot be fully grasped without examining in detail this engagement; from the beginning, Aron thought *against* Marx, and much of his enormous corpus of work is concerned with the critique of Marxist ideology. (As we will see, Aron also thought *with* Marx more thoroughly than most Marxists.) From *Opium of the Intellectuals* to *In Defense of Decadent Europe*, Aron sought to demystify the Marxist inspiration relentlessly.[9] Aron's disenchanted defense of freedom, liberal democracy, and political reason in an intellectual context marked by radical egalitarianism, hyperrationalism, and political Manicheanism is all the more impressive when we realize, as we saw in the last chapter, that he felt, like so many of his generation, the emotional appeal of Marxism in his youth.

For this reason, we will in the following pages analyze Aron's critique of Marxism, and assess some of the principal concepts and methods he employed while carrying out that critique, including the important idea of "secular religion." This is of obvious historical interest, since Aron was one of the few critical spirits at odds with Marxism in the intellectual milieu described by Judt above. Why was Aron capable of resisting the "totalitarian temptation" when others of his generation, possessing similar intellectual backgrounds and gifts, were seduced? But an explication of Aron's interpretation and critique of Marxism is of more than historical interest, for it reveals, as if in a set of negative images, many of the themes of Aron's own social theory, crucial to a full comprehension of Aron's recovery of the political.

As we shall see, Aron's critique focuses on four different targets: Marxism as a "secular religion"; Marx as philosopher and sociologist; the Leninist transformation of Marx's thought; and the fusion of existentialism and Marxism characteristic of the thought of Jean-Paul Sartre and Maurice Merleau-Ponty.[10] After looking at each of these critiques in turn, we will conclude the present chapter with an appraisal of Aron's efforts to articulate a nonideological approach to political theory, drawing in part on Aron's 1955 essay "Fanaticism, Prudence, and Faith," where, in a search for a reasonable politics, he turns to Leo Strauss's reflection on natural right as a prudential alternative to the irrationalisms and hyperrationalisms of French intellectual life.

This debate with Marxism—in all its variations—concerned what Allan Bloom correctly referred to as the fundamental "issue of our time"[11]: the opposition between Western freedom and Soviet tyranny. The essence of Aron's thought on Marxism is contained in several books: *The Century of Total War, Opium of the Intellectuals, Main Currents of Sociological Thought, In Defense of Decadent Europe,* and *Marxism and the Existentialists* (a translation of a much longer book, *Marxismes imaginaires*) and in several important shorter essays. Unfortunately, Aron never wrote the comprehensive or synoptic book on Marx and Marxism he had often hoped to write. But the outline of such a book exists, scattered in these various places. We will range freely over them all in the effort to convey its basic teaching.

## 1. SECULAR RELIGION

Aron distinguished the inspiration behind the Marxist project, which was philosophical and bound to the historical transformations of modernity, from the ideas Marx set out as a social scientist. It was the former, the Marxist inspiration, that provided the source of Marxism's popularity in the twentieth century, not the esoteric doctrines of *Capital,* which he believed were of interest only to economists, sociologists, or professional philosophers. Our analysis in this section will thus begin with Aron's understanding of the Marxist inspiration before turning to Marx as a philosopher and sociologist. Aron's concept of secular religion, which, it will be argued, has its main derivation in his appropriation of the thought of Vilfredo Pareto, takes on its central importance at this time.

The key to conceptualizing the authority of Marxism as a popular belief, Aron wrote in his 1954 study, *The Century of Total War,* lay in recognizing Marxism as a "Christian heresy."[12] Aron believed that Marxism was a form of millennialism, with the Kingdom of God lowered from the heavens and situated within human temporality, "due to arrive after an apocalyptic revolution in which the old system will be engulfed."[13] The catastrophic revolution will be the outcome of fatal contradictions within capitalist society, and the oppressed, suffering souls haunting capitalism will be the dynamic agents of change: the proletariat will achieve salvation, redeeming man in the process. Three themes, Aron observed, formed the core of this ideology.

The first Aron refers to as the *Christian* theme: religions of salvation inevitably call for the revenge of the humble and downtrodden, offering them compensation in this world or the next. As Aron emphasizes, Marxism strikingly mirrors the traditional pattern of a religion of salvation:

> Marxism makes possible a sort of belief in the victory of slaves. For are not the industrial workers the true creators of wealth? Is not the elimination of the parasites and monopolists, who appropriate an exorbitant share of the collectivist income, irresistibly demanded by an immanent logic? Thus incorporated in a materialist dialectic, the idea of the overthrow of the hierarchy dissembles its true origin: The Christian aspirations, which atheism has not distinguished, or the more or less sublimated resentments of those who are relegated to the bottom of the social scale.[14]

Disguised with scientific camouflage, Marxism drew on deep spiritual longings for its popular success.

Second, Marxism expressed a *Promethean* theme. Prometheanism was, as Aron frequently pointed out, partly constitutive of the nature of modernity.[15] Although for Aron Prometheanism would later come to entail more, including the hubristic project of mastering society, in *The Century of Total War*, he views it as the potentially unlimited extension of human power over *natural* forces. The widening of the concept of Prometheanism, which would receive its fullest expression in the 1965 book *An Essay on Freedom*, was anticipated in 1954 by a third theme Aron believed made up the core of Marxism's popular appeal: *rationalism*. Aron tersely captures its basic idea in the following sentence: "Societies develop spontaneously: they need to be reconstructed rationally."[16] Because Marxism would reveal the laws of historical becoming, the future could be anticipated and the redemption of man and the mastery of nature could be known in advance. Society could be remade from the ground up, with all of history's contingencies, all undesired social differences, all social opacity eliminated by the newly sovereign collective subject, in control, at last, of its destiny.

Together, these three themes formed the unstable matrix of Marxism as a popular ideology. Each, taken alone, would not have sufficed to make of Marxism a "secular religion." Faith in the scientific enterprise by itself, Aron noted, would lead only to a form of "messianic expectancy"—a belief that, over time, modern science would triumph over injustice and poverty; revolt, taken in isolation, "would only revive illusions so often proved false."[17] It was necessary for these elements to be brought together and synthesized in a global vision of historical development in order for Marxism to be transformed into a substitute religion in the popular imagination.

The idea of secular religion was developed by Aron during the Second World War as a way of capturing what was historically unprecedented in the phenomena of Nazism and Communism. Returning to his 1944 essay "L'avenir des religions séculières" ("The Future of the Secular Religions") we can discern more clearly what Aron means by this philosophical and political category. There, he defines it in the following way: "I propose to call 'secular religions' doctrines which, in the souls of our contemporaries, take the place of vanished faith, and situate here below, in the distance of the future, in the form of a social order to be constructed, the salvation of humanity."[18]

Secular religions, then, were substitutes for the presumably exhausted traditional religions, participating in the same energies, giving voice to the same hopes that had been the trust of the Jewish and Christian revelation. But the young Marx had seen in religion only so much alienation: once man had asserted mastery over his own works, satisfaction would not need to be postponed to an afterlife; instead, the aspirations of man, long frustrated, would be realized in *this* world, in the *real* community.[19] As Aron underscored in the 1944 essay, however, this antireligious imperative, by seeking on Earth hopes previously placed beyond the end of time, dialectically transformed itself into a kind of religion, albeit one without a transcendent object of faith.

Psychologically, the affinities between religion and secular religion were considerable. Even without a transcendent object of faith, both Nazism and Marxian socialism were capable of inspiring devotion, where the faithful would put all of the resources of the spirit in the service of the cause. Both doctrines fixed "the final goal, the quasi-sacred goal in relation to which is defined good and evil,"[20] a lamentable fact when translated into politics, where nothing was sacred outside or beyond the demands of the movement.[21] Aron summed up the resemblances: the secular religions structurally reproduced characteristic traits of the older religions; they gave a global interpretation of the universe (or at least of the historical world); they explained the meaning of the misfortunes which made human life tragic; they instilled discipline and sacrifice in the present and separated, if only in the realm of theory, the individual from the anonymity of mass society, giving meaning to lives often without hope.[22] The secular religions were, in short, what Aron would come to call ideologies, and against them the liberal democracies were often at a severe disadvantage.[23]

There were, of course, differences between the Marxist revolutionaries and the Nazis. The Marxian socialists dreamed of a universal society, open to all; the Nazis of a particularized, closed utopia, open to members of the selected race only. In Aron's words:

> The dialectic which leads to socialism presents a type of intrinsic rationality. History, as the Hitlerians saw it, was dominated by the struggle between races, comparable to that which brings into opposition beasts of prey. The final objective has nothing in common with the accomplishment of the human vocation; rather it tends to be reducible to the victory of one species over another.[24]

But Nazism, like Marxian socialism, had proven seductive to the anomic masses of the twentieth century, torn by the dramatic transformations of modernity from their certainties, nostalgic for past glories or hopeful of radiant futures. Modern science and the recognition of religious plural- ism had resulted, as Aron believed and as Weber had hypothesized, in the "disenchantment of the world." But this disenchantment had not appeased the spiritual hunger of a dissatisfied humanity; in fact, Aron reasoned, nothing would appease that hunger except "a plenitude com- parable to the one that had been promised to them."[25]

The secular religions, products of modernity itself, filled a spiritual void with false teachings and empty promises, offering a community, however impoverished, to millions of individuals desperate to believe. As Aron warned in 1944, "Every crisis, economic or political, which would uproot these multitudes, would deliver them, once again, to the joint temptations of despair and enthusiasm."[26] But it was not just the masses hearing the siren call: intellectuals, confronted with the fragmen- tation and complexity of knowledge in the modern world, often suc- cumbed to the desire for systematization, and Marxism in particular but Nazism as well, as the example of Heidegger shows, provided order and a supreme principle of authority when all other such principles were collapsing.

There was a dark and somewhat paradoxical figure lurking in the shadows of Aron's analysis of secular religion, a figure that both attracted and repulsed Aron: the disenchanted modern Machiavellian, Vilfredo Pareto.[27] The influence of Pareto on Aron's early writings was consider- able, as can be seen by attending to the posthumously published work Aron wrote, but never completed during the first part of World War II, *Machiavel et les tyrannies modernes.* Here we find a series of studies on Machiavelli and Pareto dedicated to utilizing their views on politics in the analysis and critique of the antiliberal totalitarianisms. Aron discov- ered in Pareto's *Treatise on General Society*[28] a theory of the circulation of elites along with a partial explanation of the human need for collective identification. Like the American philosopher James Burnham, Aron saw in the pessimistic politics of Pareto (and the Machiavellian tradition) what Stuart Campbell has called "a meaningful antidote" to the threat of Communist millennialism.[29] Pareto argued in the *Treatise* that all soci- eties will inevitably be divided into a small elite and a majority who, in turn, will be led. The members of the elite will either be "foxes," adept at acquiring the consent of the governed through manipulation, or "lions," willing and capable of using force against those who would dare oppose their rule. Political history tended to be the story of conflicts between foxes and lions for the spoils of power; but the distance separating the elite from the majority would remain, whatever the outcome of the struggle for power.[30] Marxism as a doctrine of collective salvation disguised this immemorial fact of human social life; as Aron was to note many years later, while discussing Pareto, the latter reminds us that the "modern class struggle, insofar as it is a struggle between the proletariat and the bourgeoisie, will result not in the victory of the proletariat but in the victory of those who speak in the name of the proletariat, a privileged minority no different from the elites that have preceded or will succeed it."[31] Aron felt that Pareto's demystifying cynicism, while in many respects exaggerated, was a salutary influence when used to confront the claims of modern ideologies; it was a bracing reminder that the realm of the political was distinguished by certain constants and that the dreams of the revolutionaries were either naive or hypocritical. They were, in short, unrealizable.

Second, Pareto divided human actions into logical and nonlogical (which, it is important to add, does not mean illogical) conduct. The bulk of social action, on Pareto's view, fell into the latter category, which meant that human behavior was directed by forces which were prerational. These prerational forces, "residues" in Paretian terminology, would give rise to "derivations": rationalizations and justifications that changed according to the circumstances of time and place, but which were rooted ultimately in certain constants of human behavior. The need for religious identification, on the Paretian view, was residual, while the derivative forms that identification might take could differ significantly. In the twentieth century they had taken the degraded form of the political religions of Nazism and communism. Aron, writing at a time of collective fanaticisms, found in Pareto's pessimistic conception of human nature a confirmation of what he was witnessing in the bloody confrontations of the century:

> The majority of minds, in the 19th century, were dominated by the idea of a unique, irreversible movement. In a climate of rationalist optimism, this idea was an idea of progress. No one puts in doubt the accumulation of knowledge, and, consequently, the increase in man's power over nature. But the economist has correctly drawn our attention to the fact that, although the standard of living of the worker in

the United States may be closely equivalent to that of Louis XIV, neither the nature of man nor the organization of societies are necessarily changed in depth by the turbulence of technology. But that is the essential point.[32]

In politics, in other words, *plus ça change, plus c'est la même chose*. But Aron did not follow Pareto all the way through to a historical philosophy of Machiavellian cynicism. He recognized that there were unprecedented elements at work in the ascendancy of the secular religions which needed to be met on their own terms, the explanation of which had to have recourse, therefore, to the *particulars* of ideology. History could not be so easily reduced to the natural oscillations of warring species of elite. That said, Pareto's theory of elites and his emphasis on the prerational component of social life were ideas Aron found useful in the analysis and critique of the secular religions. They contributed *partial* tools in the conceptualization of a complex historical, political, and social phenomenon. Aron's reliance on interpretive pluralism, which we considered in the previous chapter, can be seen at work in the appropriation of Paretian ideas. Pareto did not ask, however, what were for Aron the most important questions: What were the relations between the dominant minority and the many? What principles of legitimacy, what justifications, were proffered by the ruling elites? How did elites retain hold of the reigns of authority? How much mobility existed between the many and the elite? In other words, was the elite permeable? It was along the versant established by these questions that the crucial distinctions between democracy and totalitarianism opened up.[33] The political problem *par excellence*—and it was a problem, *pace* Marxism, without a permanent solution—was that of making the relations between the few and the many as humane and permeable as possible; it was, in short, the avoidance of evil. In this recognition, what we previously described as Aron's Montesquieuean "liberalism of fear" found its deepest meaning.[34] Such a conception of liberalism is based less on a strict construal of human nature, inevitably conflictual because based on metaphysical controversy, than on a *political* understanding which seeks to devise institutional ways of avoiding the often ruinous consequences of what, in a religious setting, might be termed original sin. It acknowledges that while we might disagree profoundly about what constitutes the good life for man, agreement surrounding what is morally repugnant, or threatening to the basic shared goods of a common human world, is easier to achieve.

How useful, or accurate, was Aron's category of secular religion in capturing the essence of ideological politics? Certainly, it helped bring out what similarities existed between Marxism, fascism, and Nazism, and what separated each from the more prosaic, but far more humane nature of liberal democracy. But it risked blurring what distinguished the various antiliberal ideologies from each other and therefore had limits as an analytic tool. The political theorist John Gray has argued that calling Marxism a "religion" is degrading to the true religions, which carry a much richer spiritual and intellectual weight. As he puts it, "If Marxism is a religion, it is only in the sense that occultism and theosophy— modern forms of magical thought which seek an abatement of tragedy and mystery through a sort of rationalistic gnosis—are religions."[35] But Aron's Paretian employment of the concept of secular religion stopped far short of directly equating real religious belief and its *doppelganger* in the political faiths of our age. In *The Century of Total War*, Aron states this unambiguously:

> It is enough to grasp the basis of religious feeling to recognize the essential difference between Stalinist fanaticism and a genuine religion. Communism points out to its adherents enemies to hate and a future to build. It arouses passionate devotion. But it offers nothing to love.[36]

Finally, then, Aron's use of the concept is best seen as part of an effort to demystify the millennial promises of ideological politics, to make the political more mundane, more prosaic, to disenchant what had been falsely enchanted. In short, it is best seen as a method of avoiding the worst, necessary during a time when the totalitarian temptation was at the height of its seductive powers. By focusing on the affinities "scientific" Marxism shared with the religions it despised, and by reminding his readers of the eternal constraints of the political, Aron helped, particularly in France, to bankrupt the Marxist enterprise in intellectual circles as thoroughly as fascism had been foreclosed on the battlefields of World War II. He thus helped open the way for a renewal of a *political* liberalism in a context that had long been resistant to political moderation. But what of the Marxism of Marx himself?

## 2. THE MARXISM OF MARX

In Aron's view, Marx was "essentially—if not exclusively—a *critical analyst of capitalism* as he observed it in mid-nineteenth century Britain and the *prophet of a catastrophe* which, after an interlude of dictatorship of the proletariat, was to usher in an end to exploitation of man by man and, therefore, socialism."[37] The idea that Marx was, above all, the critical analyst of the capitalist system, something stressed by Aron on several occasions in his writings on Marx, helps us to distinguish Aron's Marx from rival interpretations.

In emphasizing *this* vision of Marx, which implies that he was a sociologist and economist situated in a particular historical context, Aron is distancing himself from the tradition of Marxist thought associated with Georg Lukacs that took its bearings not from Marx's mature writings, the dense works of political economy culminating in the three volumes of *Capital*, but rather from his youthful, more "humanist" works.[38] Marx's earlier thought is characterized by a degree of moral fervor that is somewhat submerged in *Capital*, as well as a far more explicitly philosophical or metaphysical approach than found in Marx's later writings.

This is not to say that Aron perceives an "epistemological break" in Marx's thought between Hegelian philosophy and the "science" of history as expounded by the last major French Marxist, Louis Althusser.[39] Philosophical themes of Hegelian inspiration can still be found in *Capital*; the concern with history and the concrete existence of man is already present in Marx's earliest essays. But Marx *himself* saw his crowning achievement as *Capital*. He believed that he had scientifically discovered and demonstrated the laws of historical development. One of Aron's intellectual virtues was the principle of interpretive charity, closely linked to the notion of fairness or equity we looked at in the previous chapter. He refused the position of *external* critique as much as possible, preferring to move inside the thought of the other, determining strengths and weaknesses from within. This virtue led Aron to attempt to understand the other on the other's *own* terms. There are, subsequently, few straw targets in Aron's pages. If Marx felt the essence of his thought could be found in his mature work, Aron concluded, it would be eminently sensible to take Marx at his word and try to understand what it was that was expressed there.

Aron's exposition of the "Marxism of Marx," then, presented most thoroughly in *Main Currents of Sociological Thought*, centered around three of Marx's texts: *The Communist Manifesto*, the preface to the *Contribution to a Critique of Political Economy*, and, of course, *Capital*.[40] Each book was associated with certain paradigmatic Marxist theses. Three "clusters" of theses were of significance for Aron: from *The Communist Manifesto*, the idea of class struggle; from the *Contribution*, the general theory of Marx's economic interpretation of history, historical materialism; from the three volumes of *Capital*, Marx's substantive theory of capitalism—how it functioned, what its structure was, where it would go. Most of the ideas drawn from these works, which we will present when appropriate in what follows, contained fundamental ambiguities the sum of which can be linked directly to the role Marxism played in the twentieth century as a secular religion. They provided a degree of flexibility to Marx's thought which bordered on the protean, making it notoriously difficult—if not impossible—to falsify Marxism when taken globally, as Karl Popper has shown.[41]

Aron's criticism of the Marxism of Marx explores two kinds of these ambiguities: ambiguities of a philosophical stripe, on the one hand; sociological ambiguities on the other. The principal philosophical ambiguity ties in with our concerns of the last chapter and relates to the nature of historical law. There are, Aron relates, at least two distinct ways of thinking about historical law to be found in the Marxist tradition. Historical law can be viewed as *objective*, as being, that is, in correspondence with the broad outline of history. From the available historical data Marx selected what he felt to be of the greatest importance in the construction of the laws of historical transformation. But it is crucial to highlight the fact that Marx indeed *selected* the data. As we saw in the last chapter, this fact of selection necessitates the presence of the historical observer and the inevitable presence of a degree of subjectivity in the constitution of the object of historical study. While historical reality is not itself constructed, the observer's philosophical, political, and moral concerns will influence what aspect of it will be brought to the surface.

Aron also draws our attention to another difficulty with the conception of objective historical law: that it fails to detail with any specificity the events of the future. That is, although Marx asserts with confidence the inevitability of the self-destruction of capitalism and the advent of a nonantagonistic, postpolitical society in its wake, he has nothing to say about when these catastrophic upheavals are to occur. As Aron frequently emphasized, in Marx's thought the "future . . . is partially undetermined in that the moment and the modalities of fulfilment are not foreseeable and are not, perhaps, rigorously determined."[42] Marx's conception of historical law, if understood in the objectivist sense presented here (as ontological), thus suffers from a radical indeterminacy. An historical law of this kind bears little relation to the laws of the natural sciences because it is utterly lacking in predictive power.

Aron referred to this combination of confidence in the expected occurrence of the catastrophe and radical indeterminacy as *prophetism*, and the religious current surging through the scientistic scaffolding is hard to deny. The indeterminacy of the future cataclysm proved extremely useful to twentieth-century revolutionary regimes by granting them flexibility in their relations with the external, nonrevolutionary world. Capitalist regimes could be bargained with, even, on occasion, accommodated ("peaceful coexistence"), while the masters of the revolution waited for the final denouement, biding time before the historically conclusive struggle.[43]

An objectivist understanding was not the only way of conceiving of the nature of historical law within the Marxist tradition. In the *dialectical* conception of historical law, extremely popular for a time on the Parisian left bank, the Marxist vision is seen as the articulation of the reciprocal action between the world of history and the subject of consciousness. On this view, there is also reciprocal action between the different spheres or sectors of historical reality: society affects the economy, the economy affects the political, and so on. But this points to a problem: while Sartre and Merleau-Ponty (left bank representatives *par excellence*) retain Marxist categories in their philosophical writings, they have no pretense of revealing historical laws as the natural sciences reveal natural laws. The condition of those living under the sway of capitalism can be philosophically articulated, but that is all. As Aron explained, however, a dialectical interpretation does not of necessity lead to the advent of the nonantagonistic society. Nor does it of necessity lead to finding the condition of man as exploited or alienated, as the Marxist vision commands. While Aron shares the *premises* of the dialectical interpretation, he resists the conclusions derived from it by Sartre and Merleau-Ponty. In fact, the conclusions the latter derive seem at odds with their premises: If, as both Sartre and Merleau-Ponty hold, the individual subject conceives of history from his own position, why is the Marxist perspective deemed superior? The Marxist totality fragments into innumerable sources of knowledge, each with a seemingly legitimate claim to be taken seriously.

Aron locates a second group of philosophical ambiguities, and these are related to the connection between science and prescription in Marx's thought. Aron poses the question, Is Marx the inheritor of Kant or Hegel? A Kantian Marxism would stress the separation of fact and value, the "is" and the "ought." Marxism would be, on this view, a science bereft of moral implications. A reading of *Capital* would tell us all we need to know about surplus value; the desire for socialism would be another matter entirely, requiring an ethical imperative irreducible to the factual revelations and lawlike generalizations of Marxist "science." A Hegelian Marxism, on the other hand, would be a monism of ethical imperative and scientific truth. The "is" and the "ought" would not be separable; the subject who seeks knowledge of history is immersed in history, while socialism would emerge and must emerge from the antagonistic capitalist society. The historical observer is led inexorably from scrutinizing the real to the desire for what is not yet born, but which gestates in the womb of the present. As Aron explains, each of us is, for the Hegelian Marxist, part of history. We take our frame of reference, our conceptual bearings, from our historical situation. We grasp reality based on our contact with it, but by denying the real we express our desire for another, superior reality. The "is" and the "ought" are inextricably intertwined. Between these two alternatives, where, Aron asks, did Marx situate himself? He was, Aron argues, at the same time scientist and revolutionary. While, as a good child of the Enlightenment, he would refuse to recognize the dependency of his scientific interpretation of capitalism on a moral decision, Marx was at the same time convinced of the moral degeneracy of capitalism. To analyze it was indeed to hope for its destruction.

The twentieth century saw these two alternatives brought together in an unlikely and horrifying synthesis: dialectical materialism, the official philosophy of the Soviet Union. Its original source was Friedrich Engels's *Anti-Duhring*, where a crude metaphysic was propounded at length. The content of this metaphysic is presented by Aron as containing the following assertions: the law of reality itself was dialectical; there was a hierarchy in the various species of the world, with the human being at its apex; and a reworking of the Hegelian thesis that quantitative change at a certain point becomes qualitative. But what was the *extent* of dialectics? Was it applicable to the natural world, organic and inorganic, as well as to the human? In the historical world, Aron maintains, societies constitute in a certain sense totalities. One could legitimately make the effort to explain the different sectors of social reality in terms of one essential element, such as the economy, as long as one understood the partiality of such an approach. But could such an effort be undertaken in the analysis of nature? The answer was obviously no. Aron felt, however, that one could easily abandon the dialectics of the material world and still remain a Marxist: "Logically and philosophically, the economic interpretation of history and the critique of capitalism in terms of the class struggle have nothing to do with the dialectics of nature."[44]

While the philosophical equivocations were profound, Marx's sociology was also characterized by conceptual ambiguities. It is in elaborating on these ambiguities that Aron's fundamental disagreements with Marx become most clearly visible. The most important distinction Aron makes, and it is a distinction that regularly appears in his work, is that between the *methodological* use of concepts and their *ontological* extension. As mentioned earlier, it was the latter that Aron held to be one of the sources of Marxist dogmatism.[45]

Aron argues that the *critical* use of the Marxist conceptual battery—notions such as the forces and relations of production, infrastructure and superstructure, class relations, etc.—is "unquestionably legitimate."[46] Indeed, Aron himself utilized them in many of his analyses of modern societies, including his trilogy on industrial society.[47] But Aron used these concepts methodologically, and such use does not sanction their extension into a full-fledged philosophy of history. One need only consult historical experience in order to recognize that these ideas captured no essence, that they were not grounded in the inherent structure of the real in the way envisioned by the Marxists. As Aron puts it, "one risks finding at the same degree of development, productive forces may correspond to different relations of production."[48] Private property could correspond to an advanced development of the productive forces, collective ownership with an inferior development. Marxism, understood as a philosophy of history ontologically extending its central concepts, presupposes a correlation between the development of the productive forces and the transformation of the relations of production, bringing in its wake an intensification of the class struggle. What happens, Aron asked, when the class struggle, instead of intensifying, is lessened with the development of the forces of production, as had obviously been the case with the history of capitalism? The Marxist philosophy of history runs aground against the reef of actual historical experience. However much dialectical subtlety Marxists have subsequently employed in order to obscure this truth, it remains the single most damning refutation of Marxism as a system of thought, both sociologically and historically.

For Marx, societies are to be understood on the basis of their infrastructure (state of productive forces, science and technology, organization of labor, etc.). To shift from a critical analysis to a determinative one, *determined* relations between infrastructure and superstructure and between the forces and relations of production must be affirmed. But because most Marxist thinkers have acknowledged that determined relations appear too rigid, the notion of determination has often been replaced with the idea of "conditioning." The problem with this substitution, however, as Aron underscores, is that "conditioning" is as vague as determination is rigid. In a given society, any sector at any given moment conditions another sector. This reciprocal conditioning, which we discussed in the previous chapter, is for Aron the "very law" of social reality. There is a mutual conditioning of all the different sectors: economic on the political, the political on the social, and so on. The discernment of this interconnectedness of social reality was one of the dimensions of Montesquieu's thought that Aron admired greatly.[49] But the flexibility of the concept of conditioning raises questions about its usefulness. Something in between determination and conditioning was needed. That said, it was hard to escape the paramount significance that the idea of determination held for Marx himself.

As Aron explains, Marx saw the various kinds of society observable in history as all being marked by a certain mode of relation between owners and laborers: "Marx believed he would find the specific characteristics of a historical state in terms of certain characteristics which in his eyes were fundamental."[50] The problem with Marx's vision was that the facts he deemed inseparable were, in fact, separable. History had rendered its verdict, and no amount of dialectical sophistication could successfully reassemble the original Marxist unity after its disarticulation.

Aron's critique of Marx's sociological thought is organized into six areas of conceptual difficulty. Keeping in mind Aron's distinction between the methodological and the ontological utilization of concepts, an elaboration of these areas will allow us to finally get to the kernel of his rejection of Marxism.

1. *The class struggle.* The idea of the class struggle is at the center of Marx's thought. In *The Communist Manifesto*, the renowned polemic where Marx's core themes were presented for the first time, we see the entire pageantry of historical experience reduced to the war between classes: "free men and slaves, patricians and plebeians, barons and serfs, master artisans and journeymen."[51] In each instance what confronts us is the antagonism between oppressor and oppressed. As Aron describes it, the first fundamental idea for Marx was that "human history is characterized by the struggle of human groups which will be called social classes whose definition remains for the moment ambiguous, but which are characterized in the first place by an antagonism between oppressors and oppressed and in the second place by a tendency toward a polarization into two blocs and only two."[52]

At the heart of capitalism for Marx were the familiar figures of the bourgeoisie and the proletariat, locked in mortal combat. What distinguished the bourgeoisie from all previous exploiting classes? It was, Marx asserted, the need, driven by economic competition, to permanently revolutionize the tools and frameworks of economic production. This permanent revolution unleashed unimaginable energies, creating wealth on an unprecedented scale. This wealth was in the possession of fewer and fewer people, however, and the vast mass of the working proletariat would grow both in size and in impoverishment. But just as the productive forces which brought about the emergence of capitalism grew within the body of feudalism, so, Marx held, within capitalism were growing the productive forces which would give rise to the socialist regime, allow the expropriation of the expropriators, and spread the wealth hoarded by the bourgeoisie to the laboring masses, thus ending the reign of capital on a funeral pyre of its own making.

At the basis of the antagonism between bourgeoisie and the laboring classes was the antagonism between the forces and the relations of production, equivocal concepts which we will critically examine with Aron's help below. But fundamental to the *Manifesto*, Aron believed, were two assertions: the idea that capitalist society is *essentially* antagonistic, with this antagonism polarizing social relations; and, second, the important but dangerously misconceived notion that political power is the manifestation of class domination and nothing more. This *reduction of the political*, unfortunately still with us in other guises, was entirely in keeping with the scientistic eddies and flows of nineteenth-century intellectual life. Such currents saw politics as epiphenomenal, pulled along by deeper, more important subpolitical determinations, usually located in economic and social phenomena.

The refusal to grant autonomous status to the political realm brought with it more than explanatory inadequacies. It led Marx to the illusion that the elimination of conflicts rooted in economic life would render politics redundant. The political realm would disappear, "wither away," after the triumph of the working class, bearing the aspirations of universal humanity as its historical sword. As the political theorist Claude Lefort captures the radicality of this "leap" beyond politics, "the history of humanity, which unfolds in its entirety before the eyes of the Communists, leads to a society *without ideas*, to a society which coincides with itself to such an extent as to preclude the possibility of judgment being formulated within it."[53] In Aron's estimation, this theoretical error has been the basis for the failure, by virtually the entire Marxist tradition, to think in political terms.

While Marx did not invent the category of class conflict (we can find it in Aristotle), his originality lay in the assertion that the existence of classes was attached to specific historical phases, and that the nonantagonistic society destined to replace capitalist society would be without class relations.[54] As Aron frequently observed, however, the notion of social class is equivocal, and Marx's writings on the subject share in the equivocation. What is a social class?

Marx offers several different ways of understanding the idea of social class in his copious writings. One definition, found primarily in Marx's theoretical work, stipulates that a class occupies a fixed location in the production process. This place is both technical and legal. In Marx's historical studies, however, we see an enumeration of classes somewhat at odds with his more theoretical work.[55] The theoretical writings often advance the notion that, with the development of capitalism, class relations become simplified. The culmination of the process of simplification is the polarization of class relations, with, as we have seen, only two classes, the proletariat and the bourgeoisie, remaining. There is, Aron believes, despite appearances, no contradiction here with Marx's historical work, where this process of simplification gives way to a more varied phenomenology of historical existence and the human world. In the historical studies, Marx was analysing which groups had influence over political events in *specific* historical circumstances. But, that said, the transition from the Marxist theory of class, based on sources of income, to the observation by the historian of specific social groups, is not easy to make. What does seem to be necessary for the existence of a social class is a "certain psychological community"—a sense of unity, a capacity and need for common action.[56]

According to Aron, we have in Marx two parts of a working definition of social class, one part based on sources of income, the other rooted in a sense of psychological community. A third part, more political, can also be discovered in Marx's texts. This third component requires a class to possess a "consciousness of unity, a feeling of separation from other social classes, and even a feeling of hostility toward other social classes."[57] Combined, Aron professes, these three categories of Marxist texts provide not a complete theory, but a "sufficiently clear" political and sociological theory of social class.

Aron raises two basic objections to Marx's theory of class. The first rests on the disanalogy between the rise of the bourgeoisie and the supposed rise of the proletariat. The bourgeoisie did indeed bring with it new forces of production within feudal society. It was a privileged minority performing socially dominant functions within the old order. But, as Aron points out, in a capitalist society, the proletariat is not a privileged minority; rather, it is the great mass of unprivileged workers. Nor does it establish new forms or relations of production. The analogy Marx establishes between the rise of the two social categories thus has no basis in fact. It is, ironically enough, a myth, something Marx wanted to dispel from the analysis of the historical and political world.

Second, the minority that comes to rule in the name of the bourgeoisie is the bourgeoisie itself. It is drawn from the bourgeois class and legitimately represents bourgeois interests. They are the leaders of society, controlling industry and commerce. But after the proletarian revolution, Aron contends (and as we have explored above in our discussion of Pareto), it is individuals *claiming* to represent the proletariat who come to power. How could the proletariat itself become the privileged and dominant minority, structurally required by any complex society? This is, for Aron, "the central, immediately obvious error of the entire Marxist vision of history, an error whose consequences have been considerable."[58] The "proletariat in power" was a lie and always would be a lie until the Marxist project finally imploded several years after Aron's death.

2. *Infrastructure and superstructure.* Aron poses the question: What are the components of social reality which belong to the infrastructure? Or, on the other hand, to the superstructure? The infrastructure should, it seems, at least as Marx had laid out the distinction in *Contribution to a Critique of Political Economy*, refer to the forces and relations of production—the economic bases of society which determine the legal and political institutions, religions, philosophical beliefs, all of which seemingly reside in the superstructure. But what, exactly, are the forces of production? Aron describes them as being a function "of scientific knowledge, technological equipment and the organization of collective labor."[59] The technical apparatus of society cannot, however, be separated from the level of scientific knowledge. How could it be? But the latter would seem to belong to the sphere of ideas, which should, according to Marx, derive from the superstructure.

Thus, Aron argues, there seems to be already present in the infrastructure elements which should derive from the superstructure. It is extremely difficult to isolate what belongs to each. The forces of production, in addition, depend on the way labor is collectively organized. But this in turn depends on the laws of ownership, which belong to the legal domain, which belongs to the state, which belongs, apparently, to the superstructure. Once again, the difficulties in separating out what belongs to each sphere of social reality are evident. While these concepts may, Aron notes, retain legitimate use as instruments of analysis, when dogmatically extended and made determinative, insuperable complications inevitably follow. The differentiation of infrastructure and superstructure has proven to be a knotty and confused area of Marxist theory, spawning swarms of analyses which seek to refine or further clarify this conceptual distinction, all of which have seemingly come to naught.

3. *Forces and relations of production.* There was for Marx a *mechanism* of historical movement, the product of the contradiction between the forces and the relations of production. We have just seen what make up the forces of production. The *relations* of production consist of both property relations and the distribution of national income. At a certain point in time, according to the Marxist schema, the former grows too powerful for the latter to contain, resulting in a fundamental transforma-

tion in their relationship. At a certain stage of development, for example, private property represents an impediment to the future development of the productive forces. With the coming of Marx's postcapitalist regime, the collective control of society's productive capacity would be initiated through the socialization of the means of production, through, that is, the elimination of private property and its replacement with collective ownership.

There is a grain of truth to this analysis, Aron contends, for if you look to the emergence of the great enterprises, it is clear that the size of many modern companies has rendered individual ownership obsolete. But if the great enterprises are seen as the very essence of capitalism, then we can readily demonstrate that the Marxist view on the contradictory nature of the forces and relations of production is false. Aron is telling us that Marx is, at least in part, a product of his time. Looking to Marx to find solutions to problems he did not even conceive of can easily give way to historical anachronism, or even mythologization, if this fact is not taken into account.

Marx makes another, somewhat different, argument about the development of the forces of production. This argument posits that the distribution of ownership, which determines to a large extent income distribution, is such that capitalist society cannot absorb its own production. Purchasing power consequently remains lower than the demands of the economy require. As a result, capitalist societies will be disrupted by constant crises. Yet, Aron responds, if this contradiction were true, then it has been at work since the onset of capitalist economic relations, while the productive forces continue to grow. If Marx's thesis had substance to it, then historical experience would have provided the evidence necessary to support it. But history has not provided such evidence, so it can be said with some measure of confidence that Marx's hypothesis has not been demonstrated. We do not know when, or if, a capitalist economy will produce such an excess that its absorption will be impossible. We have no reason to believe that it will happen any time soon, or at all. More important, from Aron's vantage point, is the fact that Marx's theoretical approach to historical explanation is based on the analysis of "supraindividual structures." Implicit in such an approach is a lack of concern for the intentions and self-perceptions of historical actors—what in our previous chapter we looked at under the heading of interpretive understanding. Given that Aron held this latter method to be crucial in the examination of the political and historical realm (enabling him to adopt the commonsense perspective of citizen or Prince), we can immediately identify one of his essential disagreements with Marx or any other theorist focusing solely, or even primarily, on what takes place behind the backs of men and women. Such conceptions deny the ability of individuals (or nations, through their political representatives, as we will see) to determine their destiny, and thus commit a fundamental error of philosophical anthropology by denying the partially free status of the human person. They also fall prey to forms of functionalist explanation which can easily find themselves relying on reified anthropomorphic forces—History or Capital—acting as if they *themselves* had agency.

4. *The relationship between sociology and economics*. In Aron's view, there are numerous difficulties in Marx's articulation of the respective roles of the economic and the sociological. First of all, the capitalist regime functions only if there is a group of individuals in possession of available capital. But how does this group come to be? What is the formative process of capital accumulation? This cannot be explained in solely economic terms. Extra-economic phenomena have to be introduced in order to provide the conditions for the regime's functioning. This is a problem which manifests itself at the outset of Marx's theory.

Second, Aron affirms, the same problem appears at the conclusion of Marx's enterprise. Marx proffered any number of reasons for believing capitalism would function poorly, ravaged by internal antagonisms and countless economic and social crises.[60] But there is no *economic* demonstration of the self-destruction of capitalism on the basis of these antagonisms and crises. In order to theorize the self-destruction of capitalism, one would have to have recourse to *political* and *sociological* factors.

A third problem located by Aron concerns surplus value. Every modern economy (by which Aron means economies that have begun the process of industrialization) needs to accumulate a share of the annual production in order to expand the productive forces, a fact recognized by Marx.[61] Striking a Comtean or Saint Simonian note, Aron noted how the pursuit of productivity constituted the modern project as distinctively as the spread of democracy. Our age was characterized above all by the "monstrous development of technology and industry."[62] It was necessary to show, however, how the capitalist mechanism of saving and investment differs from other historical possibilities found in other

modern economies. A true Marxist would seek to analyse "the peculiari-
ties of a modern economy of another type."[63] This was a task carried
out by few twentieth-century Marxist thinkers, who remained content
to find wisdom in the writings of their master, and thus, paradoxically,
betrayed his legacy.

5. *The relation between the political regime and the economic system.* For
Aron, this is one of the weakest elements of Marx's sociology. As we
have seen, the state is considered by Marx to be an instrument of class
domination. After the proletarian revolution, and following a period of
dictatorial rule by the representatives of the proletariat, the state will no
longer be necessary. Classes having been eliminated, the *raison d'etre* of
the political will be lost, and the state will disappear. Aron's criticisms of
this dangerously wrong idea are manifold, and reveal Aron's political
sensibility.

Aron's first objection seems obvious, but it is important to remem-
ber the subsequent influence of Marx's naive conception of the political.
We can often see it echoed in the fanciful projects for participatory democracy advanced by more recent thinkers. Aron's point can be summarized as follows: a complex industrial society cannot do without an
administration centralized in certain important respects. A planned
economy requires centralized mechanisms that increase state power ex-
ponentially. In the absence of a free market, the coordination of economic life by political authorities inevitably and ironically leads to the
*absolute* primacy of politics, not its disappearance. A capitalist economy,
whatever inequalities it may generate, is partially defined by a decentral-
ization of decision-making power that decreases the role of the state in
the lives of its citizens. We can see evidence of the qualities of Aron's
conservative liberalism in this critique of Marx's abolition of politics, a
liberalism of an older and richer vintage than the modern *statist* liberalism
still dominant in the Western academy, if less so in Western political life.

What conceivably does disappear after the proletarian revolution is
the class makeup of the state. As Aron maintains, one can imagine the
state becoming the expression of society as a whole. But is the state in
the capitalist regime to be defined solely in terms of the power of a given
class? How could there ever be a society without antagonism? There
will be, in a postcapitalist regime just as in any regime, individuals who
exercise power in the name of the masses. There will be a state carrying
out the direction of the economy and the administrative functions nec-

essary in any complex society. There will still be antagonistic relations, between horizontal as well as vertical groups. Aron argues that one cannot establish the basis for a nonantagonistic society on the elimination of private ownership of the means of production: intergroup antagonisms have grounds other than private property. In fact, as John Gray has observed, the Marxist project, as it was realized in the Soviet Union, China, and elsewhere, gave birth to unprecedented social antagonisms, where almost all positions of success were *positional goods* (goods that cannot be possessed by all, that are, in fact, mutually exclusive).[64]

Aron's third criticism of Marx's conceptualization of the relationship of the political to the economic system is closely related to the two previous observations. It is a *global* rejection of Marx's economism, his reduction of the political, and much else besides, to the economic. The political is, on the Aronian view, irreducible to the economic. The *political problem* still remains, regardless of the social or economic regime. The political problem consists of determining who governs, how leaders are chosen, how power is exercised and what the relationship of consent or dissent is between the governing and the governed. It is, as Aron put it in the essay "Fanaticism, Prudence and Faith," to "reconcile the participation of all men in the community with the diversity of tasks."[65] These are questions that all political regimes must respond to, whatever the time, wherever the place. Marx's *postpolitical* utopia would be forced to answer them just as every other collective has had to answer them across history. Politics are as essential and relatively autonomous as the economic order. Between them there is, as we have seen at several points during the course of this chapter, a reciprocal relation. This is one of Aron's integral themes.

6. *Ideas and ideologies.* In the Marxist doctrine ideas belong to the superstructure, the outgrowth, the reflection, or the support of social class. Ideology, for Marx, was the province of false consciousness. He held that a class cannot see beyond its own condition. Aron offered two relevant objections to Marx's theory of ideology. The first asked the question: If, because of its particular situation, a class is confused by false consciousness, how did a member of this class find himself capable of clearing away the cobwebs? And, in addition, if every class can only think from within its class-determined perspective, how is truth possible? How could we say whether one ideology is better, or more true, than another? The only reply Marx (or gender theorists, race theorists,

and poststructuralists) could logically make is that one conception has more purchase on the real than its rivals. One class, or one gender, or one race sees the world for what it *really* is. For the Marxist tradition, the proletariat alone (or, really, a few intellectuals) holds the key to unlocking reality. But, as Aron acutely perceived, this is a weak argument: Why would the proletariat alone be capable of freeing itself from prejudice? The same objection—how is the theorist himself capable of reaching the truth?—might be addressed with some justice to any poststructuralist.

Aron's point was to stress that different intellectual constructs relate to the social milieu in varying ways. It is important to discern carefully the ways these divagating constructs, from painting to mathematics, relate to social reality. This is essential to safeguarding the possible universality of certain scientific truths and the universal value of certain works of art, as well as certain moral goods. Marx was far too intelligent to consistently reduce scientific truth or cultural expressions to epiphenomena of class. But in order to ward off the disintegrating force of modern nihilism, Aron avows that it is necessary to recognize, on the one hand, that there are domains where the thinker *can* arrive at a universal truth and, on the other, acknowledge that there are regions in which artistic and intellectual creations have value that transcends the bounds of culture or temporality. In other words, it is necessary to reject the Marxist theory of false consciousness.

We have followed the trajectory of Aron's reading of Marx closely, and the essence of his critique of Marx's thought should now be clear. Two themes tie together the various criticisms. The first, which reveals Aron's "elective affinity" with more politically and historically minded thinkers like Montesquieu and Tocqueville, remains the resistance to hubristic, totalizing theories in the study of human phenomena. Marx's economic theory of historical interpretation is perhaps the paradigmatic example of such a global theory. The distinction between the ontological employment of concepts, as manifested in Marx's work, and the critical, methodological use of concepts, which Aron favors, must be seen as one of the fundamental motifs of the latter's thought. The second theme is Aron's refusal to regard the political as a manifestation of phenomena external to the political. Politics is a specific sphere of social reality, autonomous and sometimes primary in the constitution of the historical and social world. In this, too, Aron looks to Montesquieu and

Tocqueville, both of whom stressed the importance of politics. Marx did not believe this to be the case, instead forwarding a theory of economic determination which saw the economic sphere as primary and the political as merely epiphenomenal.

But what of Marxism's fate in the twentieth century? How did Aron interpret the cataclysmic events which rocked Russia during the First World War, culminating in a tyranny lasting for much of the century? What was the role of Lenin in these terrible events? How did he adapt or transform the thought of Marx? We will now turn to this third part of our look at Aron's struggle against Marxism and ideological thought.

### 3. LENIN AND THE TOTALITARIAN STYLE OF THOUGHT

Lenin's contribution to the corpus of Marxist thought consists in several ideas that unquestionably bear a strong measure of responsibility for the horrors of Marxism in practice during the twentieth century. Although, as Leszek Kolakowski and others have suggested,[66] one can find the seeds of totalitarianism in the writings of Marx, Lenin was instrumental in constructing the system within which they grew to maturity. Aron, in his various discussions of Lenin's thought, stressed the import of four of these ideas.

The first, and the one with the most practical significance for the history of the Russian Revolution, was advanced in Lenin's polemic *What Is to Be Done?*: *democratic centralism*. Democratic centralism was justified by Lenin as a tactical response to the tendency of the European working-class movement to seek reform through trade union activity rather than armed revolution. Lenin was confronted with a working class that was seeking betterment in the here and now, rather than placing its hopes in the revolutionary transformation of reality. This rejection of the revolution was, to Lenin, the equivalent of the "ideological enslavement of the workers by the bourgeoisie." Unless trade union action bound itself tightly to revolutionary Marxism-*Leninism*, it would drift inexorably into the capitalist camp. The upshot of Lenin's argument was that class awareness, the *political will* to revolution, had to be imported into the working class from an outside source. Lenin was not leaving Marx's inspiration behind with this admission, for Marx also saw the necessity for intellectual leadership. But for Lenin, as Aron avers, "the worker alone, without the intellectual, can never determine the meaning of his mission."[67] The outside source, of course, was the professional revolutionary. As Lenin had described it,

> the organization of revolutionaries must consist first, foremost, and mainly of people who make revolutionary action their profession . . . In view of this common feature of the members of such an organization, *all distinctions as between workers and intellectuals*, and certainly distinctions of trade and profession, must be *utterly obliterated*. Such an organization should be not too extensive and as secret as possible.[68]

The revolutionary organization would discern the correct route. It would represent the *true* interests of the working class, despite the fact that the working class might not recognize itself in its "true" interests. And it would operate with dramatic, even ruthless efficiency: once a decision had been reached, no pluralist dissent would be sanctioned. Democratic centralism was, as Aron strongly put it in 1977, using language borrowed from Alexander Solzhenitsyn, "the first example of the institutionalized lie."[69] It was, in fact, the exact *opposite* of true democracy.

Democratic centralism rests on a *metonymical displacement* that Aron also discovered in Marx, as we saw earlier in this chapter. It was a process of reasoning that carried grave dangers for the subsequent history of the Russian Revolution. Aron describes its strange logic in the following passage from *In Defense of Decadent Europe*:

> It was a structure adapted to clandestine action but conceived, also, as a continuing prerequisite of effective action. The critique formulated by Trotsky at the time—that the Central Committee takes the place of the party, the Politburo of the Central Committee and, in the last analysis, the secretary-general of the Politburo—found shattering and tragic confirmation in reality. By a chain of serial delegation, the first link was the substitution of party for proletariat in the name of the Marxism of intellectuals, and the final link was the substitution of one man for the party.[70]

A second "contribution" made by Lenin to Marxism had less to do with revolutionary tactics and organization and more with explaining the failure of Marx's historical prophesies. How were the European masses improving their condition? Why was capitalism not leading, as had been anticipated, to pauperization? Why were workers identifying with their nations rather than their class? Lenin attempted to answer all of these questions with his theory of *imperialism*, developed in *Imperialism, The Final Stage of Capitalism*, a pamphlet "as poor scientifically as it was effective as a piece of propaganda."[71] It was this text more than any other that Aron felt to be at the origin of Marxism–Leninism as a theoretical system.

What had occurred on the Leninist view was the betrayal of the international working class by the workers of the wealthy countries. They had, in the form of higher wages, "sold out" their exploited overseas comrades. Capitalist regimes had been able to share with their workers some of the profits made on the sweating backs of foreign workers: European wealth could be explained on the basis of the overexploitation of colonial labor. This was the reason, in Lenin's characteristically unhistorical view, that members of the European working class remained staunchly chauvinist in their national identifications. With the rallying of the various socialist parties to their respective nations at the onset of World War I, Lenin, as Aron dryly noted, "became, finally, the sole embodiment of the world proletariat and of socialism."[72] This fit perfectly with the chain identification legitimated by Lenin's theory of democratic centralism that we have just described.

The war posed a major problem for Lenin, but he found an explanation for it, too, in his catch-all theory of imperialism. Not only could Lenin provide an account of working class betrayal, but his malleable theory was deemed sufficient to demonstrate the historical inevitability of World War I. Marx was aware of the tendency of capitalist societies to expand imperialistically, but his position was more nuanced. He was an unqualified supporter of the forces of modernity that capitalist expansion brought in its wake. Wiping out ossified traditions and circumnavigating the globe, capitalism would liberate energies to be captured and more effectively utilized in the postcapitalist society to come. But both Marx and Lenin, like so many rationalist thinkers deriving their inspiration from the Enlightenment, underestimated the strength of nationality and tradition. These forces altered the nature of capitalism as it encountered them.

Aron exposed this lacuna in the thinking of the founding fathers of Marxism–Leninism with the following observation: "Marx, too, had an occasional tendency not to distinguish between the *concept of capital-*

*ism*—an economic system defined by private ownership of the means of production and by commercial exchange—and the *concrete historical entity* constituted by those countries in which a system of this order is more or less imperfectly realized."[73]Aron reminded himself, however, that when Marx wrote about war, he often did so in the fashion of many historians, referring to "territorial ambitions, calculations of relative strength, concern with the balance of power or as the more or less aggressive behavior, on the part of various states, as a function of their political system."[74] In his historical writings Marx's blind spot regarding the power of nationality and history partially cleared. Lenin's explanation of World War I, on the other hand, was solely economic. It exhibited the same reductivism we earlier noted in Marx's theoretical work, but with a crudeness seldom found in Marx. As Aron captured it:

> Lenin could have interpreted the war of 1914 as Marx had interpreted the war of 1870. The European states had warred among themselves for centuries before they acquired capitalist economies, as Lenin knew well. But the authors R. Hilferding and, in particular, J. A. Hobson provided him with another possible way to interpret the war: to demonstrate not only that the French, British, and Germans who had carved up Africa among themselves all deserved to be called *imperialists* (as was undoubtedly the case), but that they were destroying each other in an unforgiving struggle *because of their imperialism*.[75]

War, on the Leninist view, was not being fought for the reasons its protagonists assumed—national interest, historic rivalries—but in order to find and protect scarce markets to consume goods capitalist regimes were overproducing. The spark of the European conflagration was to be found in the tinder of the colonial world. Interimperialist rivalry was the result of a nationally based monopoly capitalism, seeking unfair protection for its markets. Unending conflict was guaranteed by the decree "that the competing expansionism of national capitalistic systems did not allow any friendly division."[76] The war that broke out in the Balkans had as its real stake the division of the world.

Lenin had shifted the meaning of the concept of imperialism away from its traditional, *political* meaning of conquest and domination to "a vague and grandiose meaning, by equating it with *a world economic system* into which the industrialized countries integrate the other countries, subjecting them to the will of the industrialized nations."[77] Imperialism was a ravenous monster, swallowing ever-increasing portions of the world in its quest for satiety. It *was* monopoly capitalism. But the fact that capitalism was a world system meant that revolution could break out anywhere, including in Russia, a primarily feudal economy just setting forth on the road to modernization. A "proletarian" revolution in Russia would, in Lenin's dialectical imaginings, strike a blow at the weakest link in the imperialist chain of the capitalist system.

Yet Lenin's monopoly capitalism remained a vague concept. Like imperialism itself, with which it was equated, monopoly capitalism lumped together disparate phenomena. As Aron perceived, Lenin could not be bothered with attention to detail. He took his examples from different countries at different stages of economic development, "as if the structure of capitalism were the same from one country to another, and as if the concentration of production between financial groups involved *ipso facto* the elimination of competition and the rule of the monopolies."[78] And he failed to ask the crucial question: Was colonial conquest carried out in order to shut out foreign financial groups for the benefit of the banks, or could it be explained as the outcome of extra-economic factors? Lenin assumed what he needed to prove, and in so doing abandoned the political.

Lenin regarded imperialistic conflict as an inevitability: no sharing of the spoils between the various exploiting economies was possible. The chief reason he offered for this inevitability—the uneven growth of the national economies—did not hold up under scrutiny. As Aron argued, "the modification of the relations of economic forces . . . is a permanent factor in modern economics and probably in all periods of history, and it constitutes one element of diplomatic instability but is in no way a cause of explosion or of military confrontation."[79]

But Lenin's theory of imperialism was more thoroughly refuted by the course of the twentieth century than by conceptual incoherences. In the aftermath of World War II, Europe divested itself of colonial possessions. The result was not the breakdown of capitalism but a dramatic and sustained period of economic growth unmatched in European history. As Aron emphasized, the fact that living standards rose in nations which "fell victim" to decolonization led to two conclusions, both of which directly contradicted the Leninist theory of imperialism: first, capitalism did not *require* colonial conquests (colonial conquests were, again, driven more by *political* than by economic considerations); second, the increased prosperity of the working classes witnessed even in Lenin's time was not the result of the imperialistic exploitation of Europe's colonies but instead the increased productivity of labor.

It is interesting to note that in spite of the superficiality of Lenin's analysis, modern theories of imperialism have not moved too far from the orbit of its basic theses. The attempts made to explain global economic inequities and justify condemnation of the rapacious, greedy West are perhaps more sophisticated in appearance, but ultimately derive from similar questionable premises. Instead of the direct imperialism of monopoly capitalism, more recent theorists like J. Galtung have sought to condemn the *structural inequality* of the world economic system. Imperialism is now seen as the product of exploitation by foreign capitalists refusing to reinvest their profits in their host countries and taking advantage of the low labor costs they find there. In fact, transactions between the industrialized and nonindustrialized world are rejected by the structural theory as intrinsically imperialistic because of the higher productivity of the industrialized world's economies, which leads to the exchange of less labor for more. According to this argument, the world is divided into exploiting "centers" and exploited "peripheries," with the imperialist centers cultivating and maintaining rulers sensitive to their economic needs in the peripheral zones.[80]

Aron correctly felt this vision of the world rested on a series of questionable assumptions: "that the ruling minorities of all countries (except the socialist countries) oppress the masses, that Third World countries remain a part of the world economy only out of class interest, and that the ruling minorities of the industrialized countries play on the class interest of the ruling minorities in the dependent countries."[81] Such an explanation of the world economic system still kept faith with its Marxist-Leninist inspiration in that political factors were absent from the analysis. Both economic impoverishment and the corruption of local political life were attributed to the pernicious influence of the greedy, capitalist West, rapaciously exploiting the Third World. The reality of the "Third World" and its inhabitants, and their dignity as nations and individual agents, disappears in an ideological haze.

The continuing appeal of the idea of imperialism, even for many non-Marxists, may be attributable to the ease with which it moves from the explanatory to the exculpatory. It serves to provide a total explanation for what are in reality complex, disparate phenomena. But this does not make the structural theory of imperialism any more accurate than Lenin's, as Aron indicates:

> to put the imperialist label on industrialized countries which have no colonies amounts to twisting the ordinary meaning of words, and to ordaining, without any examination, the oppressive and spoliatory character of the relations between the industrialized and industrializing sectors of the world economy. The diversity of this economy is a legacy of centuries, and it derives from a historical process in which conquests by force mingle with exploitation by exchange. That the Europeans often extended their own civilization by fire and sword, from the sixteenth century onward—that they were the "aggressors"—is a fact which no one ignores and no one contests.[82]

And, as Aron was to comment in one of his more memorable phrases,

> the rise of Japan and the fall of the United Kingdom are reminders to the shallow minded (who cannot think in terms other than of some determining 'system') of the inconstancy of fortune, in both its senses. Wealth, like the favor of destiny, is never permanent.[83]

Aron's argument was based on the evidence of history. The example of the vigorous growth of the capitalist Asian economies, which were clearly entwined in the net of the world economy, clearly reveals the weaknesses in the theory of structural imperialism.

Lenin's theory of imperialism enabled him to reconcile the rising standard of living of the masses in the most advanced capitalist countries with the Marxist theory of historical development. It enabled him to locate the horrible experience of war within the historical framework of capitalism. It supplied Lenin with a reason for working-class trade-unionism. Finally, it allowed Lenin to see capitalism as a world system, raping and pillaging the globe. If capitalism was indeed an integrated world system, then the idea of revolution could be held on to: it was inevitable, even in Russia, despite the example of European trade unionism. But as Aron ironically put it: "The theory had everything—it lacked only truth." This holds as well for more recent theories of imperialism which seek simple answers for complex phenomena, following, in spite of everything, in Lenin's footsteps. The negative economic consequences of the idea of structural imperialism, for example, have been considerable, particularly in Latin America, which has only recently begun to extricate itself from their impact.[84]

Another dark legacy left by Lenin to the twentieth century is what might be called the *totalitarian style of thought*. The essence of this way of thinking can be found in Lenin's *Materialism and Empirocriticism*, a crude work which offers a materialist metaphysic linking the organic and inorganic with the historical. This book would be unexceptional, Aron believed, were it not for a frightening idea lurking in its pages: "any metaphysical deviation implies political deviation." As Aron explains, Lenin's "system of thought established in advance the system of total discipline he later practiced." Disagreement with the "correct" line was, in Lenin's mind, tantamount to heresy. The correct line was, of course, set down by Lenin himself in his works of "philosophy" and later in practice, as he moved to establish the absolute power of the Bolsheviks over the Russian people, and eventually over a large part of the world. Combined with Lenin's notion of democratic centralism, this violent style of argument and fanatical mode of thinking laid the foundations for Stalin's butchery. Aron, "the last of the liberals" in Bloom's evocative formulation, would always steadfastly reject such forms of intellectual coercion, retaining a faith in human liberty—and the human capacity to attain the truth through reason—often as lacking in contemporary theorists as in the ideologists of Aron's time.

Finally, in Aron's view, Lenin's book *The State and Revolution* presented a dangerous mixture of Machiavellian realism and utopianism in its conception of the role of the state after the revolution. Lenin's book brought together two ideas—the substitution of the dictatorship of the proletariat for the dictatorship of the bourgeoisie and the dismantling of the state apparatus with the hope of its eventual disappearance—that were to have lasting consequences. As we saw above, this "squaring of the circle" can be found in Marx as well, but Lenin gives it full and somewhat ludicrous expression. Here is Lenin's utopian formulation of the postrevolutionary role of the state apparatus:

> Capitalist culture has created large-scale production, factories, railways, the postal service, telephones, etc., and on this basis the great majority of the functions of the old "state power" have become so simplified and can be reduced to such exceedingly simple operations

of registration, filing, and checking, that they can be easily performed by every literate person.[85]

Lenin, like Marx, equated the management of the entire economy with the management of a business, a "radical misappreciation" of the representative roles of economy and state. Dialectical sophistry alone was able to conceal the monstrous nature of the omnivorous state Lenin bequeathed to the world as a result of this "misappreciation."

Marxism-Leninism, then, was no conceptual improvement on the Marxism of Marx, and was in many respects a betrayal of Marx's economic theory of history. Lenin was not a sophisticated thinker, whatever his talents as an organizer and tactician. The result of his handiwork, one of the most repressive regimes in human history, exhibited a fascination for many thinkers on the left, even when few of them actually belonged to the Communist Party. This *sinistrisme*, as Aron calls it—the systematic application of double standards in judging the Soviet Union against the West—was particularly prevalent in French intellectual life. We now turn to the final section of our discussion of Aron's critique of ideology: his encounter with the "existentialist" Marxism of Sartre and Merleau-Ponty.

## 4. EXISTENTIALIST MARXISM: A SQUARED CIRCLE?

Aron's critique of ideology, while comprehending, as we have seen throughout this chapter, the entire range of Marxist and Leninist phenomena, was often aimed at a target closer to home: the "fellow travellers." These were radical intellectuals who usually aligned themselves in public debates with Marxism and the Soviet Union, without actually belonging to the Communist Party.[86] There was a personal element at work in this choice of targets on Aron's part, for the most prominent of the fellow travellers in France were former friends, philosophers and writers who had largely come from the same formative experience as Aron. The two most notable subjects of Aron's criticisms were also two of the most influential thinkers in postwar Paris: the existentialist philosophers Jean-Paul Sartre and Maurice Merleau-Ponty. There were close ties binding Aron to this Parisian milieu, as he was to explain:

Although I have disagreed radically with Sartre, by education and interests, I belong to the same universe he does. It is by placing myself
on the ground common to Marxism and existentialism that I am able
to engage in discussion with friends of my youth, adversaries of yester-
day, and colleagues of today. It is by using the same concepts and
referring to the same values that I try to convince them of their errors.[87]

Aron wanted to convince Sartre and Merleau-Ponty that their chosen course was wrong, that their own philosophical positions were ultimately incompatible with Marxism. More broadly, Aron was concerned
with rejecting the *twin nihilisms* that dominated postwar French intellectual life: The Marxist nihilism that, as we have seen, eliminated freedom
in historical determinism; and the Sartrean nihilism, which was based on
a conception of freedom "stripped of all contents,"[88] and alienated in
the real—an alienation to be overcome only by means of revolt. The
link between Sartrean and Marxist nihilism was not as paradoxical as it
first appeared. As Aron observed, "Marxists and followers of Sartre do
not reject the values of the humanist and rationalist tradition; if both
groups are just as able to accept terror in the name of freedom, it is
because by reducing men to action or by subordinating the individual
to history, they have deprived themselves of the means of rejecting the
unacceptable."[89]Aron's critique of ideology attempted to find, as an alternative to these twin nihilisms, a prudential, morally grounded politics,
where "ethics judges politics as much as politics judges ethics."[90] We
will, in this final section, explore what Aron saw to be the tensions
between the existentialist project, broadly characterized, and Marxism;
then, to conclude this chapter, we will make an effort at teasing out the
content and implications of such a nonideological political reflection.

First of all, how did the existentialists justify their connection to
Marxism? As Aron observed, both Sartre and Merleau-Ponty felt that
existentialism would provide a better philosophical foundation for the
revolution than the regnant Marxist materialism, which was, Sartre believed, a crude mockery of Marx's own thought. While Merleau-Ponty
was to eventually abandon this intention, Sartre did not. In a sense it
can be seen as the animating force behind Sartre's last major work of
philosophy: the massive, and massively grim, *Critique of Dialectical Reason*.[91] From the outset, Aron understood clearly the existentialists'

"offer" to Marxism, as evidenced by this passage from the 1946 essay "Sartre and the Marxist-Leninists":

> If we refer to the philosophical writings of Sartre and Merleau-Ponty, the question arises in approximately these terms (at least they raise it in these terms): We are in agreement, they say, with the revolutionary aim of Marxism, we accept its inspiration and desire, but Marxism also takes the form of a materialism which is self-contradictory and inconceivable, and we cannot accept a doctrine which would oblige us to dismiss reason. Existentialism is the true philosophy of revolution, and if the Marxists yielded to our philosophical arguments there would be nothing left to divide us.[92]

In Aron's view, four basic ideas were at the heart of Sartre's efforts to link existentialism and Marxism, making of the former the "true philosophy of revolution."[93] The first idea concerns the primacy of subjectivity. The existentialist notion that thought is "in situation" posits a consciousness capable of extricating itself from the dull weight of the institutions, ideas, and distortions that make up the historical and social world with which it is surrounded. This extrication was possible, although by no means assured, because men could gain an overall perspective of their environment by the very act of seeking to move *beyond* that environment. Materialism attempted to provide the knowledge required for this act of revolutionary self-transcendence, but, as Aron accented, Sartre held that "this double relation of knowledge and transformation" was best provided by "thought in situation," the basic formula of existentialist thought.[94]

The second idea advanced by Sartre rested on the *demystifying* role played by existentialism. Materialism achieved much of its appeal from its power to explode metaphysical rank in social life, showing it to be sheer hypocrisy. Beyond the false distinctions of class, we were all organically akin. As Sartre asserted, however, existentialism could perform this function as well. According to the Sartrean doctrine, Aron writes,

> man is purely contingent, he is "thrown there" without knowing why, without reason or immediate purpose. By arriving at this existentialist consciousness, man will no longer be the victim of the mystifications of the upper classes. Just as well as and even better than the materialist, the existentialist will explain that these rights to which the

privileged classes tend to give a metaphysical substance are merely the expression of a social situation. Existentialism will demonstrate the historicity of values as such, and in so doing it will make it possible to go beyond them.[95]

Existentialism was also superior to materialism, Sartre believed, in its articulation of the relationship between determinism and freedom. Materialism, while it revealed the brute fact of determinism to the worker as he struggled against the natural order, did not do enough to preserve the precious margin of freedom available to the human subject. Existentialism, by reminding the subject of his freedom, preserved a certain consciousness, an awareness of man's capacity to transform the existing order of the world.

Finally, Sartre recognized an affinity between materialism and existentialism in the way both doctrines conceptualized history. Materialism ripped history down from the clouds, grounding it in the palpable, in the processes of life and the struggle to achieve human ends. In a similar way, Aron explained, Sartre's existentialism assumed the action of the subject and the thick resistance of things. In other words, it analyzed "the dialectic of man and obstacles."[96] Thus in every important respect, Sartre was convinced that existentialism upheld the cardinal achievements of Marxist materialism while at the same time securing a conception of freedom that materialism would inevitably eclipse.

Merleau-Ponty, too, averred the compatibility of existentialist and Marxist themes. Merleau-Ponty's existentialism, Aron noted, by attempting to go beyond both idealism and materialism, was in keeping with Marx's early thought. At the origin of Marx's historical vision was the concrete human being, laboring on the environment and creating by so doing the conditions of human existence. By beginning with this image of concrete man, Aron writes, Merleau-Ponty thought it was possible "to give a more reasonable and more satisfying interpretation of Marxist formulas."[97] Marxist formulations that were riddled with conceptual holes, such as the supposedly determinative relation that held between infrastructure and superstructure, were, on Merleau-Ponty's view, more readily understandable starting from *this* standpoint. In Aron's words, "if man is seen *primarily* in relation to nature and if this relation involves a certain form of appropriation of natural forces, then it is possible to understand all the activities of an individual or a group in terms of this original attitude and this fundamental impulse."[98] It was, then, no longer a matter of recognizing an exclusively determined relation between a primary sector of social reality and all the other sectors it affected. Rather, for Merleau-Ponty, each sector would be understood on the basis of a reference to the totality.

Second, by beginning with concrete human existence Merleau-Ponty could more convincingly interpret the relationship between the individual and society. In Marx's theory of history, social being is the ossified product of human actions; each succeeding generation finds itself confronting this ossified product as if it were a natural force. By recalling the human subject to its freedom, however, Merleau-Ponty, like Sartre, was certain that existentialism would prevent the varied circumstances of social life from being seen as final. As Aron glossed it, "a situation is never definitive, it is always being remade both by the gaze which contemplates it and by the will which transcends it."[99]

There was also an affinity between the Marxist critique of ideology and Merleau-Ponty's quest for what was fundamental to the human subject. Marx had sought to explain the myriad alienations which surround men and women—the human creations, ideas, and beliefs which eluded the grasp of their creators. By explaining them, Marx thought he could reach the essential reality of the human world, a reality consisting in the relations between man and nature and between man and the other. Merleau-Ponty saw in existentialism a similar demystifying tendency that would bring lightness to the darkness of bad faith and return "to the choice which man authentically makes of himself."[100]

Thus both Sartre and Merleau-Ponty argued that existentialism was a superior foundation for revolutionary Marxist philosophy than the suffocating materialist straitjacket in which it had been restrained. But how strained in turn was the linkage between the existentialist project and the Marxist enterprise? Aron insisted that the strains were such that the linkage was impossible *from the outset*, that the existentialists were fundamentally confused about the implications of their own thought. It was *impossible* to be both an existentialist and a Marxist, for the two philosophies were "incompatible in their intentions, their origins, and their ultimate ends."[101] Existentialism could never be extended to the point where it included or reached Marxism without at the same time ceasing to be existentialist. What were Aron's arguments in support of this position?

There were certainly elements, Aron admitted, common to existentialism and Marxism. These elements were the result of the common source of both Marxism and existentialism: Hegel's philosophical anthropology. But while Sartre and Merleau-Ponty highlighted certain shared features of the human condition, Aron explained, the reconciliation of existentialism and Marxism required the importation of "other ideas, of which some might conceivably be assimilated by existentialism," while others would remain permanently outside the existentialist orbit.[102] The reasons for this were obvious to Aron. In order to take up arms within the Marxist camp, it was necessary to accept a fundamental initial premise: *work* was the essence of man. The relationship to nature, through which man masters natural forces and creates his living conditions, is the preeminent relationship within the Marxian framework. Was this conception of human nature, of what was *primary* for human existence, compatible with the existentialism of Sartre and Merleau-Ponty? Aron's answer inclined toward the negative:

> The point is debatable; but there is no doubt that strictly speaking, the idea of work as the essence of man plays no role in the existentialism of Sartre. This idea might conceivably be added to it, although I think it gives the doctrine an entirely different slant from that of *Being and Nothingness*.[103]

Sartre's famous book was more Pascalian than revolutionary, according to Aron. Its themes dealt with the relation of the solitary individual to a Godless universe: "The Marxists and the existentialists come into conflict at the point where the tradition of Kierkegaard cannot be reconciled with that of Hegel: no social or economic regime can ever solve the enigma of history; individual destiny transcends collective life."[104] This bleak situation of solitary man faced with a meaningless universe was the most important question for the early Sartre, and hence can be seen as the existentialist question *par excellence*. If this question was primary, however, if it in fact defined the human condition, then, as Aron made clear, "men must inevitably be diverted from what, in the eyes of the Marxist, is of primary importance, namely revolution."[105]

Moreover, Sartre's *Being and Nothingness* presented a despairing image of human interaction, where the struggle between individual consciousnesses was envisioned as seemingly eternal—as hard-wired into human existence. This raised a question of crucial importance for Aron: Was this struggle indeed a permanent aspect of man's plight or was it rooted in history? One *could* start with existentialism and then move on to describe the struggle of consciousnesses occurring in history, producing the "works and regimes of civilization."[106] But the evidence of *Being and Nothingness* suggested that Sartre viewed the struggle between consciousnesses as overriding—that each being *wished the death of the other.* In order to reconcile existentialism with Marxism, then, it would be necessary to move from the dialectic of the solitary individual to that of history. History would have to be invested with meaning, and this meaning would have to be both creative and progressive. Referring to the literature of Simone de Beauvoir, however, which he clearly viewed as a stand-in for Sartre's more explicitly philosophical work, Aron argued that the existentialist vision seemed at odds with this understanding of history. History was instead seen as the history of failures: "In the writings of the existentialists the accent is placed much more on the essential and inevitable character of failure in all human enterprises than on the idea of a creative dialectic or the possibility of reconciliation."[107]

Marxism also implied, as we have seen above, a *final solution* to the enigma of history. History would ultimately be the realization of philosophy. The human vocation could be fulfilled when the dreaming images of the philosophers were engraved on the palimpsest of the social. Revolution would present the engraving instrument. Revolution, for the young Marx and old, was not an accident; it was charged with philosophical significance. But, as Aron demurred, it was unclear how the proletarian revolution could ever solve the dilemma posed by *Being and Nothingness*: "Obviously, it is permissible to favor the Communist revolution for a particular political or economic reason, but one could annex the doctrine of revolution as solution to the philosophical problem only by inverting the basic assumptions of *Being and Nothingness*."[108]

Marx reached the conclusion that revolution would solve the philosophical problem on the basis of two basic themes, both developed in his early writings (which were keenly influential on the mind-set of the existentialists). The first was the Hegelian idea of the unity of the particular and the universal. Hegel had counterposed the status of the individual of civil society, caught up with the needs and appetites of private life, with that of the political being, the individual who participated in the universality of the state. As Aron explained, however, Marx differed from Hegel in seeing in the bourgeois regime no existent unity between the concrete, particularized individual and the citizen, "who dwells in the empyrean of ideas and whose participation in the state is not embodied in concrete life."[109] The working individual was trapped in particularity, cut off from the universality expressed in the state. As a citizen, the subject might participate in universality, but only on those rare occasions when called to vote. This participation remained foreign to the material life of civil society, where the laborer toiled for his survival. In order to bridge the gap between particular and universal, between civil society and the state, Marx avowed the necessity of the proletarian revolution. The revolution would end this dualism by socializing the means of production; doing so would enable the concrete individual to participate *directly* in universality: instead of working for another individual, he would work immediately for the state. As Aron put it:

> This is what determines the end of history, according to Marxism. This determination of the end assumes that Marx retained the whole of Hegel's system of thought and that he was trying to translate Hegel's idea into reality.[110]

The second theme relied on by Marx to advance the hypothesis that revolution would solve the problem of philosophy was that of alienation. In capitalist society, human subjectivity is permanently divided from itself. Both human capacities and the products of human action elude the subject. This alienation holds not just for the worker, who sees the product of his labor taken from his grasp, but also for the entrepreneur, "who sees the products he places on the market carried away by the anonymous movement of economic forces which nobody controls."[111] Marx wanted to end alienation in order to make the torn subject whole again: "The culmination is to be total man, who would actually enjoy the wealth he has created for himself throughout history."[112] Once again, it was the philosophical idea that judged history and that at the same time discovered the meaning of history. And in fact, it was *only* philosophical knowledge that, through its disclosure of the meaning of history, could inform the proletariat of its world historical meaning.

Marx's philosophical conceptions, as taken up by the existentialists, held two difficulties for Aron. First, while there might be a rational necessity for communism if its historical truth was to be established, this did not imply that the advent of communism would inevitably occur. As Aron stressed, "Since there is an alternative, there may be a rational necessity for revolution from a philosophical point of view, but no causal necessity."[113] Or, alternatively, if a Hegelian perspective was adopted, one would be asserting that the meaning of history had been revealed before the completion of history.[114]

But if these considerations posed problems for the coherence of Marx's project, approaching history from an existentialist direction, bereft of a theory of society or the state, led one into even greater difficulties. In *Humanism and Terror*, a book written before he had largely abandoned his Marxism, Merleau-Ponty had, for example, taken the position that if history had a meaning, then that meaning was the one given to history by Marxism. He argued for a *privileged state* which would determine the meaning of the past in its entirety. The meaning of history, on Merleau-Ponty's account, would be universal, valid for all, and would consist in the realization of a homogeneous society marked by the mutual *recognition* of all. But as Aron objected in "The Adventures and Misadventures of the Dialectic," the status of such a privileged state "was so formalized and generalized that it was impossible to relate it to a particular society."[115] The institutions and ideas Merleau-Ponty *did* recommend as criteria for judging the meaning of history—the socialization of the means of production; the growing role and self-consciousness of the proletariat; and the tendency toward greater internationalism— were not linked in any necessary fashion in actual historical experience. A particular historical event, Aron observed, might satisfy one of the criteria but not another. This point of view, he concluded, was not equivalent to that of the true Marxist.

The first difficulty for Merleau-Ponty was that, as an existentialist, he wanted the worker to be a true revolutionary; he wanted the oppressed worker to truly *want* to abolish his servitude. In other words, he wanted to discover the meaning of history in the actual *experience* of the working class. As Aron maintained, though, the Marxist would hold no such romantic notions about the proletariat. This held for Marx himself, as well as Lenin.[116] The existentialist, then, without a philosophy to realize, attempted to locate the meaning of history in the *experience* of oppression or the *experience* of the working class as it struggled against its heavy chains. For Aron, the solution was "no more Marxist than it is satisfying.''[117] It was, Aron reasoned, impossible to determine the end of history on the basis of the proletariat and its *alleged* experience. Aron's conclusion was decisive:

> What will always prevent the existentialist from being a Marxist is that revolution will not solve his historical problem, that of the individual with the absence of God in atheist existentialism, and with God in the existentialism of the believer. Outside of this dialogue one may take an interest in the lot of the unfortunate and join the revolutionary party for some perfectly valid reason, but one will never arrive at the equivalent of a Marxist philosophy.[118]

A true Marxist, Aron went on, would not avoid asking difficult questions about the present historical conjuncture. But it seemed that neither the existentialists nor the more doctrinaire Marxists were willing to analyze the complications that arose when Marx's prophecies were compared with the development of history as it actually occurred. The existentialists wanted to be revolutionaries, but were ignorant of the fundamental economic and sociological facts influencing modern industrial society. As Aron tersely put it in *History and the Dialectic of Violence*: "A century after the publication of *Capital*, Sartre has nothing to say about the socio-economic structure of our epoch."[119] The existentialists wanted to float above the fray, philosophers of "commitment" who refused to take up "a concrete historical and political attitude," while the dogmatic Marxists parroted the Party line.[120]

A final, failed effort at a synthesis between existentialism and Marxism was undertaken by Sartre long after Merleau-Ponty, shaken by the Korean War, had distanced himself from the Marxian line. The attempted synthesis found expression in Sartre's mammoth, complex book, *The Critique of Dialectical Reason*. This book, first published in 1960, alternately fascinated and revolted Aron, and he dedicated an entire study, the above-mentioned *History and the Dialectic of Violence*, to exploring its paradoxes and implicit dangers. In the *Critique*, Sartre suggested a form of dialectical reason by means of which the projects of each and every individual will coalesce as part of the totality of history. In the process of developing this idea of dialectical reason, Sartre worked out a phenomenology of the life world—the everyday world of human interaction—where the prosaic and mundane is transformed, as if in a reverse alchemy, into a universe of alienation, purposelessness, and bad faith. Only in revolt, forever threatened with betrayal by institutions, is human freedom possible. In an early public response to Sartre's book, "Sartre's Marxism," Aron observed four judgments passed by Sartre on Marxism at work in the *Critique*. In the first, Sartre once again vehemently rejected a materialist metaphysics. "However strong his desire to cooperate with Stalinists may have been," Aron wrote, "he has never made any concessions at the expense of the principles of his own philosophy."[121]

In addition, as we have already seen, Sartre took as self-evident the truth of Marx's economic and sociological assertions. Marx's sociological and economic work, even though it was what was essential to Marx himself, was of little interest to Sartre. Aron quoted a telling passage from the *Critique* in order to emphasize this unflagging but facile acceptance:

> None of these remarks relating to form can, of course, claim to add anything at all to the self-evident truth of the synthetic reconstruction achieved by Marx in *Das Kapital*; they are not even intended to be a marginal commentary on that reconstruction which, precisely because of its self-evident truth, does not admit of any commentary.[122]

Third, Sartre had never actually been a Marxist, Aron continued, if by being a Marxist one meant being a militant member of a communist party. Sartre had always been, with the brief exception of a short-lived party he founded himself, a fellow-traveller. This did not stop Sartre from practising sinistrisme. In Aron's account, to the agents of sinistrisme, "It matters little what a man of the Right actually says, his views will be rejected in advance."[123] Sartre's partisanship always benefited the Soviet Union relative to the Western liberal democracies; even when he criticized the Soviet Union, Sartre would always condemn the West in the same breath. Aron was piercing in his irony:

> The significance of torture or concentration camps has varied according to the nature of the regime or the party in power. For his own sake, one would have liked the philosopher of freedom to denounce the personality cult before Chairman Khrushchev did so. In spite of his non-conformism, Sartre has not altogether avoided left-wing conformism.[124]

The final aspect of the problem was, in Aron's estimation, bound up with the concepts of historical materialism and the class struggle. The aim of the *Critique* was the renewal of Marxism by the reintroduction of existence, "taking the individual consciousness as the starting point."[125] In *History and the Dialectic of Violence*, Aron was to call this approach a "Marxism of understanding."[126]

Sartre's hubristic enterprise was, as briefly noted above, to demonstrate the possibility of a *single* history on the basis of individual consciousnesses. The "Being-for-itself" of *Being and Nothingness*—the solitary consciousness in pursuit of its desires, wants, and needs—was now referred to by Sartre as the *individual praxis* or the *constituting dialectic*, but the affinity underlying the two Sartrean vocabularies was not missed by Aron:

> The individual praxis, like consciousness, is a pro-ject (a throwing forward), at once a retention of the past and a self-translucid transcending of it in the direction of the future, a total apprehension both of the situation and the aim. History would be perfectly dialectical, that is perfectly comprehensible, if it were the history of a single man. It remains intelligible because it is made up of human actions, each of which is comprehensible as an individual praxis or translucid act of consciousness.[127]

On the basis of individual freedom, however, how could the emergence of a *single* history take place? The *Critique* did not answer this question, and, indeed, postponed it for the future (a second volume that was never finished), remaining content with a redescription of the human world as a place of scarcity, struggle, violence, and the inevitable alienation of freedom in petrified institutions which form the misery-laden history of oppression. How could freedom be maintained in the Sartrean universe? Only through *terror*—the terror of the *oath* as the rebel guaranteed his future obedience by surrendering his rights to the revolutionary "fighting group." This "freedom"—really a form of fascistic violence—was constantly threatened with a slow decay into bureaucracy and institutionalization. Sartre truly gave himself—and man—no exit from either permanent revolution or Stalinism. The possibility for a moderate and moral politics, rooted in the goods of a common world (the possibility, in other words, for political reason) was foreclosed in the Sartrean phantasmagoria.

For Aron, Sartre and the existentialists were embodiments of the literary spirit in political reflection, and they combined the worst of modern intellectual tendencies: on the one hand, a nihilistic conception of freedom, where "Man's freedom is the capacity of self-creation, although one cannot make out, at least in *Being and Nothingness*, what law this creation should obey or toward what object it should tend"[128]; on the other a historicist doctrinairism where the City of God is to be realized on the Earth below, as the result of the necessary development of history. Following the analysis of Leo Strauss in *Natural Right and History*, Aron showed that, in embracing an empty freedom, by reducing human nature to pure *negation* (man conceptualized as the capacity to transcend his determinations, and nothing more), the existentialists were defenseless when confronted with the promises of the engineers of human souls, particularly when the former remained willfully ignorant about the basic truths of political economy.[129]

Although he did not develop his insights into a full philosophy of human nature, preferring to remain on the terrain of political theory, Aron underscored that a philosophy rooted in the tradition of "virtue or wisdom" was preferable to, and more capable of preserving the varied goods of the human world than, a philosophy based on "freedom, choice, and invention."[130] The latter, when severed from a natural order transcending the individual will, offers no "moral law," no reasons for living, no "hypergoods" (to borrow Charles Taylor's phrase)[131] which might give meaning and substance to human liberty. In conclusion to this chapter, then, let us say a few more words about what constitutes, for Aron, *responsible* political reflection—a reflection based on "virtue and wisdom"—in contrast to this kind of literary or ideological politics we have been exploring in detail. Is a nonideological political theory possible?

Aron was frequently criticized for being too "negative," for refusing to succor the hopes of men, instead offering them one demolishment after another of their sacred idols. While much of what we have looked at in this lengthy treatment of the critique of ideology *has* been critical, it should be increasingly clear that Aron's method is not without a positive understanding of the role of political thought. Indeed he saw the critique of ideology as, in a sense, "a negation of the nihilism which is implicit in a certain kind of Marxism or a certain kind of existentialism."[132] We have already looked at a few such positive lessons: political thought should be multifactorial, rather than monistic; the political, as a realm where human will can be exercised, has an autonomy and even a primacy often neglected or abstracted away from in modern accounts; there is a condition of political scarcity, an antinomical structure of the political world, so that all human goods cannot be combined.

In "Fanaticism, Prudence, and Faith," one of the most important essays Aron ever wrote, he responded to the criticism that his thought was not "constructive" by detailing further his understanding of political reason:

> Many of the writings that are termed "constructive" are just as futile as plans for a universal state or a new organization of business. The term "constructive" is applied even to projects that are unrealizable, and the term "negative" to analyses which tend to delimit what is possible and to form political judgment—a judgment which is *essentially historical* in nature and which must *focus on the real* or set itself an *attainable objective*. One is sometimes tempted to invert the hierarchy of values and to take the term "negative" as a compliment.[133] (Italics added)

Too often political thought attributes a universal value to a particular doctrine—and this is not a sin solely of Marxists or fellow travellers, Aron emphasizes, but often of liberals as well—leading to the neglect of "the wisdom of Montesquieu."[134] That wisdom tells us that the same laws are not good everywhere: one cannot disregard the circumstances of time or place. It is this attentiveness to the *hic et nunc* that Aron is recommending when he asserts that political judgment is essentially historical. It is not relativism—Aron is unafraid to assert the existence of universal principles—but rather a wise acknowledgment of the complexity of the world, the structural limitations of political life, and the difficulty of translating principle into practice. There is a certain patience involved in Aron's reflection. He captures it nicely in the following epigram: "Political analysis gains by divesting itself of all sentimentality; lucidity demands effort: passion automatically goes at a gallop."[135]

One must also, Aron recounts, be open to "the plurality of considerations on which political or economic action must depend," adding that "the reconciliation of justice with growth requires a compromise between equality and the adjustment of retribution to merit." In other words, if one focuses on the real, the antinomical structure of the political world will soon be unveiled. Man is subject to "the irreducible plurality of the dimensions that characterize his existence."[136] But if that discernment is made, a politics which ignores the condition of political scarcity can be rejected as immoderate, as jettisoning *prudence*, the "god of this world below."[137] This insight is one many contemporary theorists might profitably learn, for what is evident about recent political thought—particularly in its liberal postanalytic version—is its belief that through a particular methodology (usually one form of "rational choice" or another) the political problem can be "solved." Aron's political reflection correctly eschews any permanent solution to the problem of ordering our lives together.

Both Marxists and existentialists refused to focus on the real and blindly ignored both matters of feasibility and the condition of political scarcity, thus giving birth to an unreasonable politics, a politics based on an historicist doctrinairism or on an irrational commitment to revolution, but ungrounded in any systematic reflection on the world or human nature. As Aron was to suggest in his book *The Industrial Society*, knowledge of the present, based on a "reasonable comparison of the economic, social, and political advantages of the various regimes,"[138] paralyzes utopian thought. The massive development of productive forces that modernity has bequeathed did not put an end to the "dialectics of man and his achievements, the very stuff of history."[139] An anti- or nonideological politics accepts "this dialectical conflict" and is "resigned, not to present forms of 'alienation,' but to the endless renewal of alienation in some form or other."[140] Prosaic wisdom, but wisdom nonetheless, Aron's critique of ideology, while doing battle with the political monsters and secular religions of the bloody twentieth century, has taught us how to think about politics, with both eyes open, with hope, without illusion. It is now time to turn to the life of nations, where politics is unavoidable, yet where Aron's lessons have seldom been heard.

## NOTES

1. See Fukuyama, *The End of History and the Last Man*, pp. 287–339; and, more recently, *Trust: The Social Virtues and the Creation of Prosperity* (New York: Free Press, 1995).

2. Manent's discussion of this problem, which he correctly links to the *neutrality* as between differing conceptions of the good increasingly prominent as the self-understanding of modern liberal democratic regimes and the regnant normative thrust of contemporary liberal theory, can be found in his essay "Situation du liberalisme," the introduction to the two-volume collection of liberal writings he edited for Hachette: *Les libéraux*, vol. I (Paris: Hachette, 1986), p. 7–40. See also John Gray's criticisms of neutrality in *Enlightenment's Wake*, pp. 18–30. Aron's lengthiest treatment of democratic decadence can be found in *In Defense of Decadent Europe*, pp. 169–297.

3. On the systematic effort to destroy civil society in the former Soviet Union, see the work by Aron's student, Alain Besançon, *The Rise of the Gulag: Intellectual Origins of Leninism*, trans. by S. Matthews (New York: Continuum, 1981). Besançon's penetrating treatment of the ideological dimension of Soviet tyranny led to a subtle shift in Aron's understanding of totalitarianism, as explained in the new introduction to *In Defense of Decadent Europe*.

4. Elsewhere, I have referred to this as the "Aronian Renewal." See my review article of that title in *First Things*, March 1995, pp. 61–64.

5. For Elster's most thorough critique of Marx's thought, see *Making Sense of Marx* (Cambridge: Cambridge University Press, 1985).

6. Jean-Paul Sartre, *The Critique of Dialectical Reason*, trans. by A. Sheridan Smith (London: Verso, 1976).

7. See Maurice Merleau-Ponty, *Humanism and Terror*, trans. by J. O'Neill (Boston: Beacon Press, 1969).

8. Judt, *Past Imperfect*, p. 38.

9. None of the existing studies of Aron's thought have offered a detailed exploration of Aron's work in this area.

10. One might add a fifth tangent—the critique of the "structuralist" Marxism of Louis Althusser, but Aron's criticisms of Althusser add nothing to the other four. He saw Althusser—for whom he had little respect as a philosopher—as ignoring questions of feasibility and eclipsing human subjectivity, in short, as jettisoning political reason. See Aron, *D'une Sainte Famille à l'autre*, pp. 69–276.

11. Bloom, *Giants and Dwarfs*, p. 259.

12. Raymond Aron, *The Century of Total War* (Lanham, MD: University Press of America, 1985), p. 116.

13. Ibid., p. 116.

14. Ibid., p. 117.

15. On Prometheanism, see Aron, *An Essay on Liberty*, chs. 2 and 3. We will return to the theme of Prometheanism in our final chapter. Prometheanism also figures prominently in the analysis of Aron's book *Progress and Disillusion: The Dialectics of Modern Society* (New York: Praeger, 1968), pp. 3, 4, 216, 218, 219,

221. There he sees that the "Promethean ambition and the egalitarian ideal share [a] common origin in rationalism" (p. 3).

16. Aron, *The Century of Total War*, p. 117.

17. Ibid., p. 118.

18. Aron, "L'avenir des religions séculières" in *Une histoire du vingtième siècle*, p. 153. (All translations of this essay are my own.)

19. See, e.g., Karl Marx, "On the Jewish Question," *The Marx-Engels Reader*, ed. by R. C. Tucker (New York: Norton, 1978), pp. 26–52.

20. Aron, *Une histoire du vingtième siècle*, p. 153.

21. See the recently published book, written but never finished by Aron during the "phony war" (the period before the German invasion of France) between September 1939 and May 1940, *Machiavel et les tyrannies modernes* (Paris: Fallois, 1993).

22. Aron, *Une histoire du vingtième siècle*, p. 155.

23. The most severe disadvantage is that the liberal democratic regime cannot be transformed into a secular religion, that it is, essentially, deprived of a state truth. Liberal democratic regimes do not pretend to offer their citizens the meaning of life. This is both the greatest strength of the democracies, central to their preservation of human flourishing, and their greatest weakness, since it leaves them vulnerable when confronted with a more committed enemy. Second, such regimes, as noted by many commentators, are basically pacific, and are often hesitant to take the necessary steps to ward off or defeat external threats until danger looms. This was a consistent theme of Aron's work, most thoroughly explored in *In Defense of Decadent Europe*, pp. 169–263. Aron was to modify his understanding of ideology over the years, but the most cogent usage was his earliest. He describes it in his *Memoirs*: "an ideology would be a global representation of society and its past, a representation announcing salvation and prescribing a liberating course of action." p. 282–83.

24. Aron, *Une histoire du vingtième siècle,* pp. 159–60

25. Ibid., p. 163. Political theorist Marcel Gauchet, following Aron's lead, has drawn a sharp connection between the process of disenchantment (which he sees as irreversible) and modern totalitarianism, which seeks to restore a lost social unity. See his challenging book *Le désenchantment du monde* (Paris: Gallimard, 1985).

26. Aron, *Une histoire du vingtième siècle*, p. 164.

27. For an analysis of the ambivalence Aron exhibited toward Pareto, see Stuart Campbell's "The Four Paretos of Raymond Aron" in the *Journal of the History of Ideas*, 1986, pp. 287–98.

28. Translated as *The Mind and Society*, trans. by A. Livingston and A. Bongioro, 4 volumes. (New York: Harcourt Brace, 1935). Along with Aron's book on Machiavelli mentioned above, see the clear exposition of Pareto's thought in

*Main Currents of Sociological Thought*, vol. II, trans. by R. Howard and H. Weaver (New York: Basic Books, 1967), pp. 99–176.

29. Campbell, "The Four Paretos of Raymond Aron," p. 290. James Burnham was a former Trotskyite who broke ranks and became a conservative political theorist. Many see him as one of the earliest "neoconservatives." His most important work is *The Machiavellians* (Chicago: Regnery-Gateway, 1943).

30. See Aron, *Machiavel et les tyrannies modernes*, pp. 84–118, 263–67. For Machiavelli's own discussion of "foxes" and "lions," see Bk. XVIII of *The Prince*, trans. by H. Mansfield (Chicago: University of Chicago Press, 1985), pp. 68–71, where Machiavelli writes: "since a prince is compelled of necessity to know well how to use the beast, he should pick the fox and the lion, because the lion does not defend itself from snares and the fox does not defend itself from wolves, so one needs to be a fox to recognize snares and a lion to frighten the wolves."

31. Aron, *Main Currents of Sociological Thought*, vol. II, p. 154.

32. Aron, *Une histoire du vingtième siècle*, p. 169.

33. Aron, *Main Currents of Sociological Thought*, vol. II, p. 175. See also "Democratic States and Totalitarian States" in *Thinking Politically*, pp. 325–47.

34. For a typically erudite discussion of the "liberalism of fear," see Judith Shklar, *Ordinary Vices* (Cambridge: Harvard University Press, 1986).

35. John Gray, *Post-Liberalisms: Studies in Political Thought* (London: Routledge, 1993), p. 255.

36. Aron, *The Century of Total War*, p. 147. See also the discussion of Christian belief and "doctrinairism" in *Marxism and the Existentialists*, pp. 106–8. In the latter book, Aron expressed his "horror" at the collapse of sacred and profane: "What horrifies me about secular religions is the breakdown of the distinction between the profane and the sacred, between one class and the messiah, between one regime and the kingdom of God" (p. 15).

37. Aron, *In Defense of Decadent Europe*, p. 2.

38. The *locus classicus* of this strand of Marxist thought is of course George Lukács, *History and Class Consciousness* (Cambridge: MIT Press, 1971). It is not determined, however, whether Lukács had access to Marx's early writings, which, at the time of the publication of his famous book (1923) had not yet seen the light of day.

39. Althusser's major work is *Reading Capital*, with sequel by E. Balibar, trans. by B. Brewster (New York: NLB, 1970). The notion of "epistemological break," borrowed from the French philosopher Gaston Bachelard, is elaborated in Louis Althusser, *For Marx*, trans. by B. Brewster (New York, NLB, 1969), pp. 32–33. Again, Aron's critique of Althusser can be found in *Marxismes imaginaires: D'une Sainte Famille à l'autre*. See also Stephen Launay, *La pénsee politique de Raymond Aron*, p. 108.

40. See the summary of Aron's 1976–1977 College de France seminar of that title, "Le marxisme de Marx," in *Le Débat*, No. 28, January 1984, pp. 18–29.

41. See Karl Popper, *The Open Society and Its Enemies* (Princeton: Princeton University Press, 1950), pp. 274–397. See also *The Poverty of Historicism* (London: Routledge, 1957).

42. Aron, *Marxism and the Existentialists*, p. 86.

43. Aron offers a detailed historical account of "peaceful coexistence" in his *Peace and War: A Theory of International Relations* (New York: Doubleday, 1966), pp. 672–75.

44. Aron, *Main Currents of Sociological Thought*, vol. I, p. 154.

45. This distinction between the methodological and ontological use of concepts has been central to the work of Luc Ferry and Alain Renaut. See their *Political Philosophy III: From the Rights of Man to the Republican Idea*, trans. by F. Philip (Chicago: University of Chicago Press, 1992), pp. 123–28. For the Kantian source of this distinction, see the *Critique of Pure Reason*, trans. by N. K. Smith (London: Macmillan, 1933), pp. 310–11, 426–27, 451–52.

46. Ibid., p. 155.

47. See *Democracy and Totalitarianism*; *Les lutte des classes* (Paris: Gallimard, 1964); and *18 Lessons on Industrial Society*.

48. Aron, *Main Currents of Sociological Thought*, vol. I, p. 155–56.

49. See Aron, *18 Lectures on Industrial Society*, pp. 54–55.

50. Ibid., p. 157.

51. Ibid., p. 114. As Marx himself put it, "the history of all hitherto existing society is the history of the class struggle." *The Communist Manifesto* in Karl Marx and Friedrich Engels, *The Collected Works*, Vol. 6 (London: Lawrence and Wishart, 1975), p. 482.

52. Aron, *Main Currents of Sociological Thought*, vol. I, p. 114.

53. Claude Lefort, "Rereading the *Communist Manifesto*" in *Democracy and Political Theory*, trans. by D. Macey (Minneapolis: University of Minnesota Press, 1988), p. 158.

54. Marx readily acknowledged this: See his letter to J. Weydemeyer, March 5, 1852, in Marx and Engels, *Selected Works in One Volume* (New York: International Publishers, 1968), p. 679. I owe this reference to Douglas Moggach.

55. As in *The Eighteenth Brumaire of Louis Napoleon* in *Collected Works*, vol. 11, pp. 99–197. Aron's analysis of this text can be found in *Main Currents of Sociological Thought*, vol. I, pp. 235–60. As Jon Elster notes, "Marx never defined what he meant by class." *Making Sense of Marx*, p. 319.

56. For a concise discussion of this conception of social class, see Aron's 1968 book *Progress and Disillusion*, pp. 5–24.

57. Aron, *Main Currents of Sociological Thought*, vol. I, p. 163.

58. Ibid., p. 166.

59. Ibid., p. 119.

60. See vols. II and III of *Capital* (New York: International Publishers, 1967).

61. See Raymond Aron, *The Industrial Society: Three Essays on Ideology and Development* (New York: Praeger, 1967), for a comprehensive analysis of modern industrialism. Marx's discussion can be found in his "Critique of the Gotha Program" in Marx and Engels, *Selected Works in One Volume*, pp. 322–23.

62. *Marxism and the Existentialists*, p. 97.

63. Ibid., p. 168.

64. See Gray, *Post-Liberalisms*, pp. 16, 53.

65. Aron, *Marxism and the Existentialists*, p. 103.

66. See, for a classic account, Kolakowski's *Main Currents of Marxism*, vols. I, II, and III (Oxford: Oxford University Press, 1982). There are numerous affinities between Aron and Kolakowski concerning their respective interpretations of the Marxist tradition. See also Besançon, *The Rise of the Gulag*, pp. 189–291.

67. Aron, *Marxism and the Existentialists* , p. 36.

68. V. I. Lenin, *What is to Be Done?* (Peking: Foreign Languages Press, 1975), p. 138. See Aron, *In Defense of Decadent Europe*, p. 16.

69. Ibid., p. 117. For more on Solzhenitsyn's impact on Aron's thinking, see the introduction to the new edition of *In Defense of Decadent Europe* by Daniel J. Mahoney and Brian C. Anderson, pp. x–xiii. See also the essay "Alexander Solzhenitsyn and European 'Leftism' " in *In Defense of Political Reason*, pp. 115–24, where Aron contrasts the moral witness of Solzhenitsyn with the "sinistrisme" of Sartre.

70. Aron, *In Defense of Decadent Europe*, pp. 17–18.

71. Ibid., p. 134.

72. Ibid., p. 17.

73. Ibid., p. 17.

74. Ibid., p. 134.

75. Ibid., p. 18.

76. Ibid., p. 18.

77. Ibid., p. 134.

78. Ibid., p. 137.

79. Ibid., p. 137.

80. See, as representative of this view, the works of Immanuel Wallerstein, *The Modern World System*, vols. I and II (New York: Academic Press, 1974, 1980); and *The Politics of the World Economy* (Cambridge: Cambridge University Press, 1984).

81. Ibid., p. 143.

82. Ibid., p. 144.

83. Ibid., p. 134.

84. For a discussion of the influence of a "vulgar Marxism" in Latin America, see Michael Novak, *This Hemisphere of Liberty: A Philosophy of the Americas* (Washington, DC: AEI Press, 1992), pp. 49–62. Compare with Aron's analysis of the "Marxist Vulgate" in *In Defense of Decadent Europe*, pp. 2, 27, 102–04.

85. Lenin, *The State and Revolution*, quoted in Aron, *In Defense of Decadent Europe*, p. 21.

86. They were characterized by, in the historian Paul Hollander's formulation, "displaced patriotism." See his *Anti-Americanism: Irrational & Rational* (New Brunswick: Transaction Publishers, 1995).

87. Aron, *Marxism and the Existentialists*, p. 11.

88. See Raymond Aron, *History and the Dialectic of Violence*, trans. by B. Cooper (New York: Harper & Row, 1975), p. 44. See also pp. 15, 26, 34.

89. Aron, *Marxism and the Existentialists*, p. 16. See also pp. 81–85.

90. Ibid., p. 16.

91. For an excellent treatment of Sartre's enterprise in the *Critique*, which he calls a "totalitarian dungeon," see Roger Scruton, *Thinkers of the New Left* (London: Longman Group, 1985), pp. 183–91.

92. Aron, *Marxism and the Existentialists*, p. 21.

93. For a representative early essay of Sartre—in this case responding to various charges made by communists—see the 1944 essay translated as "A More Precise Characterization of Existentialism" in *Selected Prose Writings of Jean-Paul Sartre*, vol. 2 (Evanston, Il.: Northwestern University Press, 1974).

94. Aron, *Marxism and the Existentialists*, p. 24.

95. Ibid., pp. 24–25.

96. Ibid., p. 25.

97. Ibid., p. 26. It is important to emphasize that Aron and Merleau-Ponty had many affinities, as underscored by Kerry H. Whiteside in his fine book *Merleau-Ponty and the Foundation of an Existential Politics* (Princeton: Princeton University Press, 1988), pp. 118–31. Whitehead also stresses the political divergence of the two thinkers.

98. Aron, *Marxism and the Existentialists*, p. 26.

99. Ibid., p. 27.

100. Ibid., p. 27.

101. Ibid., p. 28.

102. Ibid., p. 31. See also pp. 81–82.

103. Ibid., p. 31.

104. Ibid., pp. 86–87. The passage continues: "Individual consciousness always remains alone in the face of the mystery of life and death, however well organized may be the communal exploitation of the planet. The ultimate mean-

ing of the human adventure is not given by the classless society, even if this society is inevitable." For Aron, the existentialists, if they were to remain consistent, could not view the solution of the political problem as the solution of the human problem.

105. Ibid., p. 30.

106. Ibid., p. 32. This is what Sartre went on to do in his *Critique of Dialectical Reason* many years later, although there the problem of *scarcity* becomes central. See Aron's discussion in *History and the Dialectic of Violence*, pp. 33, 34, 36.

107. Aron, *Marxism and the Existentialists*, p. 32.

108. Ibid., p. 34.

109. Ibid., p. 34.

110. Ibid., p. 34.

111. Ibid., pp. 34–35.

112. Ibid., p. 35.

113. Ibid., p. 35.

114. In Aron's words: "A philosophy in which the truth of the system coincided with that of history presupposes a completion of history on the basis of which the truth of the whole past is comprehended. Marxism wants to maintain for its chosen goal, that is, for a future that is nevertheless free, the prestige of absolute truth, of that total rational truth which should be reserved for a completed history. How is one to expound a true and total philosophy of history before that history is complete?" Ibid., pp. 35–36.

115. Ibid., p. 59.

116. "Left to himself he will go no further than trade unionism. For him to become truly revolutionary, according to Lenin, there must be professional revolutionaries, revolutionary philosophers who will make the workers understand that the essential thing is not this or that partial improvement of their lot, but a desire for overall change. The philosophers will convince the proletariat that it alone is capable of this change, which will be the realization of philosophy." Ibid., pp. 36–37.

117. Ibid., p. 37.

118. Ibid., p. 37.

119. Aron, *History and the Dialectic of Violence*, p. 208. Aron would, on another occasion, be even more withering: "Much as Sartre may have busied himself with the writings of Marx, there is barely a trace of this reading to be found. Sartre alludes to the first volume of *Capital* and the theory of surplus value, but this is grist to his mill since it seems to show that the entrepreneur exploits the employee and the capitalist the wage-earner. There are no grounds for suspecting that he is even remotely interested in the relations between Ricardo and Marx or in Marx's place in the history of political economy. As for the unsurpassable philosophy of our epoch, which has incidentally been essentially sterile

for more than half a century now, Sartre summarizes it in vague, indeed almost meaningless phrases, such as, Men make their own history but on the basis of the given material conditions. Putting it differently: it was not Marxism which brought this by nature anarchistic man to the point of sympathizing with Stalin's Terror, but, on the contrary, his inclination towards anarchy induced him to accept Marxism, which remains alien to him or of which he retains only the negations and the utopia." *In Defense of Political Reason*, p. 120.

120. Aron, *Marxism and the Existentialists*, p. 40.

121. Ibid., p. 167.

122. Sartre, *Critique of Dialectical Reason*, quoted in Ibid., p. 167.

123. Aron, *In Defense of Political Reason*, p. 119.

124. Aron, *Marxism and the Existentialists*, p. 167. Tony Judt, in a recent essay reviewing Jean-Francois Sirinelli's *Deux intellectuels dans le siècle: Sartre et Aron* (Paris: Fayard, 1995), stressed that it was Aron who was the *true* nonconformist: "it seems to me that any true account of Sartre and Aron in their time has to begin with the paradoxical recognition that it was Raymond Aron who was the great dissenter of the age, the engaged intellectual against the current. What had once seemed to be his weaknesses—a recognition of the limits of knowledge, an uncomfortable search for the impossible equilibrium between understanding and judgment, the abandonment of philosophy just as it was displacing literature as the activity of choice for fashionable thinkers, a community of peers drawn from international rather than Parisian circles—seem now to have been his special strengths. And just as Sartre the existentialist, hoist on the petard of his own imprudence, would have been compelled to acknowledge the wisdom of de Gaulle's comment that talent in writing carries responsibility, so Aron the student of Hegel might smile wryly to know that in the twilight of the French intellectuals, it is he who, in retrospect, stands for all they once held most dear." "Two Dissenters," *TLS*, January 19, 1996, p. 6.

125. Aron, *Marxism and the Existentialists*, p. 168.

126. Aron, *History and the Dialectic of Violence*, p. xxv.

127. Aron, *Marxism and the Existentialists*, p. 168.

128. Ibid., p. 81.

129. See Strauss, *Natural Right and History*, pp. 319–21: "We have noted before that what appeared later on as the discovery of History was originally rather the recovery of the distinction between theory and practice. That distinction had been blurred by the doctrinairism of the seventeenth and eighteenth centuries or, what is fundamentally the same thing, by the understanding of all theory as essentially in the service of practice. . . . The recovery of the distinction between theory and practice was from the outset modified by skepticism in regard to theoretical metaphysics, a skepticism which culminated in the depreciation of theory in favor of practice. In accordance with these antecedents, the

highest form of practice—the foundation or formation of a political society—was viewed as a quasi-natural process not controlled by reflection; thus it could become a purely theoretical scheme. Political theory became understanding of what practice has produced or of the actual and ceased to be the quest for what ought to be; political theory ceased to be 'theoretically practical' (i.e. deliberative at a second remove) and became purely theoretical in the way in which metaphysics (and physics) were understood to be purely theoretical. There came into being a new type of theory, of metaphysics, having as its highest theme human action and its product rather than the whole, which is in no way the object of human action. Within the whole and the metaphysic that is oriented upon it, human action occupies a high but subordinate place. When metaphysics came, as it now did, to regard human action and its product as the end toward which all other beings or processes are directed, metaphysics became philosophy of history. Philosophy of history was primarily theory, i.e. contemplation, of human practice and therewith necessarily of completed human practice; it presupposed that significant human action, History, was completed. By becoming the highest theme of philosophy, practice ceased to be practice proper, i.e., concern with *agenda*. The revolts against Hegelianism on the part of Kierkegaard and Nietzsche, in so far as they now exercise a strong influence on public opinion, thus appear as attempts to recover the possibility of practice, i.e. of a human life which has a significant and undetermined future. But these attempts increased the confusion, since they destroyed, as far as in them lay, the very possibility of theory. 'Doctrinairism' and 'existentialism' appear to us as the two faulty extremes. While being opposed to each other, they agree with each other in the decisive respect—they agree in ignoring prudence, 'the god of this lower world.' Prudence and 'this lower world' cannot be seen properly without some knowledge of 'the higher world'—without genuine *theoria*." Quoted in part by Aron, *Marxism and the Existentialists*, p. 84.

130. Ibid., p. 82.

131. See his *Sources of the Self* (Cambridge: Harvard University Press, 1989), pp. 3–24.

132. Aron, *Marxism and the Existentialists*, p. 16.

133. Ibid., p. 91.

134. Ibid., p. 89.

135. Ibid., p. 102.

136. Ibid., p. 16.

137. Ibid., p. 108.

138. Ibid., p. 95.

139. Raymond Aron, *The Industrial Society: Three Essays on Ideology and Development*, p. 179.

140. Ibid., p. 179. Aron concludes his introduction to *Marxism and the Exis-*

*tentialists* with the following summation of his political ethics: Aron's studies, he believed, were devoted to making "man aware of the irreducible plurality of the dimensions that characterize his existence. They want to remind him of certain commonplace truths: political action is not the only form of action, revolution is not the only form of political action; submission to an alleged historical necessity may become the worst form of alienation. The fact that crimes may be forgotten by our grandchildren does not make them forgivable at the time they are committed. To substitute the future perfect for the simple future is too convenient. Ethics judges politics as much as politics judges ethics. Nobody can say in what circumstances one must prevail over the other, and everybody must decide this question for himself alone, at the risk of being mistaken. The worst error would be to fail to recognize this dialectic which determines our condition and to surrender totally to nihilism or fanaticism, either by denying all spiritual imperatives or by trusting blindly in an alleged determinism of history." *Marxism and the Existentialists*, p. 16.

# 4

# ANTINOMIC PRUDENCE

Raymond Aron's attachment to the politically real was nowhere more evident than in his reflection on the life of nations, which he made one of the central pillars of his thought, and which we will scrutinize closely in this chapter. Our focus will be primarily (although not exclusively) normative: What are the choices confronting the statesman? What means may he legitimately employ in pursuit of his vocation? Is universal peace possible or even desirable? Can foreign policy be moral? It is here, indeed, that the stakes of politics, the irreducible *facticity* of the political, are truly unveiled; one of the reasons, as the French theorist Pierre Hassner has noted, that international relations has been often neglected by the great tradition of political philosophy.[1] Hassner writes: "Whether through the corrupting influences of commerce and immigration, or through the risk of military invasion and the necessity of defense, the problem is the same for the Platonic republic or for the Stalinist 'socialism in one country': ties with foreign lands trouble the unity of the body politic and the exclusive loyalty of its citizens; the needs of defense force a change of priorities concerning not only budgets but also political and social structures, as well as moral and legal rules."[2]

The conceptually messy world found at the heart of international relations confounds the expectations of system builders and forces the philosopher to confront history in the making. Recent (and not so recent) theories of international relations, both normative and descriptive, have as a result often seemed farfetched, based as they are on abstract models of rational choice or unrealistic conceptions of human nature rather than on the observation of political history.[3] Aron's thought on the life of nations shares none of this abstractness; it begins with the recognition of a looming fact: the world of international relations is characterized by the persistence of independent sovereignties, jealous of their interests, their ideas, and their prestige—what Aron refers to as "Power, Glory, and Idea."[4] At the limit, these sovereignties maintained a right to force in the defense of their interests or dreams. Thus, the problem of *war* is unavoidable for the statesman. The political thinker who refuses to consider the problem of war and peace fails, as a consequence, in two responsibilities: that of advising the statesman and educating the citizen, on the one hand; and that of mirroring accurately, "scientifically," the political phenomena, on the other (we have seen that these are crucial components of political reason, as defined in our opening chapter). In order to fulfill the former responsibility, however, it was vitally necessary to carry out the latter successfully—there was a tight link in Aron's work between the descriptive and the normative. In seeking to think politically, therefore, Aron's reflection turned time and again to the moral problems of peace and war, and to what could be analytically or descriptively known in the field of international relations.[5] The most ambitious of these efforts to conceptualize the life of nations and map the dangerous terrain across which the statesman had to travel can be found in *Peace and War*, a lengthy work first published in 1962 in Paris, and called by political scientist Stanley Hoffmann "the greatest effort ever made by one man alone to embrace the whole discipline of international relations."[6]

A brief account of the theoretical architecture of *Peace and War* will begin this chapter in order to set the stage for a discussion of Aron's normative theory of international relations. Following that, an excursion into the history of political prudence will be taken, using as guides Aristotle, Aquinas, and Burke. Returning from our excursion, we will make close company with Aron's *antinomic* prudence, spelling out differences and affinities with the classical tradition of prudence while exploring the twin "praxeological" problems confronted in *Peace and War*: the "Machiavellian" problem of legitimate means and the "Kantian" problem of universal peace. Although *Peace and War* will provide a central focus, other works will be consulted as appropriate, including Aron's debate with Catholic philosopher Jacques Maritain on the nature of Machiavellianism. What will be clear at the end of our travels will be the profoundly *political* nature of Aron's thought, what we have called his defense of political reason.

## 1. AN OVERVIEW OF *PEACE AND WAR*

Looking back undefensively at *Peace and War* over twenty years later, Aron reemphasized its basic point of departure. Whenever one considered international relations, he held, one should begin with the following "classic thesis: the state of nature (or of potential war) between states differs essentially from the civil state in the interior of states."[7] This starting point secured, Aron believed it possible to develop certain analytic tools that would enable the observer to conceptualize the rough and tumble of the life of nations. The tools would fall under the headings of theory, sociology, history, and the aforementioned praxeology. What undergirds these four different conceptual realms? We find once again in *Peace and War*—and in all of Aron's writings on international relations, including his copious journalistic observations on history in the making—his defense of political reason. In the context of international relations, Alan Bloom referred to it as Aron's "statesmanlike prudence," seeing in it the distinctively political character of Aron's reflection.[8] As Aron accented in *Les dernières années du siécle*, "It is better to start with the visible phenomena, naively observed, before moving—perhaps—to the deeper reality of the phenomena."[9]

The visible phenomena, the *common human world* of international relations, the statesman's world of diplomacy and strategy (what Aron called "diplomatic-strategic conduct"), form the material for any conceptualization adequate to the phenomena. While for Aron the transformations wrought by industrial society and the spread of democracy had changed the historical specificity of problems in international relations, there was a deep continuity across time in the problems themselves. Bryan-Paul Frost, in a recent article, hits the essential when he stresses that Aron "always starts from and returns to the history of international relations as it has been practiced through the ages."[10]

But what are international relations? Can we conceive of a science covering the field delimited by international relations with the exactness (such as it is) of even, say, economics (to say nothing of physics)? Can the field even *be* delimited? Let us follow Aron's *Peace and War* and turn first to "theory." Our earlier exploration of Aron's epistemological work should lead us to expect a limited range of possibilities for a theory of international relations, and that expectation is fulfilled. Aron's starting point, rooted in observation of the history of the life of nations and the perspective of the statesman, allows him to propose a broad conceptual framework—"essentially schematic" in the words of Hoffmann[11]—based on *power* and *system*. The former entails a classification of the means and ends of foreign policy, while the latter concerns the possible kinds of international system. Let us first consider power as *means*. Power enables one political unit to impose its will on another. In the Persian Gulf War Iraq used its power to overwhelm the country it invaded, Kuwait, until an international coalition, led by the United States, was powerful enough to drive Iraq from Kuwait. But can power be calculated with any degree of rigor? In what does it consist? Aron isolates three components of power: territory, resources, and the collective capacity for action.[12]

The first two of these three components are relatively straightforward, and can be grasped by thinking about their influence on the destiny of the United States. Given its immense size, and the fact that it is protected on east coast and west by vast expanses of ocean, the U.S. has had the rare fortune of being a nation never to have had its territory invaded by an enemy force. Only as we have entered into a nuclear age, with the advent of intercontinental ballistic missiles, has this geographical security been threatened, attenuating to a degree the importance of territory. The resources a political body has at its disposal, on the other hand, depend in large part on its level of economic development. America's wealth has allowed it to bring pressure on allies and enemies alike in pursuit of its varied goals.[13] Both territory and resources are at least theoretically open to measurement. The third component, however, the collective capacity for action, makes any strict calculation of power impossible. Such capacity depends on a *psychological or spiritual dimension* that can be ignored by the statesman only at his peril, yet which stubbornly resists reductive treatment.

Who would have anticipated the fierce resistance of England to Hitler's vicious onslaught during the Second World War? Who would have anticipated the political and moral leadership of Winston Churchill?[14] A nation may wield more power than can be calculated on the basis of its riches or measured in the extent of its territory. Tiny and relatively impoverished Afghanistan (albeit with some outside assistance) proved indomitable in its confrontation with its gigantic Soviet neighbor. And perhaps it is in the nature of politics from time to time to bring forth in moments of crisis great individuals. But this is the very drama of history not the object of the scientist in his lab.

Moreover, *pace* those theorists who believe international relations can be boiled down to the struggle for power, or boiled down at all, Aron refuses to deny the life of nations the complexity that is its due, and that is evident—naively—to anyone with eyes to see. The question of power as means opens onto the question of ends. Nations follow many destinies. Some seek security, withdrawing from the world or adopting a defensive posture towards the outside; such has been the dream of autarky, the "undiscoverable solitude" of which Pierre Hassner has written as marking a permanent impulse of human particularity.[15] Others seek power, not for its own sake, but in order to cultivate influence, even grandeur.[16] Others will fight for a sacred ideal, a conception of the truth about man's destiny.[17] In other words, the moral life of actors on the world's stage is *irreducibly complex*. As Aron wrote in his 1951 book *The Century of Total War*, "diplomatic alignments are determined not by conditions of economic rivalry or solidarity, but by considerations of power, by racial or cultural affinities, by the passions of the masses."[18] Power, glory, and idea: Aron used this triumvirate to provide a shorthand for the unavoidable sprawl of history. To approach international relations geometrically, in the spirit of abstraction, as if one were measuring the force of atomic particles colliding, is to be condemned to grave misunderstanding; international relations can be mapped, certain probabilities can be discerned; but they cannot be explained scientifically in any rigorously predictive way. As Aron tersely states at the end of *Peace and War*, "that political science is not *operational*, in the sense in which physics is, or even in the sense in which economics are, is incontestable."[19] The probabilistic knowledge available to the analyst or practitioner of foreign policy belongs, not in the realm of Kant's determinative judgment, which places phenomena under the umbrella of a pre-existing universal, but rather in the realm of *phronesis*—practical wisdom. Indeed, Pierre Manent has suggested that Aron wished "to reconquer the field of practical philosophy or of practical reason, not by a return to the Aristotelian doctrine but by using the conceptual tools forged by those authors whom we might situate on the frontier between philosophy and social science, such as Montesquieu or Max Weber."[20] This pregnant observation describes Aron's intent in *Peace and War*, an intent captured by Aristotle, for whom a discussion "will be adequate if its degree of clarity fits the subject matter; for we should not seek the same degree of exactness in all sorts of arguments alike, any more than in the products of different crafts."[21]

Remaining on the level of theory, Aron also deems it useful to resort to the notion of diplomatic systems. What is a diplomatic system? Again, we must begin where the statesman, in his diplomatic-strategic conduct, or the responsible citizen, in his desire to think politically, must begin, with the recognition of the sovereignty retained by states, jealous of their independence. Those political actors that maintain regular relations, that would be drawn into generalized war, belong to a diplomatic system. Diplomatic systems can be heterogeneous, homogeneous, or some mixture of the two; they can be bipolar, multipolar, or in the limit case of global empire or universal rule, unipolar. By heterogeneous and homogeneous Aron points to the nature of political regimes and the goals they pursue, which, as we have seen, are irreducibly complex. It is important to highlight the accent Aron places on the classical concept of regime. Although Aron's notion of regime is drawn more narrowly than that of Aristotle (for whom the regime constitutes much more an encompassing way of life than for Aron), it shares with the Aristotelian understanding a refusal to abandon the political for subpolitical considerations.[22] The United States and the Soviet Union belonged to a heterogeneous system because the goals of their respective regimes—and their constituting principles—differed dramatically. The Western democracies and Iran today belong to such a heterogeneous system; the United States and Canada do not. During the Cold War, just as during the Peloponnesian War in the ancient world, the diplomatic system was bipolar—dominated by twin powers, tending to draw all lesser powers into their embrace. The Concert of Europe, in contrast, through balancing power in the nineteenth century between several nations, was a multipolar system.[23]

What all of this amounts to, theoretically (and this is in keeping with Aron's epistemological reflection), is that no closed, global theory of international relations is conceivable. How could it be conceived without placing within a conceptual prison the freedom of men and nations? The life of nations must be understood *on the ground*: the theorist (or statesman) might scale to a vantage point above the fray; but the fray itself, its stakes, its inner logic, its historical specificity, and the nature of the regimes involved, can be ignored only at the cost of political vacuity, or, worse, a destruction of the real goods the political world can bear when cultivated carefully to fruition.

The next stage of Aron's undertaking in *Peace and War*, after laying out the broad theoretical framework we have just examined, is sociological—the study of the multiple ways various factors contribute to or influence the foreign policy of a political body or nation. The sociologist seeks to determine the degree to which subpolitical forces control the actions of nations. While it is correct to emphasize in Aron the idea of the autonomy, even the primacy of politics, he did not ignore subpolitical forces; Aron's conclusions are, however, as we would expect with the epistemological approach examined in chapter 2, limited and probabilistic. Sociological causes can be moral and social, or they can be material and physical. Physical causes, Aron avers, can be broken down into space, population, and resources. Let us pause for a moment with physical and material causes and parse Aron's meaning.

Spatial causes are at work in the *environment*; as a *theater* within which nations engage their destinies; and as a *stake* in the struggle between nations. Following Montesquieu, Aron notes that the environment does not *determine* but might *influence* international relations.[24] Space as theater is simply geopolitics: the field upon which forces are arrayed and battles waged. As a stake of international relations, however, space is less important than it has been in the past, a shift explained by two basic reasons. First, the discovery that wealth no longer depends on land, that intelligence and the right ordering of economic life can enrich a nation bereft of natural resources (as in Japan) means space holds diminished economic importance.[25] The second reason relates to progress in military technology. Aron keyed on this transformation as early as *The Century of Total War*. The tank, as Aron observes, writing of the "technical surprise" of World War I, broke through the barriers of trench warfare, allowing heavily bombed terrain to be navigated rapidly and with frightening ease.[26] We have already mentioned the impact of intercontinental ballistic missiles in the abolition of space. Without lapsing into the often forbidding terminology of Martin Heidegger, Aron was always attentive to the role technology was playing in transforming our concepts—and the lived reality—of time and space.[27] Unlike Heiddeger-influenced thinkers (such as Paul Virilio), who view the speed of modern technology as issuing in a depoliticizing mutation—virtually anthropological—in political culture, Aron refused to jettison political reason.

The quantitative changes wrought by modern technology did not, in his eyes, eliminate the political.

Moving on from space, Aron next examines the question of number. How does number influence peace and war? Here, indetermination reigns. No solid inferences, Aron believes, can be drawn from the relationship of population and war. In an analysis of economic interpretations of history that recapitulates much of what we looked at in our previous chapter, Aron reasons that economic systems never make war inevitable. Aron's rather skeptical conclusions in this section of *Peace and War* have the effect of reinforcing the importance of politics, and hence the importance of human liberty. Subpolitical or transpolitical forces unquestionably constrained the actions of men and nations, but Aron here as elsewhere *preserves the political*.[28]

Finally, Aron attempts to discern the role of moral and social causes in international relations. Here, Aron again stresses that the nature of a political regime has a decisive impact on its foreign policy. In this, Aron's theory of international relations can be sharply differentiated from realist theories like Kenneth Waltz's, which view the nature of political regimes as irrelevant to the play of forces in the international arena—on Waltz's view, dominated by anarchy understood in an absolutely primary way.[29] Waltz held that neither political culture nor the nature of the regime had a major impact on the behavior of political actors or the nature of diplomatic-strategic conduct. Such behavior was ruled solely by the inexorable laws set in motion by the absence of an international arbiter and the willfulness of states. Yet, as Aron explains, the foreign policy of the Soviet Union was *ideologically* driven: as long as it upheld its constitutive principles, the communist regime would seek only tactical peace with its adversaries in the capitalist world. Post-communist Russia has behaved quite differently than would a still-extant Soviet Union, an observation which immediately falsifies those theories like Waltz's that abstract away from "domestic" politics. How, then, could the nature of the Soviet regime be ignored by the statesman? Waltz and like-minded theorists take a partial truth and seek to extend it too far, pushing a conceptual logic beyond its proper measure, and thus distorting reality in the process. Aron similarly rejected the idea of a nation having an inherent tendency in its political culture that would drive it to war. Nor was war a *necessary* expression of human nature. As Aron wrote:

The human animal is aggressive, but does not fight by instinct, and war is an expression, it is not a *necessary* expression of human combativity. War has been the constant expression in the course of the historical phase, starting from the moment when societies were organized and armed. It is contrary to the nature of man that the danger of violence be definitively dispelled: in every collectivity, misfits will violate the laws and attack persons. It is contrary to the nature of individuals and groups that the conflicts between individuals or among groups disappear. But it is not proved that these conflicts must be manifested in the phenomenon of war, as we have known it for thousands of years, with organized combatants, utilizing increasingly destructive weapons.[30]

To repeat what we have stated on several occasions throughout this study: Aron's philosophical anthropology was always attuned to the possibility of human liberty. He was deeply suspicious of all formulas which sought to immolate man's freedom in the fire of subpolitical forces. The findings of the social scientist can lead the statesman to understand more thoroughly his options, but they do not replace the need for prudent decision in diplomacy and strategy.

In the third section of *Peace and War*, devoted to the history of the twentieth century,[31] Aron seeks to measure the extent to which the nuclear age has affected the dynamics of international relations. He focuses on two principal developments: the technological revolution; and the related extension of the diplomatic field to the farthest reaches of the globe, a phenomenon Aron saw as marking the onset of "universal history."[32] Yet Aron was persuaded that these historical mutations, although they had changed much, had transformed neither the nature of men nor the nature of human collectivities. While what Aron called "history as process," the history of technological and industrial modernity, had often appeared as if it would sweep away every fixed station, it had not swept away the political. History as drama, made up of the conflicts between men and nations, appeared just as real in the twentieth century as it had five hundred years before the Christian era began. The hydrogen bomb had not ended history, it had not ended statesmanship, it had not ended war.

It is in the fourth and concluding part of *Peace and War* that Raymond Aron lays out his normative theory of antinomic prudence, which we will look at in depth later in this chapter. The normative argument draws on the numerous insights of the theoretical, sociological, and historical sections by which it is preceded, making this short detour necessary. Given its brevity, only the barest outline of Aron's rich treatment has been given, but hopefully it is enough to convey the range and scope of Aron's most ambitious book. What it is essential to emphasize at this stage is that Aron's normative theory is deeply embedded in his descriptive, indeed phenomenological, analysis of international relations, and thus is never severed from considerations of feasibility or the real dilemmas of statecraft. Following the method established in *Introduction to the Philosophy of History*, Aron situates himself within the role of statesman or responsible citizen in order to *think politically*. Before we take up the specifics of Aron's normative theory, however, another detour is required, this time through what can be called the "prudence tradition" in Western political thought. As we will come to see, Aron is most definitely a member of this tradition, but there are certain divergences we must highlight; in order to do so, this prior tradition must be understood in its basic lineaments.

## 2. THE PRUDENCE TRADITION

What is the "prudence tradition" in foreign policy?[33] We must first distinguish it from two rival traditions in the morality of international relations: realism and idealism. All three traditions advocate a certain way of conceptualizing the relationship of moral principles to the day-to-day struggles of the political world of foreign policy; all three have precedent in the history of ideas as well as in the realm of practice.

The realist tradition (one could place within it Thracymachus from Plato's *Republic*; the Athenian spokesmen in the Melian dialogue of Thucydides' *History of the Peloponnesian War*; Machiavelli; Thomas Hobbes; and, among many others in the twentieth century, Hans Morgenthau) stresses that morality and international relations have little to do with one another. (We are, of course, reconstructing an ideal type; there are many shadings of realism.) The realist believes that, following Machiavelli, the statesman must go to "the effectual truth of the thing"—that "he who lets go of what is done for what should be done learns his ruin rather than his preservation."[34] The effectual truth of the political, the realist imagines, is that it is riven with self-interest, struggle, extreme circumstances, and constantly shadowed by war. The demands of justice, as in Machiavelli, are reduced to requirements of necessity.[35]

A statesman who proceeds without keeping this truth in view, the realist warns, will soon find himself a statesman no more, a victim of his own naïveté and the cunning of his adversary. Whatever moral norms exist, exist *within* the political community; between nations there exist only tentative agreements, often abrogated when the "national interest" is at stake. The state is therefore seen as the only significant actor in international relations, while state power is theorized as determinative in international outcomes.[36] Thus the means at the disposal of political leaders must, at least with regard to external forces, remain as free as possible from the constraints of traditional morality. An overly fastidious concern with morality is, on the view of this tradition, "at best, inappropriate in international affairs, or worse, positively harmful if it encourages unrealistic, 'utopian' thinking."[37] Seeing things as they are leads the realist to understand that international relations is ultimately about the *power* and *self-aggrandizement* of states.

Many centuries before Machiavelli, in his history of the two-decade war between Athens and Sparta, Thucydides bore out this observation. The "Melian Dialogue" recounts the story of Athenian representatives seeking the submission of tiny Melos, a colony of Sparta that refuses to bend to Athenian power. The Athenians are quite frank in their approach to the Melians:

> For ourselves, we shall not trouble you with specious pretenses—either of how we have a right to our empire because we overthrew the Mede, or are now attacking you because of wrong you have done us—and make a long speech which would not be believed; and in return we hope that you, instead of thinking to influence us by saying that you did not join the Spartans, although their colonists, or that you have done us no wrong, will aim at what is feasible, holding in view the real sentiments of us both; since you know as well as we do that right, as the world goes, is only in question between equals in power, while the strong do what they can and the weak suffer what they must.[38]

The strong do what they can and the weak do what they must: such is the lesson of *power politics* defended or, with resignation, accepted by the realist tradition. Realists consequently have little difficulty in wrestling with the applicability of moral principle to the practice of foreign policy. Since "right" can be seen only in the harsh light of power, moral norms in international relations are thrown quickly to the ground when they conflict with the realities of practice.

Idealism, on the other hand, collapses the tension between morality and politics in the opposite direction. If realists view morality as largely inapplicable to the brute facticity of external political relations, idealists see the applicability of morality to practice as a matter of *will*. Too often, the idealist cries, sin and evil are legitimated as necessities of politics when they are in fact metastases of human corruption or unjust structures of power. The constraints of politics are *false* constraints. As Roger Scruton suggests, while realists see international relations in terms of power, idealists tend to view them in terms of "moral precepts, justice, trust and obligation."[39] They embrace human rights, not the state, as their primordial political category.

What is needed, idealists hold, are statesmen or international organizations with vision who will pursue the good or the just, not shore up the national interest; who will fight for human rights, not for *raison d'etat*. Idealists deny that the political can be cut off from moral considerations, or even that it somehow constitutes a realm where moral norms need to be mediated before they are applied. Hence idealists are often moralists, condemning ferociously the compromises of the politician. Since they favor the universality of human rights over the national interest, idealists are often suspicious of nationhood, and look to overarching international authorities (such as the United Nations or the World Court) to regulate the life of nations. In short they distrust the messy world of politics and refuse to sanction the ways of the world.[40]

The prudence tradition eschews both of these alternatives. Politics can not be divorced from morality, nor can it simply be reduced to morality. Two basic characteristics mark this tradition. The first is that it indeed acknowledges "the considerable difficulty of translating ethical intentions and purposes into policies that will produce morally sound results."[41] The second feature is that it places a strong emphasis on the statesman's character. As Alberto Coll writes:

> Character is seen as a key component in the ability to act morally in the political world. Writers concerned with prudence argue that a statesman's religious, philosophical, or ideological views provide a less

reliable indicator of his capacity for prudence than do a series of character traits and intellectual virtues. This focus on character makes the prudence tradition distinctive.[42]

Although thinkers within this tradition are attuned to the human capacity for evil, and see politics as a field where evil often holds sway, they refuse to collapse the "ought" into the "is," as does the realist tradition. At the same time, prudence theorists avoid distorting their perception of reality by projecting norms too hastily on an intransigent political world. This is one reason why prudence theorists refuse to abstract away from the political community in favor of universal humanity, although at the same time they refuse to remove the latter from ethical consideration. Moral action in foreign policy is therefore seen as feasible, but structural and human limitations make any direct "fit" rare: "Prudence is not value free; it remains under the guidance, however ambiguous or indirect, of moral principles."[43]

Aristotle has provided what is perhaps the most thorough philosophical treatment of the nature of prudence or practical wisdom, and it would be worth a few moments of our time to reconstruct the essentials of his analysis. Doing so will allow Aron's distinctive contribution to the prudence tradition, and his affinity with Aristotle, to become clear in our next section. The *locus classicus* of Aristotle's theorizing of prudence can be found in Book VI of the *Nichomachean Ethics*.[44] There Aristotle lays out his vision of practical wisdom as the highest form of excellence in political life. Prudence is exhibited in deciding well, so, as Aristotle puts it, "To grasp what practical wisdom is we should first study the sort of people we call practically wise."[45] The best place to look for prudence is in the management of households and states—for Aristotle the most important locus for practical wisdom. Such management is always resistant to what one might call "geometric" approaches; the latter distort, in Leo Strauss's formulation, "the exceptions, modifications, balances, compromises, or mixtures" of the human and political world.[46] Prudence is operative where things are inexact, where particulars loom large, where uncertainty reigns. And the management of households and states is indeed the kingdom of "might-have-been."[47] But what are the components of prudence? Aristotle deems three character traits as of utmost importance in being prudent: deliberateness, self-control, and good sense.

How do we determine if a decision has been well made? *Deliberation* is one important dimension: "good deliberation will be the type of correctness that expresses what is expedient for promoting the end about which practical wisdom is true supposition."[48] In order to deliberate, one must hesitate, reflect, engage in discussion. The means must be appropriate to the end and the end appropriate to the means. Possible consequences need to be imagined and considered. In politics, one can make a misstep all too easily. Returning to an example we have used throughout, U.S. President George Bush had originally decided to muster a nominal response to Iraq's invasion of Kuwait; upon further deliberation, and after a critical discussion with British Prime Minister Margaret Thatcher, President Bush reconsidered his original position and began to establish the preconditions for the more vigorous response that soon followed. President Bush *deliberated well*, keeping in mind as he did both the possible consequences of action or inaction, and once deciding, ensuring the means chosen were commensurate with the end sought.

A second character trait pointed to by Aristotle is self-control, a virtue not always evident in politics. To have self-control is to be aware of one's abilities *and* one's limitations. Emotion often clouds this awareness by obscuring one's capacity to make good judgments. A politician who allows a personal aversion (or attraction) to determine a course of action lacks prudence, as would be the case if President Bush acted on the basis of a deep hatred for, say, the Ba'athist movement of which Saddam Hussein is a member. Similarly, aversions and attractions can poison the sense of reality crucial to sound political decision-making. Without self-control, it is difficult to think clearly about consequences and choose the right means. One can get lost quickly in the forest of solipsism, never, perhaps, to find the way out.

The third component of Aristotelian prudence is simple "good sense." Good sense is equivalent to sympathetic understanding and has two fundamental dimensions: the ability to make correct judgment of what is fair, on the one hand; the capacity to enter into the other's understanding and forgive, on the other.[49] To make a correct judgment it is often necessary to enter as much as possible into the other's understanding—as is the case when we try to think politically, when we attempt to reconstruct the constraints and possibilities faced by the statesman or citizen. Often, as well, we must forgive or lose sight of the possibilities open to us. Great statesmen have almost always been marked by a certain magnanimity when dealing with former enemies. Political forgiveness remains one of the keys to historical peace, just as political vengeance remains one of the hardy and perpetual seeds of war.

Thus the prudent man deliberates well, is self-controlled, and has the capacity and willingness to enter into sympathetic understanding with the other. These components, in the Aristotelian discernment, run together, reinforcing each other like tributary streams flowing together into a larger river. They offer the prudent man the knowledge, not of universals or generalizations, but rather of the particular, of the experiential. As noted earlier, for Aristotle, we must seek only the degree of clarity fitting the subject matter under discussion. Practical wisdom cannot be taught from a textbook, but it can be learned from experience, if one has the right structure of virtues, the right "taste" for reality.

For Aristotle, a statesman is not worthy of the accolade "prudent" unless his actions are directed to *good ends*. Prudence is not mere "cleverness," as Aristotle referred to the faculty modern theorists call "instrumental reason."[50] St. Thomas would later call this *astuticia*. Cleverness finds the most efficient means to achieve an end, but the end itself might be perverse. Realist thinkers, when they speak of prudence, usually have in mind something akin to Aristotelian cleverness. Idealists often dismiss prudence as a moral category because they fear it is only a masquerade for cleverness, a way of putting a moral gloss on corrupted actions. As Aristotle writes, however, it is essential to distinguish the two faculties:

> There is a faculty which is called cleverness; and this is such as to be able to do the things that tend toward the mark we have set before ourselves, and to hit it. Now if the mark be noble, the cleverness is laudable, but if the mark be bad, the cleverness is mere smartness; hence we call even men of practical wisdom clever or smart. Practical wisdom is not the faculty, but it does not exist without this faculty. And this eye of the soul acquires its formed state not without the aid of virtue . . . for the syllogisms which deal with acts to be done are things which involve a starting point, viz. "since the end, i.e. what is best, is of such and such a nature," whatever it may be (let it for the sake of argument be what we please); and this is not evident except to the good man; for wickedness perverts us and causes us to be deceived about the starting points of action. Therefore it is impossible to be practically wise without being good.[51]

The noble statesman needs cleverness, but it does not suffice. There is a certain Machiavellianism in Aristotle, a prudent facing of the dilemmas of statesmanship not unlike that which one can find in Aron; but where the Machiavellian statesman would take his bearings from the absence of natural right and the existence of extreme situations (such as a state of political emergency), the true statesman, on the Aristotelian view, while never losing sight of necessity, takes his from what is morally right.[52] Aristotelian prudence is subject to a higher wisdom, a "theoretical wisdom" or intellectual virtue Aristotle called *theoria*.[53] Without this light illuminating the political world, prudence can slide rapidly into instrumental reason.

The prudence tradition, first given voice by Aristotle, has been rearticulated by other major thinkers in the West, including, most importantly, St. Thomas Aquinas, and, closer to our own time, Edmund Burke. We shall see shortly how Raymond Aron fits into this tradition and how he viewed it as capturing most adequately the nature of the political world. But let us pause for just a moment with Aquinas and Burke.

Aquinas incorporated the Aristotelian understanding of practical wisdom into the Christian dispensation as the foremost virtue among the four cardinal virtues (the other three being justice, fortitude, and temperance). For Aquinas, prudence was "right reason in action."[54] Brian Davies notes that, in Aquinas's teaching, prudence "is important since it is the virtue which actually disposes us to think well about what to do . . . it is the developed disposition to deliberate well, to decide well, and to execute actions well."[55] But, like Aristotle, Aquinas differentiated prudence from cleverness. In order to live a morally good life, Aquinas reasoned, we must know what a humanly good life *is, and* know how to translate this more general knowledge of the good into practice. Prudence is thus both an intellectual and a moral virtue:

> The role of prudence is to charge our conduct with right reason, and this cannot be done without rightful desire. And so prudence has the nature of virtue, not only that which the other intellectual virtues possess, but also that possessed by the moral virtues, among which it is counted.[56]

Aquinas saw prudence as subject to a higher wisdom—the natural law imparted by God into the structure of reality itself. In this, a significant tension with Aristotle, who held no theory of revealed natural law, is manifest. For Aristotle, natural right is *changeable*: under certain circumstances, when the very existence of society is threatened, the statesman is morally justified in acting in a way at odds with strict conceptions of justice. In Aquinas, the statesman's freedom is more tightly circumscribed.[57] Yet, like Aristotle, Aquinas acknowledged politics as the preeminent field for prudential action, concerning as it did the field where the common good was at stake. To Aristotle's more truncated list of deliberation, self-control, and common sense, Aquinas added several other components to practical wisdom: memory, intelligence, openness to the insights of others, acumen, foresight, circumspection, caution. The prudent statesman carried out moral reasoning on an uncertain terrain, rife with complexities and trade-offs.

With Edmund Burke in the nineteenth century we find a powerful restatement of the prudence tradition, but one with certain meaningful differences from that advanced by Aristotle and Aquinas. As a statesman himself, Burke saw in prudence a corrective to the failure of speculative theory to guide human action successfully. Burke was responding to the metaphysical madness of the French Revolution, a kind of hyperrationalism that sought the reordering of the human world along the lines laid down by abstract theory.[58] The statesman had *experience*, something not easily equaled by the geometric mind of the professor:

> A statesman differs from a professor in an university; the latter has only the general view of society; the former, the statesman, has a number of circumstances to combine with those general ideas, and to take into his consideration. Circumstances are infinite, are infinitely combined; are variable and transient; he who does not take them into consideration is not erroneous, but stark mad . . . metaphysically mad. A statesman, never losing sight of principles, is to be guided by circumstances; and judging contrary to the exigencies of the moment, he may ruin his country forever.[59]

For Burke, the statesman had to have principles, but the process of applying them to the complexity of the real—marked by "infinite" circumstances—was an arduous one. As Leo Strauss has demonstrated, however, Burke's prudence, grounded in tradition rather than theoretical wisdom, goes further than that of Aristotle and Aquinas in the direction of giving prudence full autonomy—that is, severing it from that which in both of the latter constrains and directs prudence, preventing it from degenerating into mere cleverness.[60] Burke's prudence, in arguing that practical wisdom trumps theoretical wisdom whenever conflict occurs between the two, moves us closer to a kind of Machiavellianism more commonly associated with the realist tradition. Burke was not unaware of this difficulty, but it remains unclear whether, within Burkean traditionalism, there is anything that offers a principled, lighted path out.

We will see in our next section what Raymond Aron's prudence, which we have called *antinomic*, consists in, and what provides its foundation. In this section our purpose has rather been to outline the main features of prudence as it has been thought about by several of the great thinkers of the Western tradition of political philosophy. We have learned that the "prudence tradition" avoids collapsing either of the poles of the morality–politics axis in international relations, maintaining itself in the tension between the demands of ethics and the demands of politics. In so doing a deeper, *political morality* is forged, one which appears at the heart of Aron's political reason. Let us now turn to measuring Aron's contribution to the prudence tradition.

## 3. THE AMORAL PRINCE?

Raymond Aron's normative theory of international relations begins from two basic praxeological problems. The first, which will be addressed in this section, can be captured in the form of two terse questions: Is foreign policy necessarily evil? What *means* may legitimately be used by the statesman "in the world as it is?"[61] We will follow Aron and call this the "Machiavellian problem." The second praxeological problem asks another question: Can we transcend foreign policy, leaving behind the quarrelsome word of nations in favor of universal empire or collective security? This is the "Kantian" problem of universal peace, and it shall be engaged in the concluding section to this chapter. Both provide us with a way of gaining entrance into the Aronian understanding of prudence.

The normative theory that Aron advanced as the most adequate, "scientific" response to the dilemmas of the political actor caught up in history in the making can be called *antinomic prudence*. It is imperative, if we are to grasp the essence of Aron's prudential position, to begin where Aron begins: the ambiguous and indeterminate *reality* of international relations. As we have seen in the first section of this chapter, the epistemological position of the statesman is limited to probabilities; no predictive or operational "science" of international relations can replace the need for prudential choice. As for such choice, Aron saw the political world confronted by the statesman as riven with antinomies, areas where the pursuit of a partial logic in a single-minded way can result in great evil or at least a corruption of the goods made possible through politics. Certain goods, sought in immoderation, are incommensurable and can even suddenly transform into evils, wreaking destruction.

This is true *within* the political community, where, say, the modern demands of equality and liberty are in profound tension. Within the ambiguous realm of international relations, perpetually haunted by war, it is even more powerfully the case: "[W]hat gives political life its somber grandeur is that statesmen come to do acts they detest because they believe themselves, in conscience and the depths of their soul, accountable for the common destiny."[62] Political wisdom, on Aron's view, must take into account the unavoidable conflict of goods and seek to balance their rivalry in the most moderate and just way. The statesman could legitimately search out both universal peace and the flourishing of the political community whose destiny he was responsible for; to assume, however, that these two goals were always commensurable would be to deny the antinomical structure of the political real. This recognition makes any rationalistic, deductive approach to international relations, either analytic or normative, intrinsically flawed.

Aron's defense of antinomic prudence, which is really a defense of political reason against its enemies, requires a detailed critical encounter with the two rival theories of the morality of international relations looked at in the last section: idealism and realism. As we have seen, realist theories generally argue that the absence of a universal sovereign justifies the rejection of any morality other than calculation in the life of nations; idealist theories, on the other hand, attempt to transcend international anarchy through a categorical international morality. In crucial ways, realist and idealist accounts are flawed; yet both contain, properly understood, aspects of the truth.

Starting, then, from the world as it is, where "history is violent and our ideal peaceful,"[63] what means are defensible? Does the absence of any adjudicating or decision-making body, capable of enforcing its decisions, give us sufficient reason to dismiss all claims of morality from consideration in international relations, as the realist recommends? Aron's first move is to point out that there is a possible antinomy between "legality" and fairness. As an example, he reminds us of the following: "If, in 1933, France had heeded Marshal Pilsudski's advice and used force to overthrow Hitler, who had just come to power, she would have violated the *principle* of non-interference in the internal affairs of other states, she would have failed to recognize Germany's *right* of free choice with regard to regime and leader, she would have been denounced with indignation by American public opinion, by moralists and idealists hastening to the rescue, not of National Socialism, but of the will of the people or the rule of non-interference."[64]

Who today, with the wisdom of hindsight, would not grant the moral legitimacy of a preemptive French strike against the growing Nazi menace? What horrors would have been avoided? As Aron underscores, this example brings to light an essential point about international relations. Given the fact that states have not refused themselves the option of taking the law into their own hands, remaining "sole judges of what their honor requires," the very survival of nations depends on the careful calculation of forces. But this gives moral weight to the statesmen's vocation: "it is the *duty* of statesmen to be concerned, *first of all*, with the nation whose destiny is entrusted to them."[65] If the state of nature rules among states, then national egoism is unavoidable, it is a *fact* embedded in the historically real. Aron thus views the idealist approach to international relations (the morality of law) naive and potentially dangerous.

Idealists, as we have seen, strive to establish a direct "fit" between morality and politics in international relations. The idealist morality of law is a moralistic reaction to the immorality of power politics as practiced by nations and regimes since time immemorial.[66] Aron offers four instances of this kind of *unpolitical* thinking: the Open-Door policy toward China earlier in the twentieth century, intended to protect China's independence and territorial integrity; nonrecognition of changes effected by force; outlawing war; and collective security. In each case, the results have been far from satisfactory and have perhaps done more moral harm than good.

In the first case, the policy adopted was unrealistic: the absence of any central government in Beijing in the aftermath of the disintegration of China's old regime made European interference virtually inevitable in the quest for influence. The lesson is simple: moral norms detached from any force capable of ensuring them are mere puffs of smoke. As for the nonrecognition of changes brought about by force, Aron makes a similar point:

> Still more futile is the principle of the non-recognition of changes effected by force. Populations annexed against their will receive no help from the refusal of the government of the United States to accept a *fait accompli.* Men know that in the long run international law must bow to fact. A territorial status invariably ends up being legalized, provided it lasts. A great power that wants to forbid a rival from making conquests must arm and not proclaim in advance its moral disapproval and its abstention from force (such is the meaning of the nonrecognition of changes effected by force).[67]

It is in the latter two instances, the outlawing of war and the pursuit of collective security, that are anticipated concerns we will address in the next section, concerns that circle around the idea of moving beyond foreign policy, perhaps beyond politics. But in the context of the current discussion—the failure of idealism as a normative foundation in international relations—several points need to be made. First, efforts to outlaw war, such as the Kellogg-Briand Pact, an international agreement which in the interwar period was promulgated at the instigation of the United States, are in essence attempts to recast the human condition fundamentally. As Aron observes, they represent "abstract propositions offered as normative, but stripped of all authority because *they do not express needs genuinely felt by men* and they are supported neither by force nor by institutions."[68] Aron adds: "[A]nyone imagining he was guaranteeing peace by outlawing war was like a doctor imagining he was curing diseases by declaring them contrary to the aspirations of humanity."[69]

There are two arguments packed into these observations from Aron, both of which are sound and central to his defense of political reason. First, reiterating the analysis made above, international norms need to be backed by institutional force, without which they are mere imaginings. If President Bush had merely condemned the Iraqi aggression against Kuwait, without mustering the force necessary to reverse it,

Saddam Hussein's territorial grab would likely have been ratified, at least *ex post facto*, leading to a probable future war between Israel and the Arab world. U.S. foreign policy under President Bill Clinton has been accused of just this kind of verbal posturing, particularly in its handling of the war in Bosnia.

Moreover, the idea of triumphing over war ignores the existence of *unjust status quos*, rooted in "needs genuinely felt by men." As Aron avers, "[I]t is difficult to condemn, morally or historically, the initiative of a recourse to force for two reasons: this initiative may be the only means of preventing an attack that will be mortal; no tribunal judging equitably is in a position to say what peaceful changes are imperative and to compel respect for these decisions."[70] Referring back to the distinction between legality and fairness, Aron gestures toward a conception of natural right transcending positive law. In a paradoxical way, idealists promote a vision that could lead to injustice, lest they make the implausible assumption that all arrangements between nations are just, and that this justice is reflected in the hearts of men. Aron would later give a personal slant to this argument in his study *Clausewitz*, where he decries the desire of idealist political thinkers to abolish the tragic from history: "What is lacking in run-of-the-mill professors is the sense of history and tragedy . . . how can I, as a Frenchman of Jewish origin, forget that France owes her liberation to the power of her allies, or that Israel owes her very existence to her arms and probably owes her future survival to her willingness—and, if need be, American willingness—to fight again?"[71] So might is not right, but neither is the abolition of might.

The idea of collective security (a notion oft-employed by President Clinton in response to the break-up of the former Soviet bloc) poses related difficulties. States must be in agreement over the nature of the aggression and the aggressor. Without such agreement, there will be no willingness to defend the status quo. Collective security thus presupposes exactly what is put in question in international conflict. On the rare occasions when it is possible, sufficient interest must exist for states to "accept possible risks and sacrifices in view of an interest that is not strictly material and that is *their* interest at most in the long run."[72]

In short, these various manifestations of the idealist inspiration are, in Aron's estimation, deeply problematic. Criticism of the "idealist illusion" is thus both pragmatic—in that it better serves the self-interest

of nations—and moral. Idealist diplomacy, Aron believes, slides toward
fanaticism by dividing nations dogmatically into good and evil camps
and exaggerating the crimes of power politics. Far better to adopt the
standpoint of prudence than to surrender to idealist fantasies:

> States, engaged in incessant competition whose stake is their exis-
> tence, do not all behave in the same manner at all times, but they are
> not divided, once and for all, into good and evil. It is rare that all the
> wrongs are committed by one side, that one camp is faultless. The first
> duty—political, but also moral—is to see international relations for
> what they are, so that each state, legitimately preoccupied with its
> own interests, will not be entirely blind to the interests of others. In
> this uncertain battle, in which the qualifications of the participants are
> not equivalent but in which it is rare that one of them has done abso-
> lutely no wrong, the best conduct—the best with regard to the values
> the idealist himself wished to achieve—is that dictated by *prudence*. To
> be prudent is to act in accordance with the particular situation and the
> concrete data, and not in accordance with some system or out of
> passive obedience to a norm or pseudo-norm; it is to prefer the *limita-
> tion of violence* to the punishment of the presumably guilty party or to
> a so-called absolute justice; it is to establish concrete accessible objec-
> tives conforming to the secular law of international relations and not
> to limitless and perhaps meaningless objectives, such as 'a world safe
> for democracy' or 'a world from which power politics will have disap-
> peared'.[73]

The idealist morality of law ignores the antinomies of international
political life, overcoming them in word but not in deed. It abstracts
away irresponsibly from the actual choices facing the statesman, and
therefore, as our introductory chapter emphasized, fails to think politically.[74] In seeking perfect justice, it neglects what can be achieved feasi-
bly; rather the Montesquieuian strategy of avoiding the worst, Aron
advises, than the idealist quest for the ideal.

But if Aron found the abstractions of idealism a dangerous misunderstanding of the antinomic structure of the political world, he did not
embrace what is often posed as the alternative to idealism: the amorality
of realism. As we have seen, the realist holds that, as a consequence of
the absence of any universal adjudicating or decision-making body capable of enforcing its decisions, combined with a pessimistic conception

of human nature, all or most claims of morality can be excluded from consideration between nations. The advocate of power politics argues that all means are potentially legitimate in the political community's relationship to the *other*: ruse, deception, political murder, the open violence of armed struggle.

Aron is frequently associated with such Machiavellian or Hobbesian thinking, and is often categorized as a normative realist in international relations theory.[75] But this is a fundamental misunderstanding of Aron's thought, and could only result from a failure to read his work, or at least not read it beyond the opening pages of *Peace and War*. As we have discovered, Aron *did* appreciate fully the persistence of independent sovereignties, and what that persistence implied. But to move from an acknowledgment of the rivalrous nature of states to an affirmation of unlimited means, to a justification of state *amorality* was, on Aron's view, unwarranted. When basing itself on an ostensibly neutral and "objective" reading of human nature and the nature of states, normative realism was, in fact, sneaking in through the back door a concealed metaphysics—an *idealism* of power politics.

A statesman who, following the advice of the idealist, ignores the state of nature between sovereign nations threatens the survival of the political community he is responsible for protecting. A certain national egoism is thus logically implied and morally defensible given the circumstances of international life. The moral duties of the statesman are accordingly owed first and foremost to his political community, and not to humanity in general. This is not, however, the whole story. As Aron argues, relations between political communities are "not . . . comparable to those of beasts in the jungle."[76] The conduct of statesmen in political history has often claimed obedience to norms, to be following moral principles. Morality is *woven into* the fabric of political history:

> [T]he . . . realist, who asserts that man is a beast of prey and urges him to behave as such, ignores a whole side of human nature. Even in the relations between states, respect for ideas, aspirations to higher values and concern for obligations have been manifested. Rarely have collectivities acted as if they would stop at nothing with regard to one another.[77]

That said, Aron saw a partial truth in the realist position, stressing that "the morality of struggle will have some meaning as long as war remains the final sanction of international relations.''[78] The realist school marked a necessary reaction against the excessive naïveté of idealism, but going too far, it demonstrated a failure to think politically every bit as ideological as what it opposed. An attention to the *phenomena* of politics themselves shows that the realist, by abandoning any shared norms between political communities, distorted the reality of human nature and the actual behavior of states toward one another. It abandoned the particularities of history, assuming one situation—an *agonistic* situation—held permanently. But this was to ignore the importance of *regime* in international relations, and hence, in a way, to ignore the reality of politics.

On the strict realist account, relations with democratic and ideologically driven totalitarian states would thus be placed on the same level; one is responsible for one's own and *one's own alone*. But it is clear that, at least for a democracy, to treat a democratic regime and a totalitarian regime the same way would be folly. Each calls for a different approach, just as would relations with nontotalitarian but authoritarian or theocratic regimes.[79] There was, in other words, a form of cultural relativism implicit within realism that Aron believed deeply flawed. As Aron pointed out, there were many *others*, a clear diversity of world cultures and dramatically different regimes; to recognize this fact, however, did not entail the abandonment of judgment as to their respective merits. Yet this is exactly what the realist did, placing "Christians" on the same level as "cannibals"; "*de jure*" states on the same plane as despotisms, in effect embracing "historical nihilism.''[80] Realism denied meaning to the accumulation of knowledge, to the emergence of man "from the structure of closed societies," to "the course of the human adventure.''[81] It denied *the aspiration to human universality*, which, as we have seen, Aron held to be inherent in human nature. Once again, the morality of prudence, sensitive to the antinomic structure of the political world and the particularities of history, yet open to a shared human nature and certain demands of universal morality, was the superior stance both with regard to the facts and morally:

> What is true in all epochs is that the necessary reference to the calculation of forces and the endless diversity of circumstances requires statesmen to be *prudent*. But prudence does not always require moderation or peace by compromise, or negotiations, or indifference to the internal regimes of enemy states or allies. . . . True realism today consists

in recognizing the action of ideologies upon diplomatic-strategic conduct. In our epoch, instead of repeating that all states, no matter what
their institutions, have 'the same kind of foreign policy', we should
insist upon the truth that is more complementary than contradictory:
no one understands the diplomatic strategy of a state if he does not
understand its regime, if he has not studied the philosophy of those
who govern it. To lay down as a rule that the heads of the Bolshevik
Party conceive the national interests of their state as did all other rulers
of Russia is to doom oneself to misunderstanding the practices and
ambitions of the Soviet Union.[82]

Only the morality of prudence, Aron stressed, could give any meaning
to power politics, by affirming what was true in idealism—its recognition of a shared humanity—at the same time as recalling that there was
a hierarchy of regimes, and that, on certain occasions, the prudent statesman had to surrender to "the antinomy of force and juridical norms."[83]
But while a kind of moderate Machiavellianism was unavoidable for the
prudent statesman, "anyone seeking to understand history must not stop
at the antinomy of force and juridical norms"; rather, he "must distinguish between the various modes according to which force has been
employed, must acknowledge the historical, if not the juridical, legitimacy of the use of force in certain circumstances."[84] The morality of
antinomic prudence was a *true* realism, in that it accounted for the whole
of reality, refusing to guide statesmanship by the "finished portrait" of
international relations as painted by realists. In sum, then, the normative
theory of antinomic prudence best preserved the real goods of the political world. It protected against both the naïveté and potential fanaticism
of idealism, on the one hand, and the historical nihilism and denial of
human nature of realism, on the other:

> The ambiguity of international society makes it impossible for a partial
> logic to be followed to its end, be it one of law or one of force.
> The only morality which transcends the morality of struggle and the
> morality of law is what I would call the morality of prudence, which
> attempts not only to consider each case in its concrete particularities,
> but also not to ignore any of the arguments of principle and opportu-
> nity, to forget neither the relation of forces nor the wills of peoples.
> Because it is complex, the judgment of prudence is never incontest-
> able, and it satisfies completely neither the moralists nor the vulgar
> disciples of Machiavelli.[85]

But is there not a chance that a morality of antinomic prudence, inherently tension-filled and as ambiguous as the reality it seeks to influence, will slide into naked Machiavellianism? That an antinomic prudence might not be sustainable? Does not Aron, in seeking to think politically, give too much autonomy to the discretion of the statesman, allowing the dictates of politics to trump the demands of morality as might be argued did Burke? Can a theory of prudence grounded in an awareness of the complex nature of the politically real measure up to a conception of prudence grounded, as in Aquinas, in the natural law? Jacques Maritain, in an important article written during the Second World War, to which Aron responded, argued that the "common good" must guide the actions of the political leader, taking up a conception of prudence that drew tighter reigns on the liberty of the statesman than Aron would regard as feasible.[86] We shall in concluding this section take a brief look at this debate between Maritain and Aron, for in so doing what differentiates Aron's prudence from that of other thinkers in the prudence tradition will become clear.

Maritain was convinced that a direct line of descent could be established from the thought of Machiavelli to the political marauders of the twentieth century; that, in other words, Machiavellianism, once unleashed, could not be restrained. Maritain advanced three arguments: first, that there was an irresistible slide from a "moderate" Machiavellianism (something Aron would allow) toward a virulent Machiavellianism that crowned political evil king; second, that politics must be subordinated to morality; and third, that, even on its own terms, Machiavellianism did not succeed, unraveling whatever short-run successes it might be responsible for in the long view of history. Aron attempted to answer the first question by replying to the second and third.

Must politics be subordinated to the demands of morality, by which Maritain meant the demands of Christianity? Aron held it essential to Christian thought not to confuse the City of God and the City of Man, an authentically Christian distinction he supported and indeed for which he provided a secular analogue.[87] But this distinction accepted, the "quarrel of Machiavellianism" remained unresolved. As Aron argued, "if . . . the art of success normally entails the use of injustice, and if morality and justice leads to the ruin of cities, one must conclude that a Christian can hardly be a statesman or that the statesman can hardly act as a Christian."[88] It was for this reason than Maritain had to show that, even in moderate form, Machiavellianism is self-undermining. In the short run, no one could deny that immoral means were efficacious; but Maritain took the long view: "I say that justice works through its own causality toward welfare and success in the future, as a healthy sap works toward the perfect fruit, and that Machiavellianism works through its own causality for ruin and bankruptcy, as poison in the sap works for illness and death of the tree."[89] In the *long run*, justice would prevail. Keeping politics tethered to morality, grounded in the common good, even if it meant sacrifice and injustice suffered in the short run, would lead to a more morally satisfying outcome on Maritain's anti-Machiavellian view.

Aron was willing to concede the dangers to the statesman and the political community of succumbing to immoral means. The political order was part of a human reality opening on to a moral world. A politics that took power as its "unique and supreme objective" would fall into nihilism: "To desire at any price and on any term power, unlimited power, is both for the individual and the collectivity to fall into the idolatry of the state, it is to consent to dehumanization, it is, ultimately, to end up with the barbarism of total wars in which the infinite resources of science assist in the perfection of the ancient violence of wars of extermination."[90] But Maritain's long view was an insufficient answer to those who would suffer *now* as a result of the statesman abjuring the precepts of Machiavelli for fear of moral compromise. And how are we to share Maritain's confidence that justice will win out eventually? As Aron wrote:

> First of all, even if the poisoned fruits of violence show themselves after the blow, the just person who has been its first victim knows *both* his sufferings and defeat and the provisional victory of his vanquisher, and not the ultimate disintegration of the nation which has followed the criminal leader. Moreover, admitting that justice in itself tends to cement the moral unity of a people and injustice to dissolve it, even admitting that by these traits themselves one tends to the success and the other to the defeat of the community, other factors of a material nature can cross this line of causality and cause even the worst communities, not the best, to survive.[91]

One could accept readily a philosophy of anti-Machiavellian inspiration, Aron reasoned, but in order to think politically (an essential requirement if one is to advise the Prince) one must confront the practical implications of one's moral views. Any justifiable political morality would therefore have to be concerned with the consequences— immediate and long-term—of action. But how do we draw the line between legitimate cunning, which Maritain does not reject, and immoral cynicism? Aron's answer will be unsatisfying to many: "it is impossible to give a general response."[92] The statesman does not always have a free choice of means and can ignore the antinomy between what Aron calls "the actual conditions of effective action" and moral imperatives only at the cost of abandoning his responsibility to secure the safety and flourishing of those whose fate has been entrusted to him.[93] Absent an explicit metaphysics comparable to Aristotelian *theoria*, Aron might seem close to Burke in his understanding of prudence. But on closer examination, it is Aristotle's natural right-based belief that, under certain circumstances, means are morally legitimate which under normal circumstances would be considered immoral, that is more in keeping with the Aronian view. Perhaps it is best, as recommended by Strauss, to "leave these sad exigencies covered with the veil with which they are justly covered."[94]

Aron's philosophy of antinomic prudence takes its bearings from a conception of human imperfection and a sustained meditation on the nature of political reality. It views both the moralism of the idealist and the nihilism of the realist as dangerous distortions of the ambiguous, and often tragic, realm of political morality in international relations. Idealism and realism alike remove the tragic from the political world, idealism by assuming politics can be collapsed into a categorical morality, realism by severing politics from morality utterly. Neither captures what it means to think politically, to defend political reason in a world where, to return to a formulation quoted above, "what gives political life its somber grandeur is that statesmen come to do acts they detest because they believe themselves, in conscience and the depths of their soul, accountable for the common destiny."[95]

Aron does not finally answer all of Maritain's Thomistic objections to the providence of evil in political affairs, because Maritain has refused to put himself in the place of the statesman; once one follows Aron onto the terrain of politics, the realization dawns that Maritain's objections are unanswerable, that a *categorical a priori* political morality is impossible. Such is the lesson of antinomic prudence.

In concluding this chapter, we must ask the other praxeological question, this one associated, not with Machiavelli, but with Kant: What are the conditions of universal peace? Or, can foreign policy be overcome?

## 4. THE UNIVERSAL AND THE PARTICULAR: OF NATIONS AND EMPIRES

The advent of atomic weapons and the ruins of the twentieth century force us to pose the question: Is it possible to leave international politics behind? While international relations have always been possessed by the efficacity of immorality, can we imagine a "historical transformation of states and their relations" so profound as to constitute the preconditions for universal peace, ending the "immemorial order of collectivities?"[96] In the final pages of his longest book, Aron asks what would be required for this to take place and how plausible it would be for these requirements to be achieved. As we reconstruct Aron's arguments on universal peace, we shall explore within his thought the tension between the universality of human nature and the particularity of nationhood, raising the question of *what is common?*[97] Once again we will encounter the deeply political nature of Aron's reflection, its refusal to collapse the tensions which characterize the human world, and by extension, the world of politics.

Aron set forth two categories through which power politics could be transcended: *peace through law* and *peace through empire*. In each case sovereign states submit their right to render justice to an external arbiter; without this submission states "cannot live within a definitive peace, unless they have changed their very nature or unless the world itself has *essentially* changed."[98] From the outset, Aron points to the unlikelihood of either approach succeeding, and their possibly self-undermining character. Industrial modernity, as noted earlier, had lessened the economic causes of war by opening paths to growth for nations independent of blood and conquest. But if we posit for the sake of argument the existence of an indisputable tribunal or irresistible political will, will not the economic and social causes of conflicts be magnified as a result? That is, if we abolish independent sovereignties in favor of a universal sovereign, do not the inequalities of economic development thereby become the responsibility of *one sovereign?* Yet such inequalities, if they exist within the political community, can lead to profound tension, even, on occasion "explode into revolution." As Aron maintains, "Why should it be different within a universal state or world federation?"[99] In other words, the very project of universal peace is predicated on the transcendence, not just of independent political sovereignties, but of the political problem itself. Keeping this in mind will allow us to view with healthy suspicion any such enterprise.

Indeed this has been the problem with various historical attempts to establish universal peace through treaty or agreement. The previously mentioned Kellogg-Briand Pact, as well as the League of Nations Covenant established at the end of World War I and the more recent United Nations Charter, have failed because they have in effect ratified the dictates of force. To find a home within the hearts of men and nations, global agreements of this kind would have to have universal assent; but as Aron stresses, "neither victors nor vanquished could have specified which status would have been just in itself, without reference to the historical right of force."[100] There is, Aron is saying, a permanent dimension of force to political life, a *permanent political problem.* Collective security agreements have been consequently largely ineffective, with states preserving their sacred right to decide whether or not a particular agreement has been breached, if their security has been threatened, or their honor maligned.

This permanence of politics has been the source for what Aron calls the "essential imperfection of international law": states do not commit themselves unconditionally *in what concerns them most* to international agreements. And it is the states themselves, the independent sovereignties at the root of the anarchic life of international relations, that define what concerns them most. This refusal on the part of the world's political communities to abandon sovereignty, at least in the last instance, "has been and is an element in the unique character of relations among states."[101] "Geometric minds" might find it shocking, Aron adds, but war is thus not illegal in international law, which thereby, in the words of Julius Stone, "provides for its own destruction by the simple force of its own subjects."[102]

What was the likelihood of political communities abandoning their sovereignty? What kind of progress has been made by international law? Aron examined three variables as measurements of such progress: the emergence of transnational society, of the international system, and of the consciousness of the human community as a whole. Writing thirty years ago, Aron could see little progress in any of these three areas. It was undoubtedly true, as we have already addressed, that the world was being covered by grids of near-instantaneous transport and communication. People were traveling on a scale never before met with; and never before had "so many men, without leaving their own country, been capable of seeing, on large or small screens, the images of countries they will never visit."[103]

But these were not, in Aron's view, valid criteria of transnational society. For every sign of growing transnationalism, one could find a counterindication, a different line of evolution. At the time of *Peace and War*, the existence of the Soviet Union and a thoroughly communist China—in other words, the heterogeneity of the international system—made any talk of transnational society premature: "Exchanges across frontiers are, in the Soviet Union, denied to private persons; they have become more international and not transnational."[104] In the aftermath of the fall of communism, with global capital markets spreading like wildfire, the Internet circling the planet instantaneously, and a growing cultural ubiquity, does Aron's pessimistic view of progress toward international law via transnational society still hold true? Writing somewhat later, in his neglected book *Progress and Disillusion*, Aron advanced an argument that holds as true today, as we open unto our post-Marxist history, as it did amidst the chaos of 1968:

> this unification, which we might call material, has less real impact than superficial observers are wont to believe. Even if all families had television sets—and this is far from the case on a worldwide basis—their interests would still be limited to a narrowly restricted social sphere. The poverty and misery of distant peoples, the daily catastrophes that occur all over the world, the strange customs the media purvey in such lively fashion—none of this, whether written or visual, affects the average viewer or reader as much as a quarrel with a neighbor or a colleague at the office, or the fluctuations of his own personal fortune.[105]

The material unification of the world, what Aron called the emergence of universal history, did not of necessity lead to a deeper unification, one which would leave politics behind. Moreover, if the heterogeneous nature of the international system during the long conflict with communism has given way to a more homogeneous system in 1997, new heterogeneities threaten to explode between the Islamic world and the West, and perhaps between various Asian societies and the West,[106] threatening to rip asunder the uncertain and partial peace of the post-communist world.

What then of a moral sense of universal humanity? Has this grown with time? Viewing the carnage of the century, Aron held it naive to assume a deepened moral sensitivity, despite the presence of an international human rights community. There *were* signs of universal human concern: "Men react to a *natural* catastrophe as to a misfortune which touches all humanity and the humanity within each man."[107] But these signs of universality, however important and hopeful, were weak beacons when confronted with the darkness of national passions, ethnic hatred, and ideological frenzy, which in our era of Bosnia and Rwanda seem as sadly inseparable from human nature as they have ever been. As Aron somberly put it, "One need merely attend a contest between national teams to realize that the identification of individuals with the group is powerful, the attachment to the human race or to the rules slight."[108]

In short, progress toward a system of international law has been insignificant, the prospects for perpetual peace through law slight. Aron held three conditions as essential for such peace to be achieved, at least in theory. First, if states were to agree to submit their external conduct to the rule of law, the rule of law must hold *within* political communities. Aron is making the Kantian argument, first set out in Kant's classic essay "Perpetual Peace," that in order for world peace to be possible, the internal constitutions of at least the major world powers must be *republican*, "based on the consent of the citizens and the exercise of power according to strict rules and legal procedures."[109]

If this first condition were to be established, the second would likely follow: the international system would be homogeneous, states would become increasingly aware of their relatedness, and a supranational community would gradually come into being. If a crisis arose, if a nation attempted to "opt out" of the supranational agreements, its fate would be isolation or worse. Even with these two conditions secured, however, Aron believed a third necessary: states must agree to renounce force, "and must agree without anxiety to submit their disputes to a tribunal, even those disputes whose object is the redistribution of law and wealth."[110] Is this *postpolitical world*, pacified by the rule of law, a world without nations, a global political community? Perhaps as important is the following question: Would this outcome be desirable?

In answering these questions of *peace through empire* or *world federation*, Aron felt the cardinal thing to be often overlooked: the persistence of politics and national identity. A world government achieved through empire unavoidably implied tyranny, particularly since, at the time Aron was writing, the Soviet Union was the more obvious candidate for carrying out the project of world unification. But the Soviet Union had a hard time keeping its own diverse nationalisms in check (how hard we have all come to see); extended across the globe, was this not a recipe for unending civil war? As Aron observed, "Let the Russian and American armies withdraw . . . and each of the European states will tend to resume its own autonomy."[111]

Aron was acutely aware of the call to community and nationhood manifest in human nature, a fact that made him dubious of all plans at creating a European "nation" or political community, let alone a world empire. Such views lost the "essential thing": that of "the community power, animated by a community desire, the state and nation, the human collectivity, conscious of its uniqueness and determined to assert and affirm it in the face of all other collectivites."[112] Political unification was not something cast up by the tide of subpolitical economic relations between political communities. Aron wrote presciently in response to the early enthusiasts of European union: "The hope that the European federation will gradually and irresistibly emerge from the Common Market is based on a great illusion of our times: the illusion that economic and technological interdependence among the various factions of humanity has definitively devalued the fact of 'political sovereignties,' the existence of distinct states which wish to be autonomous."[113]

Aron defined the nation as the conjunction of a community of culture—always pluralist in composition but never *absolutely so*—with a desire for political autonomy implying both chosen and unchosen elements. Nations were *real* and had ends in themselves, something denied by many liberal theorists, who, practicing a form of normative individualism, see only the individual and his choices as worthy of recognition. Aron even went so far as to speak of the "collective personality of a nation," something which grows and perishes across time. The nation, Aron continued:

> has many conditions of a material, physical or biological order, but it asserts itself only by consciousness, being capable of thought and choice. Participating both in nature and in reason, these national personalities express the wealth of human possibilities. The diversity of cultures is not a curse to be exorcized but a heritage to be safeguarded.[114]

The nation was not a burden, then, something "morally irrelevant" as Martha Nussbaum would have it, but the very precondition for human flourishing. To abstract away from the nation, as Nussbaum and other cosmopolitan liberal theorists do, is not only to egregiously misunderstand the nature of political life, which in our time has been as dominated by nationhood as by any other force; it is to sanction the *impoverishment of human existence*. It is to deny that which is common in the quest for what is individual and abstractly universal, thereby robbing the universal of its resting place, its ground, its historical seedbed. As Aron tellingly phrases it: "how could the individual be obligated to all of humanity without being so with regard to the nation that makes him what he is?"[115]

But if the nation was on Aron's view both an ideal and a fact, national*isms*—the desire for power and glory on the part of nations—are not by that token automatically justified. Men and women have duties beyond borders as well as duties within. There were "universal and formal rules" bound up with human nature itself, respect for which had to be antinomically and imperfectly balanced with our duties to our own political communities. Pretending this antinomy does not exist, as idealists are wont to do, gets us nowhere: "This antinomy is real, it has lasted in one form or another since the dawn of history."[116] While not necessarily eternal, it had marked the human political condition long enough to make us wary of schemes to overcome it by rhetorical slight of hand.

The theoretical solution to the antinomy between community and universality, Aron suggested, was the institution of federation, the voluntary version of empire. In a federation, the community of culture is maintained, as in Switzerland, where the Helvetian Confederation holds sovereignty but groups and individuals within the confederation retain their freedom to belong to their communities of memory. Could not humanity as a whole be recast as a giant Switzerland? Aron uses the word "Utopia" to characterize this idea of world federation. While there were and are many historical obstacles to its realization, was the Utopia *ultimately* unrealizable? Did it run against the grain of human nature? Aron turned, perhaps surprisingly, to German theorist Carl Schmitt to answer this second question.[117]

Schmitt's famous distinction between friend and enemy saw that alternative as intrinsic to political life, which would make any world federation a logical impossibility. As Schmitt wrote in his 1927 book *The Concept of the Political*, "A world in which the possibility of war is utterly eliminated, a completely pacified globe, would be a world without the distinction of friend and enemy and hence a world without politics. . . . [T]he phenomenon of the political can be understood only in the context of the friend-and-enemy grouping, regardless of the aspects which this possibility implies for morality, aesthetics, and economics."[118] Aron agreed with Schmitt in stressing the difference between the broadening of political community and the unification of humanity. While Aron did not deduce the *impossibility* of world organization from Schmitt's distinction, he admitted, with Schmitt, that hostility was natural to man, and could be moderated and controlled only within the political community. But that control, Schmitt believed, was based on opposition: in order for a political community to exist, it had to be *other*, had to distinguish itself from what it was *not*. If Schmitt was right, and Aron was sympathetic to his argument, a world federation, deprived of an external other, would soon dissolve by internal friction, "by the action of internal conflicts."[119] In an interview from the seventies, Aron nodded in Schmitt's direction once again, without attribution:

> violence has not vanished from the earth, and it is possible that violence within nations will increase, simply because larger conflicts seem to be ruled out. After all, one of the things that cement national unity is the threat from outside.[120]

Yet Aron hesitated to accede to this grim vision. To transcend the friend-enemy dichotomy, Aron mused in his most speculative mode, the universal history we increasingly live must give birth to three phenomena: the refusal to use nuclear weapons, the fair distribution of global resources, and the mutual tolerance of all of the world's peoples, nations, and creeds. Let us assume, implausibly but for the sake of argument, the first two have been achieved: will man still be wolf to man? To offer a positive answer to this question was to wager on the "conversion" of the human race; a negative answer "would leave no other hope of peace than the triumph of a race, a people, a Church, hence would enjoin us to sacrifice either peace or the wealth of diversity."[121] Peace versus the wealth of diversity: the end of history as boredom?[122]

Aron felt it best, in the face of these antinomies, to reaffirm an argument he first made in *The Opium of the Intellectuals*. To approach political life in the geometric spirit of abstraction, to expect more perfection from it than was logically possible, was not to embrace skepticism. The alternative to world federation or empire was not the endless tumult of the battlefield, the poison cup of the assassin, the death camps of Auschwitz. One must doubt the abstractions of the idealists and utopians, yes, but to doubt did not entail surrender to nihilism. Rather, Aronian doubt is based on "reasoning that confirms the imperfection of all social orders, accepts the impossibility of knowing the future, condemns the vain pretension of drawing up the schema of an ideal society."[123] It is, in short, the vision of antinomic prudence that we have sought to articulate across this chapter.

Antinomic prudence: a practical wisdom, as Pierre Manent stressed, not rooted in an explicit return to the Aristotelian doctrine but instead in the knowledge, drawn from the social sciences and sustained reflection on the antinomies of human existence, of the limits of our power to transform the human world. While Aron hints through his phenomenological exploration of the political world at a philosophical conception of natural right, he does not flesh out that hint with a philosophical teaching, preferring to remain on the terrain of politics. That said, Aron's prudence is preferable, as we have now seen, to its alternatives of Machiavellian realism and utopian idealism. It is more in tune with the structure of the political and moral universe, where the uncertainty of human action is the first certainty, and political reason the best hope for preserving the genuine human goods made possible by political practice, than its feasible alternatives. It recommends "that we gradually improve what exists" rather than demolishing what exists in the vain hope that perfection can be built from rubble. Aron's antinomic prudence is an expression of his conservative liberalism, balanced between the demands of universality and the need for community, a *political* morality for an imperfect and imperfectly knowable world. It is the voice of a modern Montesquieu that speaks through the pages of *Peace and War*.[124]

We have traveled a ways since the beginning of our study through dense jungles of epistemology, fogbanks of ideology, and battlefields ancient and modern. As a result, we now have a good sense of the major contours of Raymond Aron's defense of political reason, see how it unifies his work, and recognize what his contribution can still teach us. To complete our journey, however, we must come home, in a sense, and try to discern exactly what Aron's deeply political liberalism looks like when brought into contact with some currents in contemporary political thought. We now turn to the conclusion.

## NOTES

1. See Hassner's analysis of this lacuna—where international relations becomes a "sacrificial victim"—in the work of Plato, Aristotle, Hobbes, Rousseau, Locke, and Marx in his essay "Beyond the Three Traditions" in *Violence and Peace: From the Atomic Bomb to Ethnic Cleansing* (Budapest: Central European University Press, 1997), pp. 13–34.

2. Ibid., p. 17.

3. As in the work of Thomas Pogge, who attempts to apply the philosophy of John Rawls to the relations between nations. Yet Rawls's philosophy has been criticized sharply as having little to do with the political life of the United States, where it germinated as a theoretical defense of late-sixties liberalism—what conceivable constituency exists globally for an "original position" where nationhood would be denied all but derivative normative legitimacy? To approach the life of nations in this way is to abstract away from politics itself; in effect, a political philosophy without politics. For Pogge, see *Realizing Rawls* (New York: Cornell University Press, 1989).

4. Aron, *Peace and War*, pp. 71–93.

5. For a good overview of Aron's work on international relations, see Stephen Launay, *La pensée politique de Raymond Aron*, pp. 151–240.

6. Stanley Hoffmann, *The State of War: Essays on the Theory and Practice of International Relations* (New York: Praeger, 1965), p. 33.

7. See Aron's final book, *Les dernières années du siècle* (Paris: Commentaire Julliard, 1984), p. 18. (My translation.)

8. Bloom, *Giants and Dwarfs*, p. 261.

9. Aron, *Les dernières années du siècle*, p. 21. (My translation.)

10. Bryan-Paul Frost, "Raymond Aron's *Peace and War*, Thirty Years Later," pp. 339–61; see also Mahoney, *The Liberal Political Science of Raymond Aron*, pp. 91–110; and Stanley Hoffmann's entry on *Peace and War* in F. Chatelet, O. Duhamel, and E. Pisier, eds. *Dictionnaire des oeuvres politiques* (Paris: PUF, 1986), pp. 28–31. I am indebted to each of these treatments in this section.

11. Hoffmann, "*Peace and War*," p. 29.

12. See Aron, *Peace and War*, pp. 47–93.

13. See Aron's history of postwar American diplomacy: *The Imperial Republic: The United States and the World 1945–1973* (New Jersey: Prentice-Hall, 1974).

14. Pierre Manent notes: "If, for example, one attributes the English resistance in 1940 to the great soul of Churchill, one attributes it at the same time to chance: it was by great 'luck' that a man like Churchill found himself, at this particular moment, in the place to act. It is not necessary, in order to understand the year 1940, to 'find the cause of Churchill': it is Churchill who is the cause." *La Cité de l'homme* (Paris: Fayard, 1994), p. 86. (My translation.) Aron made a similar point: "Without Churchill, would England have stood firm all alone against the Third Reich? If Hitler had not attacked Russia in 1941, what course would the greatest of wars taken? Traditional history is action, that is to say it is made of decisions taken by men in a precise place and time. These decisions could have been different with another man in the same situation, or with the same man with another disposition. No one can fix, either beforehand or retrospectively, the limits of the consequences that some of these localized and dated decisions generate." *In Defense of Political Reason*, p. 138.

15. See Hassner, *Violence and Peace*, pp. 17–21.

16. As Aron once put it in an interview: "Every country has values more important than material wealth. The aims of Gaullist France were *l'independence* and *la grandeur*, never *la production* for its own sense." *Thinking Politically*, p. 292.

17. Aron, *Peace and War*, pp. 71–93.

18. Aron, *The Century of Total War*, p. 65.

19. Aron, *Peace and War*, p. 768.

20. Manent, "Raymond Aron—Political Educator," p. 14.

21. Aristotle, *Nichomachean Ethics*, trans. by T. Irwin (Indianapolis: Hackett Publishers, 1985), Bk. I, 1094b.

22. See Mahoney, *The Liberal Political Science of Raymond Aron*, p. 138.

23. See Henry Kissinger, *Diplomacy* (New York: Simon & Schuster, 1994), pp. 78–102.

24. As Montesquieu held, "If it is true that the character of the spirit and the passions of the heart are extremely different in the various climates, *laws* should be relative to the differences in these passions and to the differences in these

160     Chapter Four

characters." *The Spirit of the Laws*, trans. by A. Cohler, B. C. Miller, H. S. Stone (Cambridge: Cambridge University Press, 1989), p. 231.

25. This has been a recurring theme in the work of social theorist Michael Novak. See his *Catholic Ethic and the Spirit of Capitalism* (New York: Free Press, 1993), pp. 114–43. See the discussion of economic development in Aron, *In Defense of Decadent Europe*, pp. 133–60.

26. "*Militarily*, the internal combustion engine, supplying power to tanks and aircraft, seemed to have recreated the superiority of force needed for a breakthrough and its exploitations; railways and trucks seemed to have given land armies a mobility comparable with that of the naval powers." Aron, *The Century of Total War*, p. 44.

27. See Aron, *Progress and Disillusion*, p. 137, where he writes: "When civilian airlines introduce supersonic equipment it will take only three hours to fly from Paris to New York; it took Tocqueville as many weeks to cross the Atlantic; the speed of the trip will have been multiplied by a factor of 168. The means at men's disposal for travel and the transport of goods have altered our entire concept of space, while instantaneous communication has obliterated time."

28. I have written elsewhere about Aron's "preservation" of the political perspective. See my "Opium of the Intellectuals: Then and Now," *Gravitas*, Fall 1995, pp. 50–51. Aron's preservation of the political perspective has its domestic analogue in his theory of regimes: see *Democracy and Totalitarianism*, where Aron speaks explicitly of the "primacy of the political," pp. 6, 9–12.

29. See Waltz's scientistic *Theory of International Politics* (Reading, MA: Addison-Wesley, 1979). For a trenchant criticism, see Mahoney, *The Liberal Political Science of Raymond Aron*, pp. 91–94.

30. Aron, *Peace and War*, pp. 365–66.

31. Aron's full history of the twentieth century, scattered throughout his writings, has been anthologized in a lengthy single volume. See *Une histoire du vingtième siècle*.

32. See Aron's essay "The Dawn of Universal History" in *In Defense of Political Reason*, pp. 131–52; see also Aron, *Progress and Disillusion*, pp. 137–222.

33. I am indebted to Strauss, *Natural Right and History*, pp. 156–64, 294–323; and Alberto R. Coll, "Prudence in Foreign Policy" in *Might and Right After the Cold War: Can Foreign Policy be Moral?*, ed. by M. Cromartie (Washington, D.C: Ethics and Public Policy Center, 1993), pp. 3–28.

34. See Machiavelli, *The Prince*, Chapter XV, p. 61. Machiavelli adds: "For a man who wants to make a profession of good in all regards must come to ruin among so many who are not good."

35. Strauss, *Natural Right and History*, p. 162.

36. See Chris Brown, "International Affairs," *A Companion to Contemporary Political Philosophy*, ed. by R. Goodin and P. Pettit (London: Blackwell, 1993), p. 515.

37. Ibid., p. 515.

38. *The Landmark Thucydides: A Comprehensive Guide to the Peloponnesian War*, ed. by R. Strassler (New York: Free Press, 1996), p. 352. But while Thucydides in his classic narrative captures the full tragedy of the conflict between powerful Athens and defenseless Melos, and underscores that justice will be a casualty of war, he does not scorn justice. Classical and Christian thinkers distinguished between the inside and the outside of the political community, and established different sets of duties corresponding to each, but never offered philosophical or theological justification to power politics as it is understood by contemporary realists. A fully realist doctrine had to await the coming of Machiavelli and the rupture—a fundamental mutation in Western political and moral consciousness—with classical and Christian modes of considering the problem of peace and war and the purpose of politics.

39. Roger Scruton, "Idealism" in *A Dictionary of Political Thought* (New York: Harper & Row, 1982), pp. 212–13.

40. For a recent restatement of the idealist tradition, see Martha Nussbaum, "Patriotism and Cosmopolitanism," *Boston Review*, Oct/Nov 1994, p. 3. Nussbaum defends an educational project that will teach students that their "primary allegiance is to the community of human beings in the entire world," not to national identity, which is a "morally irrelevant characteristic."

41. Coll, "Prudence and Foreign Policy," p. 5.

42. Ibid., p. 6.

43. Ibid., p. 8.

44. Aristotle, *Nichomachean Ethics*, Bk. VI, 1139b–1145a. (Translation modified.)

45. Ibid., Bk. VI, 1140a. A little later, Aristotle points to Pericles as exemplifying practical wisdom: "Hence Pericles and such people are the ones whom we regard as prudent, because they are able to study what is good for themselves and for human beings; and we think that household management and politicians are such people." Bk. VI 1140b. (Translation modified.)

46. Strauss, *Natural Right and History*, p. 307.

47. Coll, "Prudence and Foreign Policy," p. 9.

48. Aristotle, *Nichomachean Ethics*, 1142b 32–35.

49. Coll, "Prudence in Foreign Policy," p. 11.

50. See Max Horkheimer, *Critique of Instrumental Reason: Lectures and Essays Since the End of World War II*, trans. by M. J. O'Connell (New York: Seabury Press, 1974).

51. Aristotle, *Nichomachean Ethics*, Bk. VI, 1144a.

52. See the remarkable discussion of Aristotle and Machiavelli in Strauss, *Natural Right and History*, pp. 161–62.

53. Aristotle, *Nichomachean Ethics*, Bk. X, 1181b.

54. St. Thomas Aquinas, *Summa Theologica*, trans. by T. Gilby and T. C. O'Brien (London: Blackfriars, 1964–1973), II–II, 47, 2.

55. Brian Davies, *The Thought of Thomas Aquinas* (Oxford: Oxford University Press, 1992), p. 242.

56. Aquinas, *Summa Theologica*, II II, 47, 4.

57. See Strauss, *Natural Right and History*, pp. 157–58.

58. For a treatment of the continuity of Burke's reflection, and his opposition to theoretical abstractions, see Conor Cruise O'Brien, *The Great Melody: A Thematic Biography of Edmund Burke* (Chicago: University of Chicago Press, 1992), esp. pp. 385–457.

59. Edmund Burke, speech delivered on May 11, 1792. Quoted in Coll, "Prudence and Foreign Policy," p. 20.

60. See Strauss, *Natural Right and History*, pp. 318–23. Strauss writes: "Whereas Burke's 'conservatism' is in full agreement with classical thought, his interpretation of his 'conservatism' prepared an approach to human affairs which is even more foreign to classical thought than was the very 'radicalism' of the theorists of the French Revolution" (pp. 318–19). By placing the standards for moral and political judgment within the historical process (in Burke's case, the history of English constitutionalism), Strauss holds, Burke opens the door to historicism and relativism. What is necessary, on Strauss's view, is a standard transcendent to history, based on a reflection on human nature.

61. Aron, *Peace and War*, p. 578.

62. Aron, "On Maritain and Machiavellianism," *In Defense of Political Reason*, p. 63.

63. Aron, *Peace and War*, p. 578.

64. Ibid., p. 580.

65. Ibid., p. 580.

66. Aron also briefly discusses another form of idealist thought, which he calls ideological idealism. This would be the effort to pursue, single-mindedly, one idea as the legitimating force behind statesmanship. As an example one could look to the Marxist ideal of proletarian revolution, which reduced all international morality to one principle. See ibid., p. 581.

67. Ibid., pp. 582–83.

68. Ibid., p. 582.

69. Ibid., p. 583.

70. Ibid., pp. 583–84.

71. Aron, *Clausewitz*, p. 412.

72. Aron, *Peace and War*, p. 584.

73. Ibid., pp. 584–85. (My italics).

74. As Mahoney suggests, the idealist morality of law is in effect a form of "literary politics." See *The Liberal Political Science of Raymond Aron*, p. 98.

75. See, as typical in this regard, Charles R. Beitz, *Political Theory and International Relations* (Princeton: Princeton University Press, 1979), pp. 27–28.

76. Aron, *Peace and War*, p. 581.

77. Ibid., p. 609.

78. Ibid., p. 609.

79. For the classic account of the pacific nature of democracies toward one another, see Michael Doyle, "Kant, Liberal Legacies and Foreign Affairs," parts 1 and 2, *Philosophy and Public Affairs*, vol. 12, no. 3/4, 1983.

80. Aron, *Peace and War*, p. 602.

81. Ibid., p. 602.

82. Ibid., p. 600.

83. Ibid., p. 605.

84. Ibid., p. 603.

85. Ibid., p. 609.

86. See Jacques Maritain, "The End of Machiavelli," in *The Range of Reason* (New York: Scribner's, 1952), pp. 134–64; for Aron's reply, see "Jacques Maritain and the Quarrel Over Machiavellianism" in *In Defense of Political Reason*, pp. 53–64.

87. See Aron, *The Opium of the Intellectuals*, pp. 265–94.

88. Aron, *In Defense of Political Reason*, p. 57.

89. Maritain, "The End of Machiavellianism," p. 308.

90. Aron, *In Defense of Political Reason*, pp. 59–60.

91. Ibid., p. 58.

92. Ibid., p. 60. See also the essay "Max Weber and Power Politics" in *In Defense of Political Reason* where Aron observes: "Weber is right to remind us that the eternal problem of justifying the means by the end has no theoretical solution" p. 45.

93. In a wonderful passage, part of which we have already encountered, Aron plays on Pascal in spelling out his vision of the prudent statesman: "He who attempts to play the angel plays the beast. The statesman *ought* not forget that an international order is maintained only on condition that it is supported by forces capable of balancing those of dissatisfied or revolutionary states. If he neglects to calculate forces, he fails the obligations of his responsibility, hence the morality of his job and his vocation. He makes an error, since he compromises the security of the persons and values whose fate has been entrusted to him. Selfishness is no virtue, but it nonetheless prevails among states, whose survival is guaranteed by no one. But anyone who would play the beast does not play the angel. The Spenglerian realist, who asserts that man is a beast of prey and urges him to behave as such, ignores a whole side of human nature. Even in the relations between states, respect for ideas, aspiration to higher values and concern for obligations have been manifested. Rarely have collectivities

acted as if they would stop at nothing with regard to one another." *Peace and War*, p. 609.

94. Strauss, *Natural Right and History*, p. 160. Strauss stresses that for Aristotle there are no solutions to such exigencies in advance: "There are no limits which can be defined in advance, there are no assignable limits to what might become just reprisals." It is the task of the historian, and God, to mete out justice in such instances. We once again see the affinity of Aristotle and Aron.

95. Aron, *In Defense of Political Reason*, pp. 62–63.

96. Aron, *Peace and War*, p. 703.

97. I borrow this formulation from Pierre Manent, "Modern Individualism," *Crisis*, October 1995, pp. 35–38.

98. Aron, *Peace and War*, p. 708.

99. Ibid., pp. 708–09.

100. Ibid., p. 710.

101. Ibid., p. 724.

102. Quoted in ibid., p. 725.

103. Ibid., p. 731.

104. Ibid., p. 731.

105. Aron, *Progress and Disillusion*, p. 138.

106. This is the true kernel of an otherwise deeply problematic book by Samuel P. Huntington, *The Clash of Civilizations and the Remaking of World Order* (New York: Simon & Schuster, 1996). For an "Aronian" critique of Huntington's cultural determinism, see Pierre Hassner, "Morally Objectionable, Politically Dangerous," *The National Interest*, Winter 1996/1997, pp. 63–69. See also Gray, *Enlightenment's Wake*, pp. 82–83.

107. Aron, *Peace and War*, p. 732.

108. Ibid., p. 732.

109. Ibid., p. 735. For "Perpetual Peace," see Kant, *Political Writings*, ed. by H. Reiss (Cambridge: Cambridge University Press, 1991), pp. 93–130. It is essential to note that Kant was far more hesitant about the feasibility of perpetual peace than many of his more recent exemplars. Perpetual peace was an *idea of reason*, a principle which can never be fully realized in history, but which serves as a regulative ideal toward which we can strive. Aron's understanding of perpetual peace is far closer to Kant than, say, Charles Beitz's or Martha Nussbaum's. See also Pierre Hassner, *Violence and Peace*, pp. 29–30.

110. Aron, *Peace and War*, p. 735.

111. Ibid., p. 737.

112. Ibid., p. 747.

113. Ibid., p. 748.

114. Ibid., p. 750.

115. Ibid., p. 751.

116. Ibid., p. 752.

117. Schmitt's most important work is *The Concept of the Political*, trans. by G. Schwab, with comments by Leo Strauss (Chicago: University of Chicago Press, 1996). For a superb commentary on this book, consult Heinrich Meier, *Carl Schmitt and Leo Strauss: The Hidden Dialogue* (Chicago: University of Chicago Press, 1996). Schmitt's central thesis, written at the time of Weimar Germany's greatest crisis, was that liberalism is fatally flawed by its unwillingness to recognize the violent heart of politics, that politics is a matter of life and death, inexorably opposing friend and enemy. The reception of this work has been tainted by Schmitt's subsequent involvement with the national socialist regime that rose from Weimar's corpse. Philippe Raynaud in an interesting essay has traced what might be called the "hidden dialogue" between Aron and Schmitt. See "Raymond Aron et le droit international," *Cahiers de philosophie politique et juridique*, No. 15, 1989, pp. 115–28.

118. Schmitt, *The Concept of the Political*, p. 35.

119. Aron, *Peace and War*, p. 755.

120. Aron, *Thinking Politically*, p. 301.

121. Ibid., pp. 756–57.

122. See Fukuyama, *The End of History and the Last Man*, Part V, "The Last Man," pp. 287–339. Fukuyama, following Kojeve, posits the possibility of history culminating in "secure and self-absorbed last men."

123. Aron, *Peace and War*, p. 757.

124. Aron opened his longest book with an epigraph taken from Montesquieu's *Spirit of the Laws*, Bk. I, Chp. 3: "International law is based by nature upon this principle: that the various nations set out to do, in peace, the most good to each other, and, in war, the least harm possible, without detriment to their genuine interests." On Aron and Montesquieu, see Simone Goyard-Fabre, "La liberalisme de Raymond Aron" in *Cahiers de philosophie politique et juridique*, no. 15, 1989, pp. 59–97.

# 5

# CONCLUSION: RAYMOND ARON AND CONTEMPORARY POLITICAL THEORY

I n our opening chapter, three central tasks were set out for this study: to reconstruct the essential ideas of Raymond Aron's conservative liberalism; to tie together the major writings of Aron with the theme of political reason; and to offer a critique of certain currents of contemporary political reflection for which Aron's thought can be seen as a corrective. While the first two of these tasks have been largely accomplished, the third, although implicit (and sometimes explicit) in earlier discussions, needs further development. Such will be the main purpose of this concluding chapter. In developing the critique of contemporary political thought further, Aron's distinctively *political* liberalism, which (as we will note below) looks back to an older, richer model of political theory, will be elucidated more thoroughly.

Our first step in what follows will be to engage what John Gray has called the "emptying of political life" in contemporary political theory with Aron's defense of political reason. Aron's thought resists Gray's criticisms and offers a conservative defense of liberalism rooted in historical reality, an awareness of tragedy, and a keen sensitivity to both the contingencies of politics and the self-undermining tendencies of the liberal democratic regime. Second, we will bring Aron's thought into dialogue with three other liberal thinkers: Friedrich Hayek, Isaiah Berlin, and Francis Fukuyama. These thinkers have not been chosen at random: each defends a position—on the role of the state, the nature of goods, and the meaning of history, respectively, positions that might at first glance be similar to Aron's; on closer inspection, the differences are

167

noticeable, and telling. We will distinguish Aron's political liberalism from the more utopian defense of classical liberalism found in Hayek; contrast Aron's understanding of political antinomies, looked at above, with Berlin's value pluralism; and criticize Fukuyama's liberal determinism in light of Aron's more prudential, and political, understanding of history. Finally, in our concluding words, we will raise the question of the political responsibility of intellectuals in the post-Marxist era opening before us.

## 1. OF LIBERALS, CONSERVATIVE AND MODERN: THE DISAPPEARANCE OF POLITICS

John Gray's critique of the main currents of contemporary political thought, particularly in its Anglo-American liberal form, is focused on several key features.[1] Each of these features, about which Gray's criticisms have much warrant, does not apply to Aron. Indeed, Aron's defense of political reason, and his conservative defense of the liberal regime, has more in common with an earlier, richer liberalism—that of Tocqueville, Montesquieu, Constant, and even Adam Smith—than it does with the more theoretically abstract thought of modern liberals Rawls and Dworkin. According to Gray, contemporary liberal thought is marked by a failure to think politically, with the result being a model of theorizing carried out at a far remove from the political and human world, rendering it too distant from common understandings, at best, and carrying a potentially destructive influence, at worst.[2]

In what follows, we shall see why Aron's conservative liberalism avoids the difficulties raised by Gray. It is important to emphasize at the outset that there is significant overlap among Gray's arguments. We will be less concerned with distinguishing them analytically than with painting a broad, and therefore somewhat imprecise, portrait of contemporary liberal political theory. Given that a lengthier treatment of Gray's critique remains beyond the scope of this study, let it suffice that I believe the main lines of his portrayal are well drawn (if occasionally exaggerated or unflattering); certain distortions are inevitable, but the essential comes through.

First, and perhaps most important, is the category of the *person* found in contemporary liberal theory. As has been argued by conservative theorists such as Richard John Neuhaus and Alasdair MacIntyre, as well as thinkers usually categorized on the left, such as Charles Taylor and Michael Sandel, this person is a cipher, stripped of history, religion, ethnicity, and absent any grounding in a conception of human nature.[3] The attachments that give meaning to our lives are relativized, pared away, as we imagine ourselves, in the Rawlsian notion of the original position, existing behind a "veil of ignorance."[4] This person has only one overriding concern, Gray holds, a concern for its own good, which it rationally pursues subject to the constraints of justice, conceived by Rawls and other recent liberals as impartiality. Yet as Gray stresses, without these attachments, which are essential to our identities, the good sought must be identical for all. As Gray puts it, the "appearance of a plurality of ciphers in Rawls's original position must be delusive, since, all of them having the same beliefs and motives, they are indistinguishable."[5] If the good sought is identical for each, however, then the basic structure of liberties Rawls argues are necessary for the pursuit of the good must be identical for all, as must the principles of their distribution. The outcome of this chain of reasoning, deduced from first principles, must be the *elimination of politics*: "It will not matter by whom we are governed, so long as governments satisfy common standards of justice and legitimacy."[6] But this is to do an end run, by theoretical fiat, around one of the most important questions of political philosophy: the question of who governs. Even a quick glance at political life today, dominated as it is by renascent particularisms, ethnicity, and religious belief, should disabuse us of any illusions about the obsolescence of this question. This thin conception of the person, shared by most recent liberal theory, emptied as it is of nature, belief, and history—in short, the very substance of the political and human world—has little to do with men and women as we encounter them daily, with their problems, aspirations, and fierce and often conflictual passions and opinions.

Aron's liberalism is far more attentive to history and culture, and indeed to the reality of political life, with all of its variegated personages and communities, than is the rationalist universalism of recent liberal theory. As we saw in our previous chapter, the relationship between the universal and the particular marks one of the basic tensions in Aron's thought. While temperamentally aligned with the Enlightenment, and a strong supporter of individual freedom, Aron was too conscious of the dangers of rationalism and too attuned to the conflictual and tragic nature of politics to be an uncritical admirer of the Enlightenment project. In an essay from the late seventies, Aron noted the *species* of Enlightenment to which he adhered:

> I belong to the school of thought that Solzhenitsyn calls rational humanism, and says has failed. This rationalism does not imply certain of the intellectual or moral errors Solzhenitsyn attributes to it. Montesquieu maintains a balance between the Eurocentrism of the Enlightenment and historicism. . . . In what sense can we decree the failure of rational humanism? The rationalist is not unaware of the animal impulses in man, and of the passions of man in society. The rationalist has long since abandoned the illusion that men, alone or in groups, are reasonable. He bets on the education of humanity, even if he is not sure he will win his wager.[7]

Aron belongs to the tradition of Tocqueville and Montesquieu, and, in our century, Elie Halevy: a self-critical, chastened Enlightenment, aware of the imperfections of man, the importance of history, the constancy of the tragic, and the *limits* of rationality. This is not the Enlightenment condemned by Solzhenitsyn and other critics of the Enlightenment project. Not only did Aron refuse to abstract away from the power of national identity as a force in modern life, he also rejected normative individualism by granting moral weight to the nation beyond the individuals with whom at any moment in time it is composed. The conflict between the ideals of the modern world could not be resolved theoretically, Aron believed, but only moderated as a result of patient analysis and balancing acts never complete, never without loss.[8] Let us pause a moment and get a clearer view of Aron's treatment of the antinomies of modernity.

In *Progress and Disillusion* Aron gives his most thorough treatment of these tensions. He sees three primary antinomies that contribute to the fractiousness and dissatisfactions of modern life, none of which can be overcome in practice. Together they give rise in our liberal democratic societies to an experience of constant becoming and indeterminacy. The first antinomy is that between the egalitarian spirit of the age and the hierarchical structure of modern organizations—what Aron refers to as the "dialectics of equality." We acknowledge that each individual has a right to equal dignity, to happiness, to citizenship, and to a "fair" allotment of the material goods produced by society. At the same time, industrial (and postindustrial) societies pursue the logic of efficiency in production. Efficiency requires *subordination* of some to others: how could a factory run efficiently without managers, or a military without strict lines of command? The demands of efficiency and the demands of equality are not fully compatible.[9]

Modernity has also brought with it the ideal of *individuality.* Confident of our worth, we seek to have our uniqueness recognized, our selves expressed.[10] As Aron accents, however, the very material wealth of modern societies, while unleashing a whole series of existential demands, is itself predicated on "a pitiless mechanism of production and growth."[11] This mechanism dominates our lives in myriad ways (thus limiting individuality) as economic growth becomes increasingly the end to which the liberal democratic regime is directed. Leo Strauss had a wonderful phrase capturing this antinomy of modern life, where individuality and conformism run in dialectical tandem: "the joyless quest for joy."[12] Aron called it, much more prosaically, "the dialectic of socialization."

The third antinomy of modernity is one we have already encountered: that between the "universal history" of technology, communication, and transport and the persistence of political and cultural difference. Moreover, as we have discussed earlier, the reduction in the "size" of the world, due to the ubiquity of modern technology (which is the source of the revolutions in communication and transportation), leads to the realization on the part of the poor nations of the world that they are poor. The realization on the part of the poor that they are poor has created division, which contradicts the ubiquity of technology.[13] Thus the "dialectic of universality" is born. In each of these three cases—the dialectics of equality, socialization, and universality—modern ideals are resisted by the reality of the human and political world, which offers unpliable material to the hands of rationalist reformers. Hence, to return to Aron's relationship with the Enlightenment, we see his affinity with thinkers who, while in some regard spiritually attuned to the goods of modernity, were suspicious of the Enlightenment's dream of a perfectly transparent and reconciled society.

A second core conception present in recent liberal theory is the idea of impartiality, which, Gray suggests, is rendered equivalent to the moral point of view. This idea denies moral standing to individual or collective projects unless they are compatible with impersonal standards of justice. In the human world, our relationships and attachments are not contingent to our well-being, but rather constitutive, and any theory of morality and politics that ignores this commonsense insight soon renders itself either irrelevant, or, worse, destructive. Any acceptable theory of morality, political or otherwise, must admit that moral claims are often in tension, that the demands of family, friendship, nation, and impartiality are often in conflict, with the attendant realization that tragedy and loss are unavoidable.[14] The extension of impartiality has been partial, and unique to Western civilization, and is limited by other important moral goods.[15]

Aron also avoids this problem of contemporary liberal theory. Impartiality as an ideal is particularly limited in the field of international relations, where, as discussed in our previous chapter, idealist theories ignore the enduring realities of nation, war, and religion—the realities of politics. Aron's universalism, Kantian in inspiration, was balanced by an awareness of the permanence of political conflict in international relations, and a Montesquieuian recognition of the richness of human cultures across the globe. As we have just seen, while modernity was bringing with it a "universal society," political and cultural differences were not in danger of disappearing and in certain ways had been exaggerated and brought to increased awareness by the ubiquity of modern forms of communication.[16] If impartiality as a moral ideal implies the abandonment of the forms of identification and duty bound up with the nation and religion—the driving forces of political life, before, during, and after the great ideological struggles that have scarred the twentieth century—then impartiality is an abstract and strangely ineffectual ideal with little resonance in the human world *or* the world of politics. As in the case of the concept of the person, Aron's disenchanted, conservative liberalism allows us to prudentially view the ideal of impartiality, understand its limits, and balance it against other goods alive in the political world.

The third core feature of contemporary liberal theory, Gray observes, is that of normative or "abstract" individualism, and it is closely related to the two previous conceptions we have addressed. It too introduces distortions into liberal theory, with the resulting measure of inadequacy on the part of that theory in capturing many of the most powerful currents and events of our time. As Gray argues, normative individualism, the idea that the individual is all that is morally relevant, ignores the strongest political force of our century: collective identification and thus the sense of injustice experienced by those belonging to an oppressed community.[17] This fact, always present to Aron (or Berlin), has been downplayed (with certain notable exceptions) by contemporary liberal theorists.[18] Human beings individuate themselves, as Gray rightly stresses, as members of historical communities with *cross-generational memories.*[19] Contemporary liberal theory adopts instead "an unhistorical and abstract individualism in the service of a legalist or jurisprudential paradigm of political philosophy."[20] The goal of political philosophy then becomes the application of the moral point of view, which, as we have seen, is restricted largely to the ideal of impartiality, to an ongoing effort to derive the ideal constitution. Political morality is thus conceived, not as an exploration of statesmanship or as a balancing of the myriad and sometimes conflicting goods and parties of the human world, but as a matter of adjudicating the claims of individuals in terms of rights and justice.

While Aron was not deaf to the claims of individuals, he held, as we have seen, a strong belief in the permanence and legitimacy of national forms of identification. In his short book on the nature of modern liberty, *An Essay on Freedom,* Aron's canvass of modern understandings of liberty included the sense of freedom experienced through belonging to a national community:

> It will be said that only an individual can be called free or not free, because freedom is a capacity involving reflection and decision, and only an individual is endowed with such a capacity. But when a group of men, acting in the name of an existing or future people, demand the right to form a nation and a state, they lend a kind of unity to the collectivity as a whole. Since this collectivity is the highest in our eyes, we want it to have a unity comparable to that of the individual. This collective person presents itself in relation to others on the international scene, it sees itself as endowed with singular traits and even as charged with a mission which none other could possible perform. More important, the independence of this collectivity is, for each of its members, the condition of certain concrete, authentic freedoms.[21]

To admit such forms of belonging, however, implies, as argued above, granting moral weight to the community beyond the individuals constituting it at any moment in time. If Aron is correct and the community is morally relevant, then normative individualism restricts unduly the scope of both morality and political reflection, and Aron's conservative liberalism cannot be squared with the apolitical normative individualism of Rawls and other contemporary liberal theorists. Aron thus avoids this charge of Gray's as well.

A practical corollary of this individualist bias in contemporary liberal theory makes up the fourth core conception treated by Gray: the supplanting of politics by law. This has been apparent particularly in the United States, where the juridical branch of government has been politicized dramatically while political life has been robbed of its substance to an ever greater extent.[22] Nothing crystallizes this political corruption of law and the dangers it holds for exacerbating social conflict more than the abortion debate. By framing that debate in terms of rights, warring factions in the United States, Gray observes, have been prevented from reaching any compromise solution, one reason the debate there is more divisive than in many other countries. The explosion of rights claims has led to the growing fragmentation of American political life and a steady erosion of democratic accountability.[23] This supplanting of the political with the jurisprudential that has so typified contemporary liberal theory is part of a much larger theoretical denigration of politics that has been carried out by modern thought as a whole. While Gray does not draw out explicitly the parallels of the jurisprudential reduction of politics in liberal theory with this larger denial of politics (which we have looked at on several occasions throughout this study), the phenomenon has been captured accurately by Allan Bloom in the midst of his commentary on Aron:

> Politics as a distinctive dimension of human life, not to speak of its being the most important one, has become extremely doubtful. It has been reduced or swallowed up by other disciplines which explain it away. Economics, anthropology, sociology, and psychology, among others, claim primacy over political science. Modern abstract notions like the market, culture, society, or the unconscious take the place of the political regime as the prime cause of what counts for human beings. Older views either denied the real existence of such things as cultures or claimed that the political is the central cause rather than their effect.[24]

The broad theoretical reduction of politics present in modern thought, nowhere more evident than in Marxism (as we have seen in chapter 3 above), was consistently resisted by Aron, who insisted on the autonomy, and occasionally even the primacy, of politics.[25] This theoretical emphasis, rooted in Aron's defense of political reason, gave his liberalism an awareness of the role, limits, and possibilities of politics absent in the later liberal tradition. That later tradition shares with Marxism and much of the movement of modern thought an impoverished understanding of the political.

It was for these reasons that Aron was not overly enamored of the rights explosion, already evident, for obvious reasons, in the aftermath of World War II. His disenchanted liberalism had a Burkean component to it, for there was no attempt in Aron's writings to articulate a definitive list of fundamental rights or liberties, which he saw as at least in part a product of cultural and political traditions. Aron's disinclination to deduce a list of fundamental rights was matched with a critical discernment of the feasible. If rights were to be confused solely with what was desirable and at the same time were to ignore the constraints of economic and social reality they could soon be rendered worthless currency, ruined by inflation.[26]

Gray offers a final core conception of contemporary liberal theory that contributes to its political inadequacy. Gray questions the desirability and even coherence of the contemporary liberal defense of neutrality.[27] First of all, Gray holds, an important distinction must be made between the older liberal idea of tolerance and the contemporary liberal notion of neutrality. The older ideal viewed tolerance as the essential precondition for any stable *modus vivendi* between imperfect human beings. It was, however, inherently judgmental: we tolerate something when we let a belief, even though we might find it offensive or pernicious, continue to exist. We tolerate scientology, for example, not because we hold that it may be in possession of the truth, but because of the inherent good of freedom of belief, a good that allows erroneous belief. Toleration thus implies that we have a sense of right and wrong, and that we have some sense, some image of the good life we share through the political community. But this means, necessarily, that the older liberalism was nonneutral in respect of the good.

For the new liberalism, however, the liberalism of the Rawlsian tradition, justice requires that government in its institutions and practices behave neutrally, not with tolerance, toward rivalrous understandings of the good life. Government, at least on a strict reading of the ideal of neutrality, is not to discriminate against *any* form of life driven by a conception of the good. To discriminate against any such view would be to violate the ideal of equality which underlies contemporary liberalism. As Gray makes clear, were this ideal to be fully implemented, government would be refused the right to favor or advance certain ways of life over others deemed substandard or even immoral. Indeed, were this ideal to be implemented fully, the result would be, in Gray's phrase, "the legal disestablishment of morality."[28] Such a regime would be undermined, either through the failure to nurture the cultural and moral prerequisites of the liberal order itself, or through the fragmentation of political life, bereft of a common culture, into warring particularisms— a paradoxical return, as Gray has pointed out in another context, to a Hobbesian state of nature, now projected onto the screen of politics.[29] Bloom has written of this fragmentation in an American setting:

> Country, religion, family, ideas of civilization, all the sentimental and historical forces that stood between cosmic infinity and the individual, providing some notion of a place within the whole, have been rationalized and have lost their compelling force. America is experienced not as a common project but as a framework within which people are only individuals, where they are left alone. To the extent that there is a project, it is to put those who are said to be disadvantaged in a position to live as they please too. The advanced Left talks about self-fulfilment; the Right, in its most popular form, is Libertarian, i.e., the right wing form of the Left, in favor of everybody's living as he pleases. . . . If there is an inherent political impulse in man, it is certainly being frustrated.[30]

In reality, the liberal regime has more severe moral prerequisites, going beyond the individualism described by Bloom in the above passage. The refusal to witness this truth among contemporary liberal theorists has left a legacy both theoretical and practical. Theoretically, the ideal of neutrality misunderstands the nature of liberal democracy and eclipses the political world. If politics refers to no common good, if it is deprived of any substantive moral task, what purpose does it serve? Practically, the ideal of neutrality, promoted, at least in an American context, through the agency of the judiciary, has the tendency to render older goods of civility, virtue, and duty moribund, emptying the political world of its moral contents. Aron's conservative liberalism, particularly, though not exclusively, in his later works, was attuned sharply to this central paradox of the liberal democratic order, what might be called "the problem of democracy."

In *In Defense of Decadant Europe*, for example, a book written in the mid-seventies, Aron warned that the liberal democratic West could not survive solely on the basis of economic growth; it needed to endorse a common way of life.[31] Without an active spirit of citizenship and a degree of Machiavellian *virtu*, the risk was great that the liberal regimes would lose what Manent has called the "instinct for political existence,"[32] especially in the face of the spiritual and military threat posed by totalitarian regimes. Aron was convinced that liberal regimes required certain shared virtues—virtues of moderation and tolerance (understood in Gray's sense) as well as more martial virtues—in order to survive.[33] That Aron saw clearly this fundamental paradox of the liberal democratic regime, that the instinct for political existence and strict neutrality are incompatible, was undoubtedly due to his deeply political nature. The apolitical theorists of contemporary liberalism, in their refusal to adopt the commonsense perspective of citizen and statesman, have largely glossed over this difficulty (we will see another example of it below with Hayek), and in this way the Aronian understanding of liberalism is superior to its more recent rivals.

In sum, following Gray's assessment of contemporary liberal theory, we have discussed five features that have characterized the Rawlsian tradition: a thin conception of the person; an overestimation of impartiality as a moral ideal; normative individualism; a supplanting of politics by a jurisprudential paradigm (mirroring the suppression of the political realm carried out by modern thought in many of its most prominent tendencies); and finally the difficulties opened up by the replacement of the traditional liberal norm of toleration with the contemporary ideal of neutrality. In response to Gray, we have argued that Aron's conservative liberalism, rooted in the defense of political reason, is superior to this later tradition in its grasp of the nature and importance of the political world.

Are these difficulties of contemporary liberal theory occasioned by a common methodological error? What has occurred in contemporary liberal philosophy has been the "conquest" of politics by abstract theory.[34] The ambiguities, exigencies, and trade-offs that make up political life are replaced with theoretical frameworks distant from the phenomena with which they are meant to be concerned.[35] There has been, as we have seen throughout, a wide-spread effort to "freeze" the political world into place, which has had an impoverishing effect on political theory. As David Miller has noted, some of what have been regarded as the most important contributions to political theory in the last two decades, by which he means the theoretical productions of the liberal tradition we have been assessing, while philosophically quite sophisticated, are "poorly-grounded empirically" and fail to bring together "the philosophical analysis of political principles with an empirical understanding of political processes in a wholly successful way."[36] These two hypotheses—that liberal philosophy has "conquered" politics and that liberal political philosophy is poorly grounded empirically—are in reality two sides of the same coin. What they inform us about is the loss of mutuality between political thought and political practice. This is in stark contrast with an earlier tradition of political thought, when political philosophers were also political economists, historians, and social theorists. Returning to Gray for a moment, he has drawn attention to this difference in approach exemplified by earlier thinkers like Adam Smith, Tocqueville, Hume, and John Stuart Mill (one could quickly add Aristotle and Montesquieu, who have authored respectively the two greatest works of comparative politics in the tradition of political philosophy), concerned "with what history and theory had to teach about the comparative performance of different institutions and the constraints of feasibility imposed on human institutions of all sorts by the circumstances of any realistically imaginable world."[37] Gray adds that when these political philosophers of an older, richer tradition were liberals, they were preoccupied with the cultural and institutional preconditions of liberal civil society. The threats to liberal civil society—threats to the stability and even the very existence of the liberal order—were manifold, and these diverse thinkers were united in their effort to understand the political reality and history of their time in order to preserve the precarious gifts of artifice, nature, and tradition that were their inheritance.[38] In Gray's words: "The strange death of this older tradition has gone oddly unlamented, as political philosophy has come to be dominated by a school that prides itself on its insulation from other disciplines and whose intellectual agenda is shaped by a variety of liberalism that at no point touches the real dilemmas of liberal society."[39]

N. Scott Arnold has also raised this criticism of contemporary liberal political philosophy, although somewhat allusively, at the conclusion of his patient demolition of Marxism, *Marx's Radical Critique of Capitalist Society.*[40] Arnold argues that Marxism fails to satisfy conditions he believes necessary for any successful radical critique of existing institutions: a "critical explanations" condition which stipulates that the ills and injustices marking the society under critique must be shown to be pervasive and rooted in the basic socioeconomic structure of the society; a "normative theory" condition that tells us why the "ills and injustices" of the previous condition are pernicious things; and an "alternative institutions" requirement (that we mentioned in our opening chapter) which demands that radical criticism describe in a plausible way how different institutions would actually function, how they will solve the problems created by the institutions they are replacing, and how they might persist as stable social forms.[41] But Marxism is not alone in failing these conditions. As Arnold comments:

> The two-decade long preoccupation with theories of justice runs a grave risk of being just so much talk. For example, John Rawls does not explain how income redistribution by the democratic state is to be effected without organized pressure groups diverting rivers of tax revenues to themselves and their constituencies. To take another example, Robert Nozick offers no explanation for why the minimal state would stay minimal. These theorists of justice ignore not only the question of how to get from here to there, which is perhaps understandable, but also the question of how changed institutions would actually function there.[42]

In other words, the failure of contemporary liberal theory, Arnold suggests, is in some ways as profound as that of Marxism, and for many of the same reasons. The sundering of theory and practice is complete, political thought left at once hubristic and somewhat barren. It is clear something has been lost.

Aron's thought, as we have seen through our extended examinations of his philosophy of history, critique of ideology, and theory of international relations, offers a model of thinking about politics, of *thinking politically* that avoids these theoretical shortcomings and that can serve as a corrective to the drift of modern theory. Aron's conservative liberalism, and his sustained defense of political reason, looks back to the older tradition of liberalism lamented by Gray, as Thomas Pangle has affirmed:

> Self-serving and self-indulgent libertarianism; bloodless and narrow utilitarianism; scientistic thinking that was at once reductionist and abstractly universal; a so-called Kantianism that encouraged liberal softness and doctrinaire moralism: each of these powerful contemporary tendencies had the effect, in Aron's eyes, of extinguishing appreciation of the irreducibly political dimension of human existence—that core of unmoralistic statesmanship and citizenship which (Aron stressed) had been most sympathetically and lucidly delineated by Aristotle, Montesquieu, Burke, and Tocqueville. Like Bertrand de Jouvenal, Aron called for and promoted a *philosophic* reflection on past and present political practice. He had in mind studies that would not try to distort sound practice by forcing it into abstract models, but that would instead attempt to clarify such practice in a respectful, appreciative, but also philosophically critical spirit.[43]

Aron's understanding of politics separates in a fundamental way his disenchanted, deeply political liberalism from the far more abstract unpolitical political theory of contemporary liberalism. But we still need to get a little clearer about the exact *contours* of Aron's liberalism, which we shall do by bringing it into dialogue with Hayek, Berlin, and Fukuyama.

## 2. ARON, HAYEK, BERLIN, AND FUKUYAMA: MODERN LIBERTY AND MODERN POLITICS

Hayek's 1960 book *The Constitution of Liberty*, considered by some to be his masterpiece, attempted to set out in the most theoretically rigorous way what might be called the foundational logic of the free society.[44] It represents a sophisticated defense of classical liberalism, restated as a series of deductive axioms flowing from a set of basic principles. Aron admired the "breadth of the construction" of Hayek's book, and observed that it was a "delight for the mind," which did not stop him from disagreeing with its conclusions.[45] While Aron found much of worth in Hayek's thought, so contrary to the Marxist-dominated spirit of the age, his liberalism was far more political than Hayek's, in whom, finally, he saw an apoliticism that mirrored, albeit in a far more noble fashion, the rejection of politics of Marx and the Marxists themselves. The question animating Hayek's enterprise is the following: What does it mean to live in a free social order? In Hayek's treatment, two conditions must be insured, conditions which imply a third. Let us look at each in turn before moving to Aron's criticisms.

First, freedom on the Hayekian view has to be understood as *non-constraint*. This immediately poses a second question: What do we mean by constraint? For Hayek, this was self-evident: "coercion occurs when one man's actions are made to serve another man's will, not for his own but for the other's purpose."[46] In order to coerce, it is, of course, usually necessary to *threaten*, perhaps with physical force. Constraint *instrumentalizes*, thus making him who suffers constraint the object of another's will, rather than the autonomous subject of his own destiny. Hayek's understanding of liberty is negative, and reminds us of how Isaiah Berlin defined such freedom: "If I am prevented by others from doing what I could otherwise do, I am to that extent unfree; and, if this area is contracted by other men beyond a certain minimum, I can be described as being coerced, or, it may be, enslaved."[47] Thus, if we are to live in a free society, Hayek reasons, we must ensure that the individual can secure for himself a realm of privacy, where all such coercion is excluded.[48]

Second, a free society must be based on strictly universal laws. Hayek draws a sharp distinction between a general law, applicable to all regardless of circumstance, and specific commands, which involve the inevitable rule of one individual over another: "The conception of freedom under law . . . rests on the contention that when we obey laws, in the sense of general abstract rules laid down irrespective of their application to us, we are not subject to another man's will and are therefore free."[49] The former is noncoercive, Hayek believes, while the latter is pernicious and necessarily intrusive. This distinction allows Hayek to preserve a margin of freedom within the life of work. If I am given a "general instruction" to edit a manuscript, or fasten a bolt on a car door in a factory, this preserves a margin of initiative and liberty that is collapsed when my boss tells me exactly how it is to be done. Similarly, Hayek holds, a free society cannot treat any class of citizen differently, say, through taxation, or policies of "affirmative action" without of ne-

cessity subjecting some individuals to the will of others, and thus reintro-
ducing "specific commands." The *combination* of these two foundational principles—the conception of liberty as non-coercion and the
Rousseauean-Kantian embrace the universality of law (along with his
anti-rationalist epistemological considerations, which need not detain us
here)—led Hayek to his support for a strictly limited state (although he
does accept the need for government provision of a minimal welfare
"safety net") and the attendant freedom for individuals to transact their
business as they saw fit. The resulting regime would secure greater material well-being and maximize the freedom of men and women; it would
be, in short, the "good society."[50]

Aron articulated a series of criticisms against Hayek's vision of the
free society, convinced that Hayek had, like so many other political
thinkers in the twentieth century, abstracted away from politics. Hayek's
abstraction is ironic, given his concern for undermining rationalism in
economic and political life; despite Hayek's sensitivity to history, and his
sympathy with the English Whig tradition, the constitution of liberty at
times risks becoming as artificial, as cut off from the political and human
world, as John Rawls's theory of justice or Robert Nozick's anarchic
minimal state.

Aron's first criticism held that Hayek's understanding of freedom
ignored other ideas of freedom alive in political history. To say that one
is free only if noncoerced and subject to strictly universal laws is to
disregard the importance of *belonging* to the sense of being free. While
Hayek was perfectly justified in definitionally restricting the use of the
term "freedom" to noncoercion, this has not been the dominant understanding across time. As Aron wrote in *An Essay on Freedom*, using the
example of the Algerian struggle for independence from colonial France:

> Let us suppose that the integration to which the Algerians had long
> aspired and which was offered them when they demanded indepen-
> dence had actually been granted them. Would they have been liber-
> ated if they had obeyed the same laws and enjoyed the same rights as
> the French people? There is no reason to believe that they would.
> Real freedom, freedom which individuals experience as such, depends
> just as much on men and manners as it does on laws . . . the formation
> of an independent nation eventually becomes for a population, even
> one that is theoretically an integral part of a liberal state, the necessary

condition for the personal freedoms in a twofold sense. The individual will not feel free even if, according to the legislation in force, he ought to experience the feeling of freedom, as long as discrimination between the ethnic group to which he belongs and the dominant ethnic group persists in *practice*. Nor will he be able to arrive at the positive freedom of political participation as long as he does not recognize as his own the state of which he is theoretically a citizen. If freedom as participation is, in our time, an integral part of freedom as we conceive of it, national liberation is an indispensable element or phase of this freedom.[51]

Earlier we had noted, following Manent, that Aron did not describe or elaborate the principles of the best regime, but instead began from within the political world, examined the actual ideals that men expressed, and sought to moderate their expression in order that such ideals might be made more compatible, more in keeping with the realities of human nature and the structure of society.[52] For many men and women of the twentieth century, being part of a nation, of a collectivity made up of one's brothers and sisters, has been inseparable from the meaning of freedom, even though, as Aron went on to acknowledge, it often seemed "everything proceeds as if the acquisition of collective freedom were made at the cost of many personal freedoms."[53] The ideals of nationhood and of noncoercion have often conflicted, but Hayek, like Martha Nussbaum and recent liberal theorists generally, did not sufficiently recognize the independence of a nation as a source of freedom and meaning in the lives of its citizenry. Not only, as we saw earlier, was Aron not a normative individualist, granting moral weight as he did to the nation, as such, above and beyond its members, he also held that freedom and belonging are tightly intertwined.

In a related way, Hayek's distinction between general prescriptions and specific commands in the workplace fails to capture the real "sentiment of liberty or oppression" experienced by the worker.[54] That sentiment is a function of many more factors than Hayek suggests, such as the solidarity of workers, remuneration, the openness of the workplace to upward mobility, and so on. Seeking theoretical clarity, Hayek sought to extirpate any such subjective impressions from his argument. Yet as Aron points out, Hayek fails to do so. Hayek's definition of freedom rested, as we have seen, on a notion of coercion, which he wanted to define objectively. The idea of coercion itself, however, requires the *sense* of being threatened. This is to sneak a subjective determination into the meaning of coercion, and hence into the meaning of freedom itself, *even within the confines of Hayek's own theory*. But if we allow subjective attitudes and understandings into the meaning of freedom, then Hayek has to find another justification for drawing the lines of liberty where he decides to draw them, both in the workplace and, more broadly, throughout Hayek's rule-governed "good society." Why shouldn't we consider the sense of belonging as a dimension of freedom? As Aron puts it, "No more than obedience to specific commands entails constraint does submission to permanent directives or general laws guarantee liberty."

Nor, Aron argued, does Hayek have room within his theory for what Locke called "federative" power, "the Power of War and Peace, Leagues and Alliances, and all the Transactions, with all Persons and Communities without the Commonwealth."[55] As we saw in the last chapter, the problem of war and peace is central to politics. Hayek's theory is silent on foreign affairs, a silence, Aron believes, that characterizes "most liberals."[56] Hayek is silent because to speak of foreign policy would force into the open the inevitable rule of "men by men and not by laws."[57] How could it be otherwise? While between states there are obligations of natural right, without a universal police force of sufficient—perhaps ultimate—power, or the abolishment of independent centers of sovereignty, the Prince decides justice. On Hayek's view, all action leading to war, all diplomatic action, would have to be seen as constraint of the governed by the governors, and therefore a denial of freedom. Aron returns to Carl Schmitt, once again without attribution, in his somber response to Hayek:

> If there are some men who do not hesitate, in a situation of necessity, to sacrifice individual liberty to the nation's freedom, we would be wrong to deny that they have intelligible motives, if not rational ones, for the preference. As long as there are wars, belonging to a political order will be equivalent to discriminating between friends and enemies. If I have to pay for the liberty I enjoy during peacetime with the obligation of fighting with brothers of the same race, or language, or nationality during war, I can resign myself, with perfect lucidity, to the loss of my peacetime freedom in order to find myself once again among my brothers the day each of us confronts death.[58]

Given the fact that there is no collectivity without foreign policy, there is no collectivity without federative power. Federative power is always exercised by men, not laws. Therefore, Hayek's constitution of liberty ignores something essential to liberty: *political* liberty. I have a right, if I am to die for my country, to know the man who sends me to my death. Hayek sought to banish *command* from the political world, a permanent temptation of liberalism. Aron's liberalism is distinctive in that it sees the role of command, the inevitability of command, and the moral legitimacy of command as part of the political and human world. Aron's liberalism is thus far more political than Hayek's, indeed far more political than most rival liberalisms.[59]

Just as Hayek, but not Aron, ignores the federative power inseparable from politics (politics being inseparable from peace and war), so Hayek, but not Aron, ignores, or refuses to give sufficient weight to, the moral and civic preconditions to the success and flourishing of the liberal regime. Aron was mindful of the tendency of the liberal democratic regime to undermine itself through the radicalization of its basic principles of liberty and equality, its dependence on certain moral assumptions and mores. Aron grants that Isaiah Berlin is right to warn, as does Hayek, of the potential dangers of equating freedom and morality.[60] But "the danger exists on the other side, too," Aron suggests, for a "society must first be before it can be free."[61] Hayek presupposes too much, in particular education in the "common life," for in order "to leave everyone a private sphere of decision and choice, it is still necessary that all or most want to live together and recognize the same system of ideas as true, the same formulation of legitimacy as valid."[62] Aron's liberalism understood that the liberal regime was not solely natural to man, but rested on an art of politics, one of the chief goals of which was civic education. Civic education, which could not be presupposed, was necessary to "instruct men, to make them capable of reason and morality."[63] Reason and morality are for Aron intrinsic to the flourishing of the free society; without them liberty risks becoming license, and license cannot support the free society.

Aron raises one more objection to Hayek's constitution of liberty worth mentioning, and it concerns what might be called Hayek's dogmatism. Hayek's rejection of all but minimal government welfare provision is deemed utopian by Aron, and unjust. It is an outgrowth of Hayek's single-minded pursuit of liberty, understood in a single-minded way. Hayek reduced the complexity of the political and moral world to only one of its "values," making that "value"—liberty as non-coercion—ultimate. Aron saw such reduction of moral and political complexity as "unacceptable"; indeed he goes on to say that it is "wrong, in both theory and practice, to refer everything to a sole objective."[64] Aron conceded the legitimacy of social rights, the so-called "real" rights to economic and material benefits demanded by socialists, although he refused to grant them the same weight as the "formal" rights (to free speech, freedom of assembly, etc.) of the liberals. The idea of social justice, Aron believed, was not as meaningless as Hayek presumed. Indeed, Aron regarded the quest for a prudential synthesis of the formal and real liberties as the goal, never to be perfectly realized, of Western societies.[65]

It was also utopian to believe that, under the conditions of modern representative democracy, welfare provision could be eliminated. Citizens in a democracy will not regard the market as somehow beyond the will of the community, a sacred grove where government dare not tread. Why would Hayek expect citizens in a democracy to accept market outcomes, if those outcomes are deemed injurious? There will always be a democratically expressed need for *some* government action as a response to human needs, although there may be great variation in the range and extent of that action, and Hayek was right to warn of the ineffectiveness of most government intervention in the economy. The welfare state might be reduced in scope, reformed for greater efficiency, perhaps even recast as a public-private venture, but on Aron's view it was inescapable, built into the logic of our modern societies. A political theory which seeks its abolition, like Hayek's *The Constitution of Liberty* or, more recently, and far more abstractly, Robert Nozick's *Anarchy, State and Utopia*, exhibits a failure of political reason.[66]

Isaiah Berlin, unlike Hayek, perceives the complexity of the human moral and political world. No one would dare accuse Berlin of reducing moral and political complexity to one ultimate "value." Indeed Berlin's liberalism, in its recognition of tragedy, its appreciation of the moral relevance of national belonging, and its attentiveness to the varied and often rivalrous goods that make up the human world, has much in common with the thought of Aron. What separates them, however, is of great consequence. Central to Berlin's project has been one overriding idea: that human goods and evils are real (i.e., objectively built into our relation to the world), multiple, and in conflict.[67] On Berlin's view, in fact, they are seldom in harmony, and on certain tragic occasions, the conflicts of goods or evils are *incommensurable*—where there is no rational, *a priori* way of deciding the conflict, and where any decision will be unavoidably antinomic in consequence. Moral and political life, Berlin holds, is fraught with such conflicts: a political choice for liberty conflicts with a choice for equality; justice and mercy can be pointedly at odds; our liberties may conflict (as in the conflict between our liberty to be left alone and our liberty to have information); a citizen or statesman may have to choose between supporting, in John Gray's words, a "murderous traditional tyranny" and a regimented, intrusive regime that suffocates economic and political liberties.[68] On at least one reading of Berlin's thought, when we are confronted with such choices reason fails us, and we are left with "groundless commitment," indeterminate and even irrational.[69] This is not far from Max Weber's "war of the gods," where everyone must choose their own gods or demons. Berlin has situated himself "against the current" of Western thought, which falls prey to, on the Berlinian view, the "Ionian fallacy"—the view that all goods are in principle commensurable and that reason can provide rationally binding solutions to our moral discords. For Berlin, Plato, Aristotle, Christianity, and Marxism fall prey to this fallacy, which yields the germ of totalitarian politics. The liberal regime is defended by Berlin as offering the most breathing room to the diversity of our moral and political understandings, as expressed in the doctrine of moral pluralism. Yet this argument ultimately fails. As Gray has shown, value pluralism cannot, if held consistently, offer anything more than contingent support for the liberal democratic regime; value pluralism subverts liberalism itself. Certain goods or morally praiseworthy ways of life—that of, say, a Japanese samurai, or an Hassidic Jew—will only flourish in non-liberal gardens. Such gardens might be preserved in liberal societies with great difficulty, and only if liberal principles are prevented from colonizing the entire human world. And if our choice for the liberal democratic regime is only a matter of groundless commitment, or if we base our choice on it solely because it is our way of life, then the liberal democratic regime cannot be privileged in any fashion. As Leo Strauss observed, despite his humanity, Berlin's doctrine of value pluralism comes to seem indistinguishable from relativism.[70]

Aron's sensitivity to the antinomic structure of the political world captures what is correct about Berlin's account: that goods cannot be maximally combined (we have looked at several such conflicts of goods throughout); that on occasion we are confronted with situations where no choice seems good (as when the statesman must choose a military action which he knows will kill innocent human beings); that dark angels inhabit the human soul. But unlike Berlin, Aron's acceptance of political antinomies does not exaggerate their incidence, nor does it surrender reason when confronting them. Aron's antinomic prudence, central to his defense of political reason, is more akin to the "classical pluralism" of Aristotle, which, while cognizant of the plurality and incommensurability of the goods alive in the city, does not surrender the necessity of prudently balancing them.[71] To balance the conflicting goods of the political and moral world is for Aristotle one of the primary tasks of the political thinker: moderation is preferable for reasons of justice and reasons of human flourishing; it is more likely to realize the common good than more agonistic alternatives.[72] The hints of a theory of natural right throughout Aron's work, although never developed philosophically, point to a more classical, indeed Aristotelian, understanding of the political and moral world than one finds in Berlin. Aron's defense of the liberal regime is thus not merely a groundless commitment to a particular way of life, but rather is rooted firmly in a moderation more in keeping with the rivalrous goods of human nature and the structure of society. The moderate position represented by the imperfect liberal democratic regime is *better* than its alternatives, something, as Gray and Strauss have both suggested (with contrary valuations), that Berlin would have trouble justifying on the grounds of value pluralism, although the spirit of humanity and moderation breathes through every page Berlin has written.[73]

Francis Fukuyama's *The End of History and the Last Man* was an audacious book, so much so that the phrase "The end of History" has become common currency.[74] Fukuyama's book, based on an earlier article of the same name, advances an interpretation of modernity that it would be only a slight exaggeration to call *liberal determinism*. Bringing to bear Aron's philosophy of history, considered in our second chapter, on Fukuyama's bold interpretation will bring our study of Aron's thought to a conclusion. Fukuyama's central argument states that History—the history of grand ideologies of the Hegelian-Marxist type—has ended. It has ended not with the establishment of a classless communist utopia but with prosaic liberal democracy. It has ended in boredom. There may indeed still be wars and revolutions, best seen as atavisms, however bloody, but liberal democracy will never be challenged again as an economic and political system. Written against the backdrop of the worldwide collapse of communism, Fukuyama's thesis brought home the failure of the radical left and the bankruptcy of its Marxist-inspired ideas. If this was not enough to excite reams of commentary, much of it angry and critical, especially on the part of left-leaning thinkers, Fukuyama's argument was justified on the basis of a directional theory of history that, paradoxically, owes a great deal to Hegel and Marx. It was as if the left's own heroes were being asked to bury them.

What does this directional theory of history consist of? Two ideas form its nucleus. The first is economic, the second moral and political. The economic engine driving history to its destination in liberal democracy is based on the growth of human productive powers—the application of technology to the satisfaction of human wants. Fukuyama summarizes this economic interpretation of history early in *The End of History*:

> The unfolding of modern natural science has had a uniform effect on all societies that have experienced it, for two reasons. In the first place, technology confers decisive military advantages on those countries that possess it, and given the continuing possibility of war in the international system of states, no state that values its independence can ignore the need for decisive modernization. Second, modern natural science establishes a uniform horizon of production possibilities. Technology makes possible the limitless accumulation of wealth, and thus the satisfaction of an ever-expanding set of human desires.[75]

Fukuyama holds that only a liberal, free-market economy can successfully answer the need for satisfaction; it does so through the generation of immense gains in economic productivity. Economic liberalism is the rational outcome of the historical process, given that all other arrangements have proven economically inefficient. It succeeds in fulfilling the desiring element in human nature.

The second part of Fukuyama's historical "Mechanism" is, as noted above, political or moral. It rests on another aspect of human nature— the "thymotic" part—which Fukuyama draws from Plato by way of

Hegel and Alexandre Kojeve. This conception of human nature sees man as striving for *recognition*. Recognition amounts to desiring the desire of the other, and hence requires the existence of society. From the beginning, we are immersed in a human world. Yet human sociability leads initially not to peaceful civil society, but to the violent struggle for prestige. Recognition is inherently unstable. The struggle between two subjects, A and B, can lead to three outcomes: the death of both A and B; the death of A or B; or a relationship of lordship and bondage between A and B. All three outcomes are unsatisfying, the first two for obvious reasons, given that recognition requires two parties. With regard to the third, the reason might not be immediately apparent: the lord wants recognition, not from a slave, but from another lord. Applying the Hegelian master-slave dialectic to the interpretation of political history, Fukuyama sees liberal democracy as an answer that satisfies master *and* slave. Only the liberal democratic regime instantiates mutual recognition, and it does so by lifting the slave to the status of lord. As for the need for recognition, "no other arrangement of human social institutions is better able to satisfy this longing, and hence no further progressive change is possible."[76] Combining the outcomes of this twin dialectic of material wants and the need for recognition leads to the realization that modern capitalist democracy is the "end" of history. There will be no further *ideological* challenges, and it will only be a matter of time that those countries still immersed in history will realize the error of their ways and catch up on the road to peace, harmony, and consumer bliss.

With what we have seen previously, both in this chapter, and earlier in our study, it should be evident that Aron's views on the intelligibility of history cannot be easily reconciled with those of Fukuyama. First, Fukuyama's reading of historical development, in at least one of its dimensions, suffers from a defect similar to Marxism. Fukuyama's economic interpretation of history is a causal monism, and too deterministic to be fully credible as an explanation of the historical transformations that have led to the state of the world in 1997.[77] As we saw in our examination of Aron's theory of the causal explanation of historical and social phenomena, stopping the causal regress at the level of economic life is insupportable. In addition, although Fukuyama includes the need for recognition as a force at work in history, thus re-Hegelianizing Marx, it is unclear at best that liberal democracy is the only answer to the requirements of that need. There *is* empirical evidence to suggest the world is becoming more friendly to liberal democracy, but Fukuyama reifies a tendency—which could easily be interrupted—into an inexorable process, and ignores countervailing evidence.

Moreover, if we attend to the breakup of the Soviet Union, what we see is that the desire for recognition is not manifesting itself in the form of the secular, universalist liberal democratic state, as Fukuyama expected it would. Instead, we see the surging forth of *national* aspirations and a renewed sense of ethnic identity. "I recognize those like me but not the other": this is at least as viable a prediction of the near future as that which would hold were Fukuyama's vision of historical development true. Aron's attentiveness to the antinomy between the universal and the particular would lead him to be less than sanguine about the triumph of liberal democracy, at least along the lines envisioned by Fukuyama. Aron's answer to Fukuyama would be the same as that he gave to Sartre, Merleau-Ponty, and other "idolaters of history": avoid speaking of an end to history, for we cannot see an end to history. We are not God, our knowledge is finite, and history has a way of returning with a vengeance. In Aron's words, written in 1961:

> Never have men had so many motives for not killing each other. Never have they had as many motives to feel themselves associated in one and the same project. I do not conclude from all this that the age of universal history will be peaceful. We know that man is a rational being, but what of men?[78]

Fukuyama's theoretical weakness is, as might be expected, practical as well. The category of "liberal democracy" is used loosely in *The End of History*, leading to a failure to distinguish regimes that differ dramatically. Are Japan and the United States truly characterized by the same kind of political and economic order?[79] Canada and Singapore? Fukuyama's lack of historical detail abstracts from the reality of politics in a way Aron would never accept. There are liberal democracies, and then there are those countries which will be liberal democracies: this is the extent of Fukuyama's sensitivity to the tumult of political history. Perhaps the most threatening challenge to freedom and democracy at present is the emergence of fundamentalist regimes opposed to everything Western (with the exception of armaments). Yet Fukuyama's end of history argument, a kind of liberal determinism, gives little notice to political fundamentalism, resolving the potential conflict between the West and Islam by stipulation. Such regimes, on Fukuyama's view, can offer no long-term solace to the souls of men; as a piece of historical observation, something that remains counterintuitive at best. Fukuyama's arguments, if taken as advice to the Prince, could result in minimizing the import of security, and a failure to know the enemy—one of the deadliest failures to think politically. The political teaching of *The End of History* is finally limited in prudential guidance. In order to defend the liberal democracies, as imperfect as they are worthy of preservation, it is of vital importance not to downplay the real dangers confronting them.

★   ★   ★   ★

As should now be clear from this extended encounter between Aron and certain representative currents of contemporary political thought, his conservative liberalism is informed with the same refined sympathy for the political perspective we have located throughout his work during the course of this study. It is a liberalism that has more in common with that of Tocqueville or Montesquieu than that of John Rawls or Martha Nussbaum. Aron's political liberalism, his defense of political reason, can inform our way of doing political philosophy by reminding us of the need to *think politically*. This is, *pace* Fukuyama, still necessary as we enter into a new, post-Marxist millennium.

To think politically, one must, as we have seen, take into account the antinomical structure of political life. Human goods cannot all be politically combined. To ignore this warning (but also to overstate it) is to endanger the moderation essential to humane political life. Too often, contemporary political thought seeks to permanently abolish the tragic from politics, rather than finding ways to moderate the permanent effects of the tragic. Aron rejected both the emancipatory narrative dear to progressives that sees the movement of history as a continual process of accumulating gains, and another, which might be called Hayekian, pessimistically regarding modern history as a story of growing state power eclipsing, absorbing, or destroying the intermediary institutions and social structures that protect liberty from centralized power. Aron's Tocquevillian view instead emphasized, as should be clear by now, the fundamental importance of human freedom and prudential wisdom:

> Regimes are not contradictory; there is no absolute necessity for a
> violent break between one regime and the next. But within each re-

gime, men are faced with different problems and as a result of this the same institutions change their meaning. Against the power of a plutocracy, men call on universal suffrage or on the State; against a fast-encroaching technocracy, men fight to safeguard local or professional autonomies.[80]

Moreover, political thought should begin from within the common human world and not lose sight of it, even though the political philosopher can inform and enlighten, moderate and disenchant the perspectives of citizen and statesman. To the idolaters of history, Aron responded that the notion of a single meaning to history was unsustainable. While the observer could find *meanings* in history—indeed, as we have seen in chapter 2, reality is rich with a plurality of meanings—the whole remained ambiguous, elusive, problematic. Nor was history a prewritten tale of subpolitical forces, with human actors reciting lines written elsewhere, behind their backs, in the grinding of gears or the clanging of coin. Again, like Tocqueville, Aron recognized the realm of freedom as circumscribed, yet saw within the circle of our liberty the immense weight of human choice. Thus the political thinker should be observant of the limits of our reason to grasp the complexities of the real and cognizant of the feasibility constraints which should run with every theoretical flight. He must try to "achieve a reasonable compromise between conflicting demands which, carried to extremes, would be totally incompatible."[81]

Such a phenomenology of the city might seem sterile to those who find the truth lacking in excitement, but it reminds the political thinker of the fragility of the liberal democratic order, our best hope in the fractious modern world, and of the need to tend to that order by bringing to mind, for liberals and democrats, the importance of civic education, *virtu*, and the essential role of the political art in tempering the excesses of liberal democracy. He should advise liberals and democrats, statesmen and citizens, that there are *enemies*, something liberal democratic regimes have often forgotten, and often at great peril to themselves. Aron's appreciation for the antinomies of politics, his taste for history and the importance of human choice amidst all of its uncertainty, his sharp awareness that every regime has a makeup to which one must adjust one's political thinking, are qualities little in evidence in contemporary political theory, which has covered over the political. Although his thought was more political than immediately philosophical, Aron was a political philosopher, a true friend of liberal democracy because he never aimed to flatter it.


## NOTES

1. Gray's criticisms are set out with most force in *Enlightenment's Wake*, particularly in the important introductory chapter, "Against the New Liberalism," pp. 1–10; chapter two, "Notes Toward a Definition of the Political Thought of Tlon," pp. 11–17; and chapter three, "Toleration: A Post-Liberal Perspective", pp. 18–30. Gray's critique has been the subject of a special issue of *Social Research*, vol. 61, No. 3, Fall 1994. See in particular his response to his critics, "After the New Liberalism," pp. 719–35. Although I think Gray's critique is a salient one, I have deep reservations about his more positive project. See my "The Abandonment of Reason" in *The Salisbury Review*, Vol. 14, No. 3, Spring 1996, pp. 46–47.

2. Gray has not been alone in making these criticisms. From very different theoretical and political perspectives, see Harvey Mansfield, *The Spirit of Liberalism* (Cambridge: Harvard University Press, 1978) and Benjamin Barber, *The Conquest of Politics* (Princeton: Princeton University Press, 1988).

3. For Neuhaus, consult *The Naked Public Square* (Grand Rapids: Eerdmans, 1984); MacIntyre's criticisms are laid out in *After Virtue*, esp. pp. 246–52; Sandel's *Democracy's Discontent: America in Search of a Public Philosophy* (Cambridge: Harvard University Press, 1996), pp. 3–24 offers a succinct restatement of his views on contemporary liberalism; for Taylor, see *Sources of the Self*, part one. These works are only the tip of a large iceberg of literature, and often at sharp variance with one another, particularly in their stance toward normative conceptions of human nature and the role of religious belief in grounding moral considerations publicly.

4. See, of course, John Rawls, *A Theory of Justice* (Cambridge: Harvard University Press, 1971). Rawls has over the years reformulated his theory in a way that has sought to address various criticisms, including some of those under discussion here. See his *Political Liberalism* (New York: Columbia University Press, 1993). As to whether Rawls has succeeded or not, the views are mixed. For a sharp criticism of the later Rawls, see John Gray, "Can We Agree to Disagree?" *New York Times Book Review*, October 1993. For an effort to reconcile liberal universalism and concerns about cultural difference, see Will Kymlicka, *Multicultural Citizenship: A Liberal Theory of Minority Rights* (Oxford: Oxford University Press, 1995).

5. Gray, *Enlightenment's Wake*, p. 4. See also Gray's "What is Dead and What is Living in Liberalism" in his earlier *Post-Liberalism*, pp. 283–328.

6. Gray, *Enlightenment's Wake*, p. 4.

7. Aron, *In Defense of Political Reason*, p. 170.

8. See Aron, *An Essay on Freedom*, pp. 49–99; and *Progress and Disillusion*, part three, "The Dialectic of Universality," pp. 135–222.

9. Aron, *Progress and Disillusion*, pp. 3–59.

10. See Taylor, *Sources of the Self*, pp. 368–90 on the "expressivist turn."

11. Aron, *Progress and Disillusion*, p. xv; see also pp. 63–134.

12. Strauss, *Natural Right and History*, p. 251.

13. Aron, *Progress and Disillusion*, pp. 137–222.

14. For a liberal treatment of partiality, see Thomas Nagel, *Equality and Partiality* (London: Oxford University Press, 1991). For a richer analysis of moral complexity, see Aurel Kolnai, *The Utopian Mind*. In his introduction Pierre Manent captures Kolnai's nuanced view of moral complexity with clarity: "It is natural to desire the incarnation, or realization of positive values. In this sense, for every significant theme of human action and for every value, it is natural to desire a coincidence between the *is* and the *ought*. But in ordinary, non–utopian life, everyone is aware, despite this desire, not only of his own inadequacies and of human inadequacy in general, but also of the tension between different positive values (not to speak of the ambiguity and indetermination of every one of them), of the way in which urgency can shift value-priority, of the weight of necessity and the role of contingency" (p. xix). The methodological approach of contemporary liberal theory, distancing itself from the common human world, ignores this moral complexity and thus abolishes tragedy.

15. On the extension of the "moral sense" beyond the similar to include the other in Western history, see James Q. Wilson, *The Moral Sense* (New York: Free Press, 1993).

16. Again, see *Progress and Disillusion*, particularly pp. 135–222.

17. See Gray, *Post-Liberalism*, pp. 286–87, 306–07, 312. See also Berlin, "The Bent Twig" in *The Crooked Timber of Humanity*, pp. 238–61.

18. For an attempt to theorize nationalism from within the methods of contemporary liberal theory, see Yael Tamir, *Liberal Nationalism* (Princeton: Princeton University Press, 1993). See also Kymlicka, *Multicultural Citizenship*.

19. See Gray, *Enlightenment's Wake*, pp. 6–7.

20. Ibid., p. 6.

21. Aron, *An Essay on Freedom*, p. 59.

22. See the controversial symposium, "The End of Democracy? The Judicial Usurpation of Politics" in *First Things*, Nov. 1996, No. 67, pp. 18–42.

23. This tendency to translate all political conflict into the language of rights was already noticed by Aron in *In Defense of Decadent Europe*, part three. See also

Mary Ann Glendon, *Rights Talk: The Impoverishment of Political Discourse* (New York: Free Press, 1991).

24. Bloom, *Giants and Dwarfs*, p. 260.

25. See Mahoney, *The Liberal Political Science of Raymond Aron*, pp. 42, 119, pp. 123–25.

26. See Aron's essay "Sociology and the Philosophy of Human Rights" in *Politics and History*, pp. 122–38; and *Les dernières années du siècle*, pp. 199–210.

27. Gray, *Enlightenment's Wake*, pp. 18–30. Gray writes: "Toleration as a political ideal is offensive to the new liberalism—the liberalism of Rawls, Dworkin, Ackerman and suchlike—because it is decidedly non-neutral in respect of the good. For the new liberals, justice—the shibboleth of revisionist liberalism—demands that government, in its institutions and policies, practice *neutrality*, not toleration, in regard to rival conceptions of the good life. Although in the end this idea of neutrality may not prove to be fully coherent, its rough sense seems to be that it is wrong for government to discriminate in favour of, or against, any form of life animated by a definite conception of the good" p. 19.

28. Ibid., p. 20.

29. See "Hobbes and the Modern State" in *Post-Liberalism*, pp. 3–17. See also the argument of Pierre Manent, "The Modern State" in Lilla, ed., *The New French Thought*, pp. 131, where Manent observes: "By subtle, indirect but infallible means, authorization comes ever more to resemble an injunction and has the same effects. The law permits the citizen to be indifferent to all the goods that have been the object of the human pursuit; and little by little it orders that indifference. How is it possible to believe that what the law, which is naturally awe-inspiring, allows is truly wrong?" If Gray sees the triumph of factionalism and warring individualism as an outcome of liberal neutrality, Manent warns against the slide toward indifference to ideals and the triumph of a kind of nihilism. It need not be stated that these two views are not necessarily incompatible.

30. Bloom, *The Closing of the American Mind* (New York: Simon & Schuster, 1987), p. 85.

31. Aron, *In Defense of Decadent Europe*, pp. 244–63.

32. See Manent's introduction to *Les libéraux*, Vol. I., p. 40.

33. As Aron put it dramatically in a 1939 address: "When one is speaking to people who profess to despise peace, one must say that, if one loves peace, it is not out of cowardice. It is ridiculous to set regimes founded on work against regimes founded on leisure. It is grotesque to believe cannons can be resisted with butter, or effort with rest. When totalitarian governments threaten them, the democratic governments must answer that they are as capable of being as heroic as they are, and as industrious; and that is what is meant, in my thinking, by stating we are capable of the same virtues. The only difference, and it is an important one, is that in the democracies, one must consent spontaneously to those necessities which are imposed elsewhere." *Thinking Politically*, p. 333.

34. The notion of a theoretical conquest of politics is borrowed from Benjamin Barber, *The Conquest of Politics*, in particular the introduction and conclusion. It should be noted here that Barber's normative ideal of strong democracy is every bit as flawed and apolitical as the approaches he criticizes.

35. On Gray's view, this is the case with "communitarian" theory as well: "the community invoked by these writers is not one that anyone has ever lived in, a historic human settlement with its distinctive exclusivities, hierarchies and bigotries, but an ideal community, in a way as much of a cipher as the disembodied Kantian self the communitarians delight in deflating. In our world—the only one we know—the shadow cast by community is enmity, and the boundaries of communities must often be settled by war. This is the lesson of history, including the latest history of the post-communist states. Communitarian thought still harbors the aspiration expressed in those forms of the Enlightenment project such as Marxism, that are most critical of liberalism—that of creating a form of communal life from which are absent the practices of exclusion and subordination constitutive of every community human beings have ever lived in. There is another irony here, in the fact that, whereas it remains committed to the Enlightenment project in one of its most primitive forms, the main current in recent political philosophy seems to be wholly untouched by the disenchanted sociological vision of Weber and Durkheim, who must be among the Enlightenment's most gifted children." *Enlightenment's Wake*, pp. 6–7. For Aron, the central problem of politics was, in a sense, making individuals live in communities. That said, community is not a simple or easy achievement. When Aron spoke of community, it was never in abstraction from the real enmities and hopes of existing communities, with all their flaws and all their accumulation of history. In this sense, even if we were to accept at face value Gray's condemnation of communitarianism (a condemnation I assent to only in part), Aron's understanding of community, as we saw in our last chapter, would be closely akin to that which Gray points toward, without the pathos.

36. See Miller's entry "Political Theory" in *The Blackwell Encyclopedia of Political Thought*, ed. by Miller, Coleman, et al. (Oxford: Basil Blackwell, 1987), p. 385.

37. Gray, *Enlightenment's Wake*, p. 10.

38. For a superb analysis of Tocqueville's contribution to, and understanding of, the art of politics, see Pierre Manent, *Tocqueville and the Nature of Democracy*, foreword by H. Mansfield, trans. by J. Waggoner (Lanham, Maryland: Rowman & Littlefield Publishers, 1996).

39. Gray, *Enlightenment's Wake*, p. 10.

40. Arnold's book, a devastating refutation of Marxism, including its analytic variant, is little different in its overall argument from Aron's treatment of the Marxist tradition, as reconstructed in chapter 3. What is different is the methodi-

cal, step-by-step approach of the other, a well-known characteristic of the analytic tradition of philosophy.

41. Ibid., pp. 4–6. Arnold adds a fourth condition, a "transition" requirement which requires an at least minimally plausible story about how the move to a different society might occur successfully.

42. Ibid., p. 291.

43. Pangle, "Political Theory in Contemporary France: Towards a Renaissance of Liberal Political Philosophy?" p. 1002. Pangle also mentions Claude Lefort, Francois Furet, and Pierre Manent—all influenced by Aron—in this short, but prophetic article. Aron's influence on the new French liberalism, as mentioned above, has been profound, although the tensions between these thinkers is growing, and will grow further.

44. See F. A. Hayek, *The Constitution of Liberty* (Chicago: Henry Regnery, 1960). For a reconstruction of Hayek's thought in its entirety, see John Gray, *Hayek on Liberty* (Oxford: Basil Blackwell, 1989); for a much shorter, but illuminating, treatment, see Pierre Manent, *Les libéraux*, Vol. 2 (Paris: Hachette, 1986), pp. 396–98, 410–11.

45. See "The Liberal Definition of Liberty: Concerning F. A. Hayek's *The Constitution of Liberty*" in Aron, *In Defense of Political Reason*, pp. 73–91, as well as editor Mahoney's discussion, pp. 67–71; see also Aron, *An Essay on Freedom*, pp. 59–63.

46. Hayek, *The Constitution of Liberty*, p. 133. The following references to Hayek are quoted in Aron, *In Defense of Political Reason*, pp. 74–78. Only the first reference shall be given below.

47. Berlin, *Four Essays on Liberty*, p. 122.

48. See Hayek, *The Constitution of Liberty*, p. 134.

49.  Ibid., p. 153.

50. Aron, *In Defense of Political Reason*, p. 73.

51. Aron, *An Essay on Freedom*, pp. 60–61.

52. Manent, "Raymond Aron—Political Educator," p. 16.

53. Aron, *An Essay on Freedom*, p. 61.

54. Aron, *In Defense of Political Reason*, p. 77.

55. John Locke, *Two Treatises of Government*. ed. by P. Laslett (Cambridge: Cambridge University Press 1988), p. 365.

56. Aron, *In Defense of Political Reason*, p. 83. Aron writes of Hayek: "He limits himself to indicating, in passing, that, provisionally, the world state appears to him a danger to individual liberty; in these conditions it is better to accommodate oneself to the plurality of states and to eventual wars." With such an ambitious theory, how can Hayek justify excluding questions of foreign policy? Once again, we see, in Hassner's formulation, foreign policy as "sacrificial victim" to an ambitious, indeed utopian, political theory.

57. Ibid., p. 83.

58. Ibid., p. 84.

59. On the permanent liberal temptation to dispense with command, see Manent, "Situation du liberalisme," the preface to *Les libéraux*, Vol. I, pp. 9–40. This text has been translated in part as "The Contest for Command" in *The New French Thought*, ed. by Lilla, pp. 178–85.

60. Berlin, *Four Essays on Liberty*, pp. 118–72.

61. Aron, *In Defense of Political Reason*, p. 86.

62. Ibid., p. 86.

63. Aron, *An Essay on Freedom*, p. 161. Particularly important is political freedom, downplayed by Hayek, for "political freedom helps to make men worthy of it, to make them citizens who are neither conformist nor rebellious, but critical and responsible."

64. Aron, *In Defense of Political Reason*, p. 89.

65. See Aron, *An Essay on Freedom*, p. 99; *Memoirs*, p. 480; and Alain Renaut, "Politique de l'entendement, politique de la raison: De Raymond Aron à Fichte," *Cahiers de philosophie politique et juridique*, no. 15, 1989, p. 37. Renaut writes: "the Aronian analyses signal the danger to which liberalism is exposed when, stripping all meaning, as did Hayek, from the idea . . . of social justice, it is radicalized, and closed off from the partial truth comprised by the tradition of social rights." (My translation.)

66. See Nozick, *Anarchy, State and Utopia* (New York: Basic Books, 1974). From its very title, however, Nozick indicated that his book was best seen as a normative thought experiment rather than a serious exercise in *political* reflection, which requires a concern for feasibility, as we have seen.

67. For the best statement of Berlin's idea of value pluralism, see *The Crooked Timber of Humanity*, p. 12, where Berlin writes "What is clear is that values can clash—that is why civilizations are incompatible. They can be incompatible between cultures, or groups in the same culture, or between you and me. You believe in always telling the truth, no matter what; I do not, because I believe it can sometimes be too painful and too destructive. We can discuss each other's point of view, we can try to reach common ground, but in the end what you pursue may not be reconcilable with the ends to which I find that I have dedicated my life. Values may easily clash within the breast of a single individual; and it does not follow that, if they do, some must be true and others false. Justice, rigorous justice, is for some people an absolute value, but it is not compatible with what may be no less ultimate values for them—mercy, compassion—as arises in concrete cases." I have in this conclusion drawn on my review of John Gray's *Isaiah Berlin* published in the *Australasian Journal of Philosophy*, September 1995, pp. 485–86.

68. See Gray, *Isaiah Berlin*, pp. 56–57.

69. Ibid., p. 142. It is important to stress that Gray's reading of Berlin exaggerates the agonistic side of Berlin's thought, and downplays the prudential, making Berlin sound more like Max Weber. Gray is correct, however, in developing the complete teaching of objective pluralism, and perhaps inadvertently pointing to a weakness in Berlin's thought. For a more nuanced treatment see Claude Galipeau, *Isaiah Berlin's Liberalism* (Oxford: Oxford University Press, 1994), esp. pp. 112–15.

70. See Leo Strauss, *The Rebirth of Classical Political Rationalism: An Introduction to the Thought of Leo Strauss*, Selected and Introduced by Thomas L. Pangle (Chicago: University of Chicago Press, 1989), pp. 13–19.

71. On classical pluralism see Manent, *La Cité de l'homme*, pp. 233–41: "The true elements of the city are the ends or motives of the action of individuals, that is to say the goods of individuals. The 'pluralism,' or, if one wants, the 'liberalism' of Aristotle does not reside in the equal rights of individuals, but in the affirmation of the simultaneous presence of diverse and unequal goods in the same city, and in the recommendation that particular groups attached to these diverse goods and thus particularly apt to produce or preserve them, participate— unequally, to be sure—in the government and in the magistratures" (p. 241).

72. See Aristotle, *The Politics*, Bk. III, pp. 206–16. In their introduction to Aron, *Thinking Politically*, the editors call attention to just this Aristotelian dimension of Aron's thought: "Aron fulfilled the chief civic function of the political philosopher as articulated by Aristotle in Book III of *The Politics*. The political philosopher aims to be the good citizen *par excellence* by moderating the already overheated and partial commitments of the various partisan camps agonistically contending in the life of the political regime. The political philosopher seeks to prevent the outbreak of civil war by educating the public toward the common good, not through preaching but by setting an imitable and humanizing example of good citizenship" p. 10. See also Mahoney, *The Liberal Political Science of Raymond Aron*, pp. 137–47.

73. As Aron observed of Weber's war of the gods, "The limits of science, the antinomies of thought and action, are authentic contributions to a phenomenological description of the human condition. The philosophy of discord (if one can use such a phrase) translates these fundamental ideas into another language and gives them a different meaning. This translation, or transposition, implies a refusal to differentiate between vitalistic values and reasonable accomplishment; its hypotheses include the total irrationality of choices between political parties or among the various images of the world in conflict, and the moral and spiritual equivalence of various attitudes—those of the sage and of the madman, of the fanatic and the moderate. . . . The choices to which historical man is condemned—because science is limited, the future is unforeseeable, and short-term

values are contradictory—are not demonstrable. But the necessity of historical choices does not imply that thought should yield to, or be dependent on, decisions that are essentially irrational—or that existence can be fully realized in the kind of liberty that would refuse to yield, even to Truth." *History, Truth, Liberty*, pp. 372–73.

74. The critical literature on Fukuyama's Kojeve-inspired book is voluminous. An excellent collection of critical essays is *After History? Francis Fukuyama and His Critics*, edited by T. Burns (Lanham, MD: Rowman & Littlefield, 1994). See in particular Fukuyama's response to his critics, "Reflections on *The End of History*, Five Years Later," pp. 239–58. For a learned and respectful treatment of Fukuyama's book, which treats Fukuyama's theoretical precursors, including Aron and Kojeve, see "The Ends of History," the book-length conclusion to Perry Anderson, *Zones of Engagement* (London: Verso, 1993).

75. Fukuyama, *The End of History and the Last Man*, p. xiv.

76. Ibid., p. 289.

77. For a criticism of Fukuyama as having misunderstood the most important political developments of our time, see Gray, *Post-Liberalism*, pp. 245–49. As Gray suggests, "the vision of perpetual peace among liberal states, which has haunted Western thought at least since it was given systematic formulation by Immanuel Kant, will soon be seen for what it always was—a mirage that serves only to distract us from the real business of statesmanship in a permanently intractable and anarchic world" p. 249.

78. See Aron, *In Defense of Political Reason*, p. 151, as well as Mahoney's commentary, pp. 127–30.

79. Fukuyama has addressed some of these problems with his recent book *Trust*, which carries out a remarkable comparison of business practices in several capitalist economies.

80. Aron, *Opium of the Intellectuals*, p. 21.

81. Ibid., p. 21.

# BIBLIOGRAPHY

## BY RAYMOND ARON

*An Essay on Freedom*. New York: New American Library, 1970.

*The Century of Total War*. Lanham, MD: University Press of America, 1985.

*Clausewitz: Philosopher of War*, trans. by C. Booker and N. Stone. Englewood Cliffs, NJ: Prentice-Hall, 1985.

*Democracy and Totalitarianism: A Theory of Political Systems*, ed. by Roy Pierce. Ann Arbor: University of Michigan Press, 1990.

*Les dernières années du siècle*. Paris: Commentaire Julliard, 1984.

*Eighteen Lectures on Industrial Society*. London: Weidenfeld, 1967.

*History and the Dialectic of Violence*, trans. by B. Cooper. New York: Harper & Row, 1975.

*History, Truth, Liberty: Selected Writings of Raymond Aron*, ed. by Franciszek Draus, with a memoir by Edward Shils. Chicago: University of Chicago Press, 1985.

*The Imperial Republic: The United States and the World 1945–1973*. Englewood Cliffs, NJ: Prentice-Hall, 1974.

*In Defense of Decadent Europe*, with an introduction by Daniel J. Mahoney and Brian C. Anderson. New Brunswick: Transaction Publishers, 1996.

*In Defense of Political Reason*, ed. by Daniel J. Mahoney. Lanham, MD: Rowman & Littlefield Publishers, 1994.

*The Industrial Society: Three Essays on Ideology and Development*. New York: Praeger, 1967.

*Introduction to the Philosophy of History: An Essay on the Limits of Historical Objectivity*. Boston: Beacon Press, 1961.

*Leçons sur l'histoire*, ed. by Sylvie Mesure. Paris: Fallois, 1989.

*La lutte des classes*. Paris: Gallimard, 1964.

*Machiavel et les tyrannie modernes*. Paris: Fallois, 1993.

*Main Currents of Sociological Thought*, Vols. I–II, trans. by R. Howard and H. Weaver. New York: Basic Books, 1967.

*Marxism and the Existentialists*. New York: Praeger, 1969.

"Le marxisme de Marx." *Le Débat*, January 1984, 18–29.

*Memoirs: Fifty Years of Political Reflection*, trans. by G. Holoch, forward by Henry Kissinger. New York: Holmes & Meir, 1990.

*The Opium of the Intellectuals*, trans. by T. Kilmartin. New York: Doubleday, 1957.

*Peace and War: A Theory of International Relations*. New York: Doubleday, 1966.

*La philosophie critique de l'histoire: Essai sur une théorie allemande de l'histoire*. Paris: Julliard, 1987.

*Politics and History*, trans. by M. Conant, with an introduction by Michael Ledeen. New Brunswick: Transaction Publishers, 1984.

*Progress and Disillusion: The Dialectics of Modern Society*. New York: Praeger, 1968.

*Thinking Politically: A Liberal in the Age of Ideology*, with an introduction by Daniel J. Mahoney and Brian C. Anderson. New Brunswick: Transaction Publishers, 1997.

*Une histoire du vingtième siècle*, ed. by Christian Bachelier. Paris: Plon, 1996.

*D'une sainte famille à l'autre: Essai sur marxismes imaginaires*. Paris: Gallimard, 1969.

## OTHER WORKS CITED

Althusser, Louis. *Reading Capital*, with a sequel by E. Balibar, trans. by B. Brewster. New York: Verso, 1970.

———. *For Marx*, trans. by B. Brewster. New York: Verso, 1969.

Anderson, Brian C. "The Abandonment of Reason." *The Salisbury Review*, Vol. 14, Spring 1996, 46–47.

———. "The Aronian Renewal." *First Things*, March 1995, 61–64.

———. "Opium of the Intellectuals: Then and Now," *Gravitas*, Vol. 2, Fall 1995, 50–51.

———. Review of John Gray, *Isaiah Berlin*. *Australasian Journal of Philosophy*, Vol. 73, No. 3, September, 1995, 485–86.

———. Review of Jon Elster, *Political Psychology*. *Perspectives on Political Science*, Vol. 23, Fall 1994, 211.

Anderson, Perry. *Zones of Engagement*. London: Verso, 1993.

Aquinas, St. Thomas. *Summa Theologica*, trans. by T. Gilby and T. C. O'Brien. London: Blackfriars, 1964–1973.

Arendt, Hannah. "Understanding and Politics." *Partisan Review*, Vol. 20, July–August 1953.

————. *The Origins of Totalitarianism*. New York: Harcourt Brace Jovanovich, 1951.

Aristotle. *Nichomachean Ethics*, trans. by T. Irwin. Indianapolis: Hackett Publishers, 1985.

————. *The Politics*, trans. by B. Jowett. Cambridge: Cambridge University Press, 1988.

Arnold, N. Scott. *Marx's Radical Critique of Capitalist Society: A Reconstruction and Critique*. Oxford: Oxford University Press, 1990.

Barber, Benjamin. *The Conquest of Politics*. Princeton: Princeton University Press, 1988.

Baverez, Nicolas. *Raymond Aron: Un moraliste au temps des ideologies*. Paris: Flammarion, 1993.

Beitz, Charles. *Political Theory and International Relations*. Princeton: Princeton University Press, 1979.

Berger, Peter L. *The Capitalist Revolution: Fifty Propositions About Prosperity, Equality, & Liberty*. New York: Basic Books, 1986.

Berkowitz, Peter. *Nietzsche: The Ethics of an Immoralist*. Cambridge: Harvard University Press, 1995.

Berlin, Isaiah. *Conversations With Isaiah Berlin: Recollections of an Historian of Ideas*, with Ramin Jahanbegloo. New York: Scribner's, 1991.

————. *The Crooked Timber of Humanity: Chapters in the History of Ideas*, ed. by Henry Hardy. New York: Knopf, 1991.

————. *Four Essays on Liberty*. Oxford: Oxford University Press, 1969.

Besançon, Alain. *Rise of the Gulag: Intellectual Origins of Leninism*, trans. by S. Matthews. New York: Continuum, 1981.

Bloom, Allan. *The Closing of the American Mind*. New York: Simon & Schuster, 1987.

————. *Giants and Dwarfs: Essays 1960–1990*. New York: Simon & Schuster, 1990.

Brown, Chris. "International Affairs." *A Companion to Contemporary Political Philosophy*, edited by Robert Goodin and Philip Pettit. London: Blackwell, 1993.

Burnham, James. *The Machiavellians*. Chicago: Regnery-Gateway, 1943.

Burns, Timothy. *After History? Francis Fukuyama and His Critics*. Lanham, MD: Rowman & Littlefield, 1994.

Campbell, Stuart. "The Four Pareto's of Raymond Aron." *Journal of the History of Ideas*, Vol. 47, April–June 1986, 287–298.

Chatelet, Francois, Olivier Duhamel, and Evelyne Pisier, eds. *Dictionnaire des oeuvres politiques*. Paris: PUF, 1986.

Cromartie, Michael, ed. *Might and Right After the Cold War: Can Foreign Policy Be Moral?* Washington, DC: Ethics and Public Policy Center, 1993.

Davies, Brian. *The Thought of Thomas Aquinas*. Oxford: Oxford University Press, 1992.

Doyle, Michael. "Kant, Liberal Legacies and Foreign Affairs," parts 1 and 2. *Philosophy and Public Affairs*, Vol. 12, no. 3/4, 1983.

Elster, Jon. *Making Sense of Marx*. Cambridge: Cambridge University Press, 1985.

————. *Political Psychology*. Cambridge: Cambridge University Press, 1993.

Ferry, Luc. *From the Rights of Man to the Republican Idea: Political Philosophy, Vol. 3*, with Alain Renaut, trans. by F. Philip. Chicago: University of Chicago Press, 1992.

————. *The Systems of Philosophies of History: Political Philosophy, Vol. 2*, trans. by F. Philip. Chicago: University of Chicago Press, 1992.

————. *French Philosophy of the Sixties: An Essay on Anti-Humanism*, with Alain Renaut, trans. by M. Schnackenberg Cattani. Amherst: University of Massachusetts Press, 1990.

Frost, Bryan-Paul. "Raymond Aron's *Peace and War*, Thirty Years Later." *International Journal*, Vol. 51, Spring 1996.

Fukuyama, Francis. *The End of History and the Last Man*. New York: Free Press, 1993.

————. *Trust: The Social Virtues and the Creation of Prosperity*. New York: Free Press, 1995.

Galipeau, Claude. *Isaiah Berlin's Liberalism*. Oxford: Oxford University Press, 1994.

Gauchet, Marcel. *Les désenchanetment du monde*. Paris: Gallimard, 1985.

Glendon, Mary Ann. *Rights Talk: The Impoverishment of Political Discourse*. New York: Free Press, 1991.

Goyard-Fabre, Simone. "Le liberalisme de Raymond Aron." *Cahiers de philosophie politique et juridique*. No. 15, 1989, 59–97.

Gray, John. "Can We Agree to Disagree"? *New York Times Book Review*, October 1993.

————."The Derelict Utopia." *TLS*, May 24, 1996, 29.

————. *Enlightenment's Wake: Politics and Culture at the Close of the Modern Age*. London: Routledge, 1995.

————. *Hayek on Liberty*. Oxford: Blackwell, 1989.

————. *Isaiah Berlin*. London: HarperCollins, 1995.

————. *Post-Liberalism: Studies in Political Thought*. London: Routledge, 1993.

Hall, J. A. *Diagnoses of Our Time*. London: Blackwell, 1981.

Hassner, Pierre. *Violence and Peace: From the Atomic Bomb to Ethnic Cleansing*, trans. by J. Brenton. Budapest: Central European Univerisity Press, 1997.

————. "Morally Objectionable, Politically Dangerous," *The National Interest*, Winter 1996/1997, 63–69.

Hayek, F. A. *The Constitution of Liberty*. Chicago: Henry Regnery, 1960.

Hoffmann, Stanley. "Raymond Aron and the Theory of International Relations." *International Studies Quarterly*, Vol. 29, March 1985, 13–27.

————. *The State of War: Essays on the Theory and Practice of International Relations.* New York: Praeger, 1965.

Hollander, Paul. *Anti-Americanism: Irrational & Rational.* Rutgers: Transaction Publishers, 1995.

Horkheimer, Max. *Critique of Instrumental Reason: Lectures and Essays Since the End of World War II,* trans. by M.J. O'Connell. New York: Seabury Press, 1974.

Huntington, Samuel P. *The Clash of Civilizations and the Remaking of World Order.* New York: Simon & Schuster, 1996.

Judt, Tony. *Past Imperfect: French Intellectuals, 1944–1956.* Berkeley: University of California, 1993.

————. "Two Dissenters." *TLS,* January 18, 1996, 6–7.

Kant, Immanuel. *Critique of Pure Reason,* trans. by N. K. Smith. London: Macmillan, 1933.

————. *Political Writings,* ed. by H. Reiss. Cambridge: Cambridge University Press, 1991.

Kissinger, Henry. *Diplomacy.* New York: Simon & Schuster, 1994.

Kolakowski, Leszek. *Main Currents of Marxism,* Vols. I–III. Oxford: Oxford University Press, 1982.

Kolnai, Aurel. *The Utopian Mind and Other Papers,* ed. by Francis Dunlop, with an introduction by Pierre Manent. London: Althone Press, 1995.

Kriegel, Blandine. "De la philosophie politique." *magazine litteraire,* January 1996, 51–53.

Kymlicka, Will. *Multicultural Citizenship: A Liberal Theory of Minority Rights.* Oxford: Oxford University Press, 1995.

Launay, Stephen. *La pensée politique de Raymond Aron.* Paris: PUF, 1995.

Lefort, Claude. *Democracy and Political Theory.* Minneapolis: University of Minnesota Press, 1988.

Lenin, V.I. *What is to Be Done?* Peking: Foreign Languages Press, 1975.

Lilla, Mark, ed. *The New French Thought: Political Philosophy.* Princeton: Princeton University Press, 1994.

Locke, John. *Two Treatises of Government,* ed. by P. Laslett. Cambridge: Cambridge University Press, 1988.

Lukàcs, George. *History and Class Consciousness.* Cambridge: MIT Press, 1971.

Machiavelli. *The Prince,* trans. by H. Mansfield. Chicago: University of Chicago Press, 1985.

MacIntyre, Alasdair. *After Virtue.* Notre Dame: University of Notre Dame, 1984.

Mahoney, Daniel J. *The Liberal Political Science of Raymond Aron.* Lanham, MD: Rowman & Littlefield, 1992.

Manent, Pierre. *La Cité de l'homme.* Paris: Fayard, 1994.

————. ed. *Les libéraux,* Vols. I and II. Paris: Hachette, 1986.

————. "Modern Individualism." *Crisis*, October 1995, 35–38.

————. *Tocqueville and the Nature of Democracy*, foreword by Harvey Mansfield, trans. by J. Waggoner. Lanham, MD: Rowman & Littlefield, 1996.

Mansfield, Harvey. *The Spirit of Liberalism*. Cambridge: Harvard University Press, 1978.

Maritain, Jacques. "The End of Machiavellianism." *Review of Politics*, Vol. 4, January 1942.

————. *The Range of Reason*. New York: Scribners, 1952.

Marx, Karl and Engels, Friedrich. *Capital*, Vols. I and II. London: Penguin Books, 1967.

————. *Collected Works*. London: Lawrence and Wishart, 1975.

————. *The Marx-Engels Reader*, ed. by R.C. Tucker. New York: Norton, 1978.

————. *Selected Works in One Volume*. New York: International Publishers, 1968.

Meier, Heinrich. *Carl Schmitt and Leo Strauss: The Hidden Dialogue*. Chicago: University of Chicago Press, 1996.

Merleau-Ponty, Maurice. *Humanism and Terror*, trans. by J. O'Neill. Boston: Beacon Press, 1969.

Merquior, J. G. *Foucault*. London: Twayne, 1985.

Mesure, Sylvie. *Raymond Aron et la raison historique*. Paris: Vrin, 1984.

————. "Objectivité theoriqué et objectivite pratique chez Raymond Aron: De l'histoire à la politique." *Cahiers de philosophie politique et juridique*, No. 15, 1989.

Miller, David, et al. *The Blackwell Encyclopedia of Political Thought*. Oxford: Basil Blackwell, 1987.

Montesquieu, Baron de. *The Spirit of the Laws*, trans. by A. Cohler, B. C. Miller, H. S. Stone. Cambridge: Cambridge University Press, 1989.

Nagel, Thomas. *Equality and Partiality*. London: Oxford University Press, 1991.

Neuhaus, Richard John. *The Naked Public Square*. Grand Rapids: Eerdmans, 1984.

Novak, Michael. *The Catholic Ethic and the Spirit of Capitalism*. New York: Free Press, 1993.

————. *This Hemisphere of Liberty: A Philosophy of the Americas*. Washington, DC: AEI Press, 1992.

Nozick, Robert. *Anarchy, State, and Utopia*. New York: Basic Books, 1974.

Nussbaum, Martha and respondents. "Patriotism and Cosmopolitanism." *Boston Review*, October/November 1994.

Oakeshott, Michael. *Rationalism in Politics and Other Essays*. London: Methuen, 1962.

O'Brien, Conor Cruise. *The Great Melody: A Thematic Biography of Edmund Burke*. Chicago: University of Chicago Press, 1992.

Pangle, Thomas. "Political Theory in Contemporary France: Towards a Renaissance of Liberal Political Philosophy?" *PS*, Vol. 20, Fall 1987, 999–1003.

Pareto, Vilfredo. *The Mind and Society*, Vols. I–IV, trans. by A. Livingston and A. Bongioro. New York: Harcourt Brace, 1935.

Pogge, Thomas. *Realizing Rawls*. New York: Cornell University Press, 1989.

Popper, Karl. *The Open Society and Its Enemies*. Princeton: Princeton University Press, 1950.

——. *The Poverty of Historicism*. London: Routledge, 1957.

Rawls, John. *Political Liberalism*. New York: Columbia University Press, 1993.

——. *A Theory of Justice*. Cambridge: Harvard University Press, 1971.

Raynaud, Phillippe. "Raymond Aron et le droit international." *Cahiers de philosophie politique et juridique*, No. 15, 1989, 115–28.

——. "Raymond Aron et Max Weber: Épistemologie des sciences sociales et rationalisme critique." *Commentaire*, Vol. 8/9, No. 28–29, 1985, 213–21.

Renaut, Alain. "Politique de l'entendement, politique de la raison: De Raymond Aron à Fichte." *Cahiers de philosophie politique et juridique*, No. 15, 1989, 27–39.

——. "Raymond Aron et la retour à Kant." *magazine litteraire*, April 1992, 61–62.

Sandel, Michael. *Democracy's Discontent: America in Search of a Public Philosophy*. Cambridge: Cambridge University Press, 1996.

Sartre, Jean-Paul. *The Critique of Dialectical Reason*, trans. by A. Sheridan Smith. London: Verso, 1976.

——. *Selected Prose Writings of Jean-Paul Sartre*, Vol. II. Evanston, Ill.: Northwestern University Press, 1974.

Schmitt, Carl. *The Concept of the Political*, trans. by G. Schwab, with comments by Leo Strauss. Chicago: University of Chicago Press, 1996.

Scruton, Roger. *A Dictionary of Political Thought*. New York: Harper & Row, 1982.

——. *Modern Philosophy: An Introduction and Survey*. London: Sinclair-Stephenson, 1994.

——. *Thinkers of the New Left*. London: Longman Group, 1985.

Shklar, Judith N. *Ordinary Vices*. Cambridge: Cambridge University Press, 1986.

Strauss, Leo. *Natural Right and History*. Chicago: University of Chicago Press, 1953.

——. *The Rebirth of Classical Political Rationalism: An Introduction to the Thought of Leo Strauss*, ed. by Thomas Pangle. Chicago: University of Chicago Press, 1989.

Tamir, Yael. *Liberal Nationalism*. Princeton: Princeton University Press, 1993.

Taylor, Charles. *Sources of the Self*. Cambridge: Harvard University Press, 1989.

Thucydides. *The Landmark Thucydides: A Comprehensive Guide to the Peloponnesian War*, ed. New York: Free Press, 1996.

Tocqueville, Alexis de. *Democracy in America*, trans. by G. Lawrence. New York: Harper & Row, 1969.

Todorov, Tzvetan. *The Morals of History*, trans. by A. Waters. Minnesota: University of Minnesota Press, 1995.

Virilio, Paul, *Speed and Politics*, trans. by. M. Polizzotti. New York: Semiotexte, 1986.

Wallerstein, Immanuel. *The Modern World System*, Vols. I–II. New York: Academic Press, 1974, 1980.

——. *The Politics of the World Economy*. Cambridge: Cambridge University Press, 1984.

Waltz, Kenneth. *Theory of International Politics*. Reading, MA.: Addison-Wesley, 1979.

Weber, Max. *From Max Weber: Essays in Sociology*. Oxford: Oxford University Press, 1946.

Whiteside, Kerry H. *Merleau-Ponty and the Foundation of an Existential Politics*. Princeton: Princeton University Press, 1988.

Wilson, James Q. *The Moral Sense*. New York: Free Press, 1993.

Yack, Bernard, ed. *Liberalism Without Illusions: Essays on Liberal Theory and the Political Vision of Judith N. Shklar*. Chicago: University of Chicago Press, 1996.

# INDEX